Venezuela

Venezuela

Hilary Dunsterville Branch
and other contributors

BRADT PUBLICATIONS, UK
HUNTER PUBLISHING, USA
DISTR. SANTIAGO, VENEZUELA

First published in 1993 by Bradt Publications, 41 Nortoft Rd, Chalfont St Peter, Bucks, SL9 0LA, England.
Distributed in the USA by Hunter Publishing Inc., 300 Raritan Center Parkway, CN94, Edison, NJ 08810.
   Distributed in Venezuela by Distribuidora Santiago CA, Apto 2589, 1010A Caracas.

ISBN 0 946983 70 4

Cover photos by Edward Paine, Last Frontiers.
Front cover: Chinak-Merú falls, Aponguano river.
Back cover, top: Playa Medina, Paria Peninsula.
Back cover, bottom: Squirrel monkey, Amazonas.
Typeset from the author's disc by Patti Taylor, London NW10 3BX
Printed by Guernsey Press

Acknowledgements

My grateful thanks to travellers and readers of the two editions of the *No Frills Guide to Venezuela* who provided information: Florence Smith, Bill Quantrill, Justine Freeth, Huw Clough, Christopher Leggett, Chris Sharpe, Oyvind & Helen Servan, Don Jacobs, Steve Whitaker, Sandrine Tiller, Lindsay Griffin, Peter Ireland, C. Sganga, Rowena Quantrill, Mark Dutton, James Mead, Andrea Bullock, Debbie Quintana, Darren Kealey, Mary Lou Goodwin, Marco Crolla, Michele Coppens, C. Nacher, Edith Steinbuch, Luis Armas, Julian Singleton, Tim Wainwright, Alison Vickers, Peter Weinberger, Sven Berge, Karen and John Whitehead, Barney Gibbs, Edward Paine, Tracey & Paul Weatherstone, Harald Baedeke, Luke Tegner and Katherine Lewis.

INTRODUCTION

Venezuela has, for some years, been one of the gateway countries to South America, with the cheapest flights to the continent routed through Caracas. Travellers may take one horrified look at this city and flee south. But Caracas has its devotees and it is always important not to judge a country by its capital. The largest Venezuelan cities, including Caracas, are located near the coast. Everything else is called the *interior*. Ninety percent of Venezuelans live in the northern ten percent of the land, so that much of the country is delightfully free of urban blight, retaining local colour and traditions. There is some excellent backpacking in a variety of mountain scenery, from cloud forest to glacier, and in some splendid national parks. Away from the built-up coast, there are still coral reefs, beaches, amazing birdlife, immense rivers, waterfalls — and a relative absence of international tourism which cannot last indefinitely.

This guide emphasises ecotourism and is not intended as a complete guide to every city and all hotels. It has grown from two editions of the *No Frills Guide to Venezuela* in response to readers' suggestions and requests, describing places of greatest interest to the more adventurous traveller.

Prices: readers should note that while the value of the *bolivar* devalues (to the advantage of hard-currency travellers) local prices rise vs. the U.S. dollar. For this reason I have given the U.S. equivalent of many fares and prices.

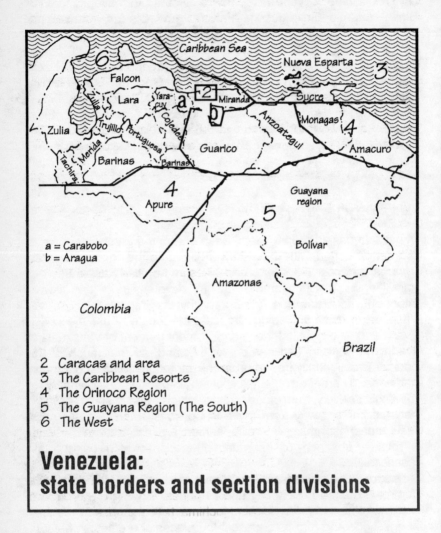

a = Carabobo
b = Aragua

2 Caracas and area
3 The Caribbean Resorts
4 The Orinoco Region
5 The Guayana Region (The South)
6 The West

Venezuela:
state borders and section divisions

Table of Contents

MAPS

Boxes

Sir Walter Raleigh

Sir Walter Raleigh (or Ralegh) was a favourite of Queen Elizabeth I, who was much pleased with his successful campaigns against the Spanish. In 1595 he sailed to 'the Indies' to explore new lands and search for gold. His journeys through the Orinoco region (present day Venezuela and Guiana) took him as far south as Angostura, now known as Ciudad Bolívar. On his return to England he wrote an account of his journeys, entitled *The Discoverie of the Large, Rich and Bewtiful Empire of Guiana*. His account of the riches of the region was at odds with the lack of material evidence, and scant interest was paid to his reports of vast deposits of iron ore (now a great source of wealth for Venezuela). After the death of Queen Elizabeth, King James condemned the unfortunate explorer to death on charges of conspiracy. However, he was released in 1616 (after 13 years in the Tower) on the proviso that he would travel again to the Orinoco, and this time he was to bring back the gold. After his son, who had accompanied him, was killed in a skirmish with the natives, Raleigh sailed home, without the promised riches, to be beheaded.

SECTION ONE

GENERAL INFORMATION

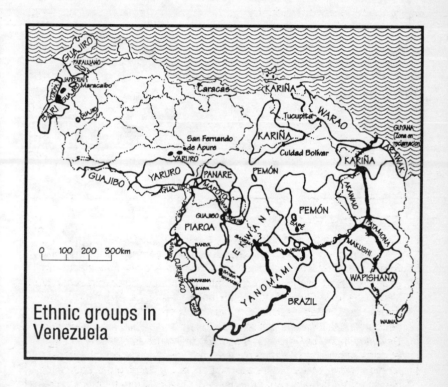

Ethnic groups in Venezuela

Jaguars are said to fish using the tips of their tails as a lure.

Chapter 1

Information for travellers

A BRIEF HISTORY

Columbus landed in Venezuela in 1498 on his third voyage and discovered Paria Peninsula. Pre-Columbian Venezuela was inhabited by disparate tribes unable to repel the Spaniards who arrived early in the 1500s. With no fabulously wealthy empire such as the Incas' to conquer, the Spaniards early established ports and agricultural settlements. The first Spanish towns were Cumaná in 1521 and Coro in 1527.

The first stirrings of an independence movement came in 1749. Then in 1806 Francisco Miranda, sailing from Philadelphia and assisted by American volunteers, attempted to overthrow the ruling powers. He was unable to land, all volunteers were imprisoned and the 10 American officers were hanged. Miranda made a second attempt in 1811 and was captured. Simón Bolívar took up leadership (more about Bolívar in the Caracas chapter) in 1813. The turning point in his struggle came when he took Angostura (subsequently renamed Ciudad Bolívar) and recruited British mercenaries and the fearless horsemen of the *Llanos*, led by General José Antonio Páez. They marched over the Andes, won the Battle of Boyacá in 1819 and took Bogotá. With only isolated pockets of the country under his control, Bolívar's revolutionary congress proclaimed Gran Colombia, made up of present-day Ecuador, Colombia, Venezuela and Peru and Bolivia. Independence was sealed at the Battle of Carabobo on June 24, 1821, and the Spanish army was finally booted out of Venezuela two years later.

The union soon broke down and Venezuela was declared an independent state before Bolívar's death in 1830, with José Antonio Páez its first president. Although Venezuela was devastated by the 12-year Independence struggle, and further sapped by a century of *caudillos* and dictators, democracy has been in force since 1958.

In 1989 Carlos Andrés Pérez was elected president for the second time (his first term in office was from 1974 to 1979). The 1990s have seen a dramatic fall in his personal popularity, and in 1992 an attempted coup was greeted with enthusiasm by many Venezuelans. Early 1993 saw another attempt to remove him from office. Where force failed the law prevailed and in June 1993 Pérez was suspended as president pending trial on corruption charges. Congress chose Ramón J. Velasquez to be interim president until the next national elections in December 1993.

The economy

Venezuela is a member of OPEC; only two countries in the world produce more oil, and this wealth has subsidised government services (such as good roads); oil held off inflation for many years. In order to combat reduced income, Venezuela is privatising ports, telephones and hundreds of state companies. Tourism and beach resorts promise to be big employers some day. In the meantime, the second industry in Venezuela after oil is Polar beer!

GETTING THERE

From Britain

For flights the specialist travel agency for South America is Journey Latin America, 16 Devonshire Rd, Chiswick, London W4 2HD; Tel 081-747 3108. At present (June 1993) their cheapest flights are with TAP (Air Portugal) via Lisbon for £387 to £433 return depending on season, and direct flights from £468 with VIASA (some of which go via Porlamar, Margarita). July, August and December are the most expensive months for air travel.

Other cheap flight specialists are Trailfinders, 42-48 Earls Court Road, London W8 6EJ; Tel 071-938 3366. They also offer a complete traveller's service — vaccination centre, a library and insurance scheme. WEXAS, 45 Brompton Road, London SW3 1DE, Tel 071-584 1133, offer discounted flights on some airlines including VIASA for members (cost: £39.58 per year). Inara Christian, a helpful Venezuela specialist, runs Columbus Travel in the Latin Centre, Elephant & Castle, 071-252 5959.

From the USA

North American travellers have a wide variety of flight options. Venezuelan airlines are growing. Two new companies flying to the United States are Air Margarita and Zuliana de Aviación, flying between Venezuela and the U.S. Zuliana's return fare between Maracaibo or Caracas and Miami was $340 (1992).

Airpass

Avensa, the Venezuelan airline, offers a 7-day no limit air pass, as well as one for 14 and 21 days. These must be bought *outside* the country.

ORGANISED TOURS

The companies listed above do some organised tours to Venezuela, which usually include the Angel Falls and trekking to the 'Lost World' of Roraima. Venezuela also features in the brochures of other adventure travel companies. The specialist tour operator to Venezuela in Britain is Last Frontiers, 20 High Street, Long Crendon, Bucks; Tel/fax (0844) 208405. They offer a range of escorted tours from the luxurious to the more rugged, and also make bookings and provide the latest advice for independent travellers.

A new company, also specialising in Venezuela, is Geodyssey. As well as tours off-the-beaten track they offer a tailor-made service for people who do not wish to join a group. 29 Harberton Road, London N19 3JS. Tel 071-281 7788, fax 071-281 7878.

More information See Chapter 10 for flights from London or the US to Margarita Island. Page 15 also has information on travelling by bus from neighbouring countries in South America. See page 16 for a ferry service from the Caribbean Islands.

BEFORE YOU GO

Visas

Travellers to Venezuela should have a passport with at least six months validity. Airlines are authorised to issue 60-day **tourist cards** (*tarjeta de turismo*), at no cost, on the spot when you buy your return ticket. Extensions for periods up to 60 days can be obtained in Caracas from the Interior Ministry: Departamento de Turismo, 2nd floor (east stairs), DIEX (Direccíon de Identificación y Extranjería), Av. Baralt opposite Plaza Miranda, (02) 4833185/3206; hours 8.00 to 12.00, 13.30 to 16.00. Each 30-day renewal costs Bs.1,005 in fiscal stamps, bought on ground floor; bring a photo and your return ticket. Consulates can issue 90-day tourist cards, also renewable. Consulates now also issue a multiple entry **tourist visa** (*visa de turismo*), valid for one year from date of issue; these may take up to 48 hours to obtain. Besides your passport, the consul may require a personal interview, a bank letter or job letter as proof of financial solidity. Cost: $2 for US citizens, $10 for UK citizens. The address of the Venezuelan Consulate in Britain is 56 Grafton Way, London W1P 5LB; tel 071-387 6727.

If you are not flying to Venezuela you would be safest to get a visa before leaving home. Border officials seldom have tourist cards and may not know the official requirements. So play safe.

Transit visas are only for passengers, airline staff and sailors who can prove their imminent departure. Cost: same as tourist visas. **'Transeunte' visas** which allow you to work or study require health and 'good conduct' certificates, prior DIEX approval, $50, and a great deal of patience. Because a *transeunte* cannot leave the country without a tax clearance, this is NOT for you.

Peter Weinberger, wishing to enter from Brazil, went to the consulate in Boa Vista. 'As far as I know everybody, regardless of nationality, needs a visa for overland entry to Venezuela. Even though I clearly asked for a 3-week tourist visa and showed financial solidity and an airline ticket to Europe, the consul issued only a 72-hour transit visa. Furthermore, the consulate gave me absolutely the wrong information, that the transit visa can be extended at any DIEX office in Venezuela. But these visas are generally not extendable and even the DIEX head office in Caracas was able to grant me only 24 hours to leave the country legally.'

HEALTH AND SECURITY

Venezuela is not a primitive country, its private hospitals are good, and no extraordinary health precautions need be taken. Travellers to the Orinoco or Amazon area should, however, protect themselves against malaria. For up to date information on the best anti-malaria regime, phone the Malaria Reference Laboratory in London on (071) 636 7921 (a tape recording listing recommended courses of pills for different areas of the world). The wisest approach to travel health in general is to visit one of the British Airways Travel Clinics (phone 071-831 5333 for your nearest one). Their information is bang up to date. Americans should contact the Center for Disease Control in Atlanta, tel: (404) 332 4559.

Stock up on anti-diarrhoea medication, and if you are venturing off the beaten track, bring a good first aid kit. The books *The Tropical Traveller* by John Hatt and *Traveller's Health* by Richard Dawood are jam-packed with useful advice.

Always carry your passport (not a copy). People found to be *indocumentado* are liable to be fined, imprisoned or at the very least harassed by officials. Carry your passport well hidden in a money belt or inside pocket.

Robbery is becoming increasingly common in Venezuela. Be sensible, keep your valuables hidden or locked in the hotel safe, and enjoy your trip.

WHAT TO BRING

Common sense will tell you what to pack: if it's a coastal holiday with swimming and snorkelling, bring lots of sunscreen, mask and snorkel, and clothes that protect areas prone to sunburn — shoulders and base of neck; bring an old tee-shirt and shorts for protection against sunburn while swimming, and old trainers to protect your feet against coral or sharp rocks or sand fleas on river banks in the 'interior'.

If you are backpacking in the Andes, remember it may drop below freezing at night, be cold and damp during the day at high altitudes and very hot at lower altitudes. You will need layers of clothes — two thin wool sweaters will be more practical than one thick one (unlike some Andean countries, there are no great sweater bargains to be had in Venezuela, so bring them with you). One sweater and a sweatshirt may be even more versatile. You'll need all the usual backpacking gear: light tent, stove (Bluet Gaz is available in Caracas), 3-season sleeping bag, thermal wear. Decent mountain gear, although expensive, can be found in sports shops in Caracas and Mérida.

Those travelling to the hinterland and on rivers should bring or buy a *fine mesh* mosquito net (the self-standing sort is unavailable in Venezuela), malaria pills, cotton mix clothes, a warm blanket for chilly tropical nights, and plastic bags to waterproof clothes. The best form of insect protection is a long-sleeved shirt and long socks (spray socks and cuffs). A hat is essential for river travel and savanna walking.

Everyone should have a rain poncho (cheap, plastic), torch (flashlight) for dodgy electricity supplies, earplugs (for noisy hotels or buses), strong needles and thread or dental floss for repairs, reliable matches, a large supply of tea which is regarded in Venezuela as a drink for sick people (or, worse, a teabag is put in a cup of hot milk), and a knowledge of Spanish or at least a good phrasebook and dictionary.

MONEY

The currency unit is the bolívar. The exchange rate in June 1993 was Bs.89 = $1; Bs.137 = £1. US dollars are universally accepted; other hard currencies may be much harder to change. Always change money (dollar bills never pounds) before leaving major cities. US$ travellers cheques can be exchanged in *casas de cambio* in most, but not all, cities and you are asked to produce your cheque purchase slip. American Express is represented by the Banco Consolidado, and Visa by the Banco Union. Thomas Cook sterling cheques should be changed in Caracas (Turismo Maso). It is useful to carry some small denomination dollar bills for emergencies. Credit cards are widely used in big cities; Visa appears to be the most popular, then American Express, Master. Although cash advances from abroad by credit card should take less than a day in Caracas, this service may be unavailable in the '*interior*'. Transfer of funds by ordinary cheque can take a month.

John Whitehead writes: 'I suggest taking American Express dollar cheques as more banks accept these. Also, avoid banks to exchange money, unless you have up to two hours to kill. They are incredibly slow.' Instead he used money change booths in airports or large cities. A charge card is a good idea. 'I had to use my Visa card on a number of occasions and, to my relief, when home I was given an extremely favourable exchange rate.'

See page 19 for more on banks.

Chapter 2

In Venezuela

ARRIVING AND LEAVING — BY PLANE

Most visitors fly into Venezuela, arriving at **Maiquetía Airport**, officially called the Simón Bolívar International Airport; it is not in Caracas but Maiquetía on the coast, some 35km from Caracas.

The International Terminal

This is large and modern, with many facilities, but travellers complain about unintelligible loudspeakers, poor information system and aggressive porters. There are no lockers for checking luggage. On the main concourse, huge departure and arrival boards announce scheduled times and changes, but they are fallible so check with your airline desk. Booths line the main concourse giving service for airport/exit tax stamps, money change, car hire and major hotel reservation. A police booth is open day and night, (031) 552498.

Upstairs, a fast-food restaurant and cafeteria take the place of a passenger lounge. It's less comfortable but nicer to sit outside on the terrace overlooking the runway. Also upstairs, the CANTV telephone office is open day and night for placing overseas calls. Well hidden in the basement is the low-price *Cafetín* where you can get a hot meal ($3) as well as fresh juices and espresso coffee, from 5.00 to 24.00. To find it, look for a rear corridor beside the customs hall, opposite the *Correos* or post office, and go down one floor to the *sótano*.

Among airport services is a round-the-clock passenger assistance number, (031) 552424, promising *atención al público*; dial 424 on house phones at either side of the customs hall. The airport switchboard number is (031) 551111; for Immigration, (031) 552670.

One service sorely lacking is a central information desk or meeting point. Since the customs hall has three doors and all are obstructed by people looking for arriving aunts and in- laws, the search may be agonizing, especially when flights are delayed. I suggest that you arrange to meet at one of the desks listed below.

Airline ticket counters   These are only open at flight time. An important exception is **Viasa** whose ticket desk is open from 5.00 to 24.00. Moreover, there is a Viasa information booth (same hours), although the girl on duty when I was there did not speak English.

Car rental   Avis, Budget and Hertz are open from 5.00 to 24.00, National is open 24 hours every day. See page 16.

Hotels/Travel   The government agency, **Corpoturismo,** (031) 551060, 552747, is open daily 6.00 to 24.00. English-speaking attendants make reservations for selected Caracas hotels, 2 to 5-star class; one week minimum with one night's deposit. Some brochures available. The **Macuto Sheraton**, luxury resort on the central coast (35 min. by car), has a booth. Also, a travel agency, **Viajes Melia**, (031) 552790/92, arranges transfers, tours, flights, translation and computer services, as well as reservations for the modern Melia Caribe next to the Macuto Sheraton.

Money change   Busiest of the three *casas de cambio* is **Italcambio**, (031) 551080, open 24 hours every day of the year (in theory). You get the best rates from such exchange bureaux, the worst rates from hotels and shops.

Taxis & buses   There is a system of taxi tickets that you can pay in advance according to a zoned map of Caracas. At the official booth opposite the main customs door, ask for a *taxi autorizado*. Be advised, however, that a 'special' list allows taxis to charge double or triple for certain hotels. Pick a general destination, not a hotel. For example, while a taxi will charge nearly $20 to the Lincoln Suites in Sabana Grande, a ride to Plaza Venezuela or Chacaito costs about $12. In the same way, a person asking for the Macuto Sheraton Hotel on the coast (which is in Caraballeda, not Macuto), pays about double the normal rate of about $10. Each piece of luggage is Bs.20. Outside the terminal, drivers of all sorts of vehicles compete noisily for your dollars; compare prices or else you will be overcharged (tips not essential). Among taxi lines giving reliable service to the airport (not only pick-up but wake-up as they ring you beforehand) are: Astrala (02) 815627, Taxitour (02) 749411, and Utac (02) 575-0053.

   Por puesto vans (pay-by-the-seat cars or mini-buses) go to Caracas for around $1.50 a seat. If you are going to Macuto or a hotel on the coast, which is called the Litoral, you can take a *por puesto* on the main road; from the upper airport concourse, walk through and beyond the parking lot to reach the road.

Bus service is good. The blue and white airport buses charge about Bs.80 to Caracas, running from 5.00 until the last flight. They park outside the east (left) end of the terminal. Once in Caracas many passengers get off at the **Gato Negro** Metro station, others continue to the terminus (Organización Ucamc, 5730612) at Parque Central on Av. Sur 17, under Avenida Bolívar. This is also the starting point for a number of airport *por puestos*. Walk 1½ blocks to the **Bellas Artes** station.

Telephones & post　International service is provided by the CANTV office on the upper concourse, open 24 hours. When dialling from the coast, remember to add 02 before Caracas numbers. See page 18. Postal services, *correos*, are provided at the Ipostel desk on the main concourse.

To Macuto　Darren Kealey writes: 'Upon arrival at Caracas airport it is a good idea to head to Macuto and stay the night at the Hotel Macuto rather than make the longer, more expensive journey to Caracas. A night in Hotel Macuto costs £5.00 per person including en suite facilities and air-conditioning. A similar hotel in Caracas costs double. From the airport walk across the car park to the main road and cross over. A *por puesto* bus will take you to Macuto, on the coast, for 15p, a taxi costs £3.00. *Por puestos* run from Macuto to Caracas about every two minutes, take ¾ hour and will cost you less than a pound. Starting your trip in Macuto saves the hassle of arriving in a large, daunting city with something of a budget hotel shortage. Macuto is a very easy-going coastal resort popular with Caraqueños at weekends.'

'Taxis to the *litoral* were around £13 (1992) and the drivers did not seem to want to barter. However the 'pirates' did and we secured a ride for £8. The Hotel Macuto is on a down, rather unclean with unreliable hot water; however, the pool is good. Cost is now around £16 double.' (John and Karen Whitehead)

Leaving

A private shuttle service links Maiquetia and Caracas. Buses leave from Parque Tolón, Calle Nueva York, just west of Av. Principal, Las Mercedes, (016) 218317, (02) 9791220. Departures on the hour 4.00 to 18.00, 7 days a week. About Bs.300.

Allow an hour or more to drive from midtown Caracas. Be prepared for heavy traffic even on weekends, when beach-goers cause blocks at tunnels (one is 2km long) on the 17km tollway or

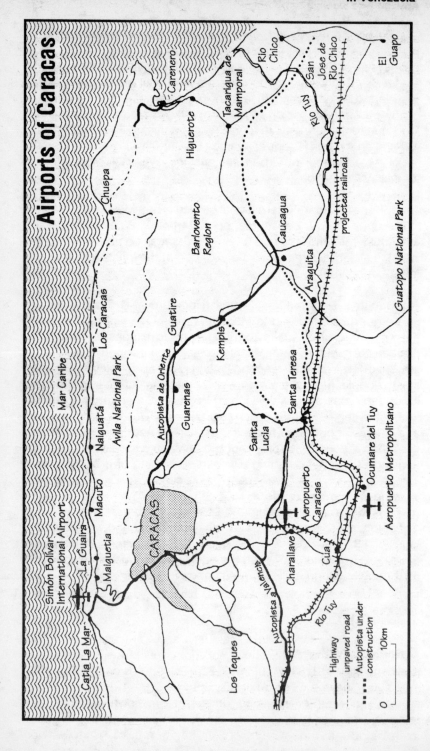

Airports of Caracas

autopista. Torrential rains and accidents produce frequent hold-ups. Passengers must be at the airport two hours before flight time or risk being bumped off over-booked flights; weekends are bad, holidays are nightmarish. If you are going standby, get a standby number from the desk at the far left of the main airport hall.

Buy the stamps for your **airport and exit taxes** and fill out the Exit card. Tourists pay a Ministerio de Hacienda exit tax of Bs.30, plus an airport tax of Bs.800 for international flights. *Transeuntes'* exit tax has gone up to Bs.1,400 plus airport tax of Bs.900. Venezuelans and residents pay an exit tax of Bs.400, plus the Bs.900 for airport departure. On domestic flights, all passengers pay Bs.40 airport tax.

Domestic flights

The National Terminal is the building to the left, and about 500m east of the international terminal. When taking a domestic flight immediately on arrival (or prior to departure) it is simplest to make the transfer on foot, if you are not overloaded, because drivers must take a circular route and there is no regular bus anyway. Avensa and Viasa have their own transfer service.

South of Caracas are two private airports, serving as base for many light planes. They are the starting point for some flights to Los Roques, the Llanos and Amazonas. In Charallave is the Aeropuerto de Caracas Oscar Machado, (02) 5724312, atop a flattened hill about one hour by car from central Caracas. It has a restaurant, taxi, telephones, but no public transportation. The Aeropuerto Metropolitano, (039) 240340, is in Ocumare del Tuy, 25km south. No air bus service.

Charter companies include: Aeroejecutivos, (02) 919286; Amazonair, (02) 2832627; Rent-a-Charter, (02) 2617480; Rutaca, (085) 22195. Airline offices are closed on weekends.

National airlines have a series of discounts which (although not stated) are given only to local travellers. Such discounts include family and tourist plans, senior citizen and student rates. You could try for these discounts; have ready a photocopy of your student/ID card. The previous phone numbers, and those below, are in the Caracas area.

Domestic airlines

Aereotuy, Edif. Gran Sabana, Boulevard de Sabana Grande, a block from Metro east exit, (02) 7618043, 7616231. Many flights to Kavac, Canaima and other Gran Sabana strips, as well as Los Roques, Margarita, Ciudad Bolívar.

Aeropostal, Torre Este, Parque Central, nivel Lecuna, (02) 5764511, 5763922-phone reservations 7am-7pm, national air terminal (031) 552828, international (031) 551300. Local and foreign destinations including Aruba, Curaçao, Cuba, Dominican Republic, Martinique, Trinidad. Popular branch offices in Torre Capriles, Plaza Venezuela, 7819198; Carmelitas a El Conde, 817174.

Avensa, Esq. El Chorro, Av. Universidad, Caracas, (02) 563366, 5623366-phone reservations day & night, national terminal (031) 551520/21, international (031) 551531. Branch office at Esquina Ibarras, Av. Urdaneta, 5633177/66. Avensa and its sister company Servivensa fly to Aruba, Bonaire, Colombia, Curaçao, Panama, Guatemala, Costa Rica, Mexico and Miami-New York.

Cave, PH, Edif. Pichincha, Av. Principal El Bosque, (02) 9522722, (031) 551054. Service on small jets and prop planes to Barcelona, Coro, Güiria, Valencia, Puerto Ordaz. Four flights daily to Los Roques, $60 return.

Viasa, Torre Viasa, Av. México opp. Hilton, (02) 5762611, resv. 2998111, airport (031) 551410/2. Flagship line gives international service to three continents. Ring Viasa's east branch in the CCCT, Chuao, (02) 959435, for information about '*pre-despacho*', 15.00 to 21.00 the day before flying. This saves time at the airport and ensures you do not get bumped, but there have been reports of missing luggage.

Zuliana de Aviación, P-10, Edif. Torreón, Calle Veracruz, Las Mercedes, Caracas, (02) 919810, Maracaibo (061) 512889. Maracaibo and Caracas to Miami, Aruba, Bogotá, Medellín.

ARRIVING AND LEAVING — BY BUS

International

Buses go to Colombia, Ecuador and Peru. A Peruvian line, Expreso Internacional Ormeño, also offers connections to Chile and Buenos Aires. Their double-decker coach leaves Caracas at 16.00 on Mondays for Bogotá-Quito-Lima ($170). Ticket booth at Aeroexpresos Ejecutivos, (02) 333601, (014) 237505. Valid passport and yellow fever vaccination required. Overland to Bogotá takes nearly three days. Many travellers to Colombia take the bus to San Antonio del Táchira, cross the border, then fly on from Cúcuta.

Domestic bus and taxi lines, car hire

Long distance Buses go from Caracas to all points of the country. The old Nuevo Circo Terminal on Av. Lecuna (near the bull ring) is to be supplemented by the new Terminal de Occidente which will serve western destinations. You can walk from **La Hoyada** Metro station across Av. Bolívar to the Nuevo Circo. **La Bandera** station on the Metro's Line 3 to El Valle is being built to serve the Terminal de Occidente. East-bound buses will soon leave from the new Terminal de Oriente, located beyond Petare.

Fares are inexpensive, about $12 to Margarita or Mérida. Once you have found the sales booth for the right bus or *Expreso*, you should buy a *boleto* an hour before departure so as to avoid sitting in the stifling rear, dubbed the *cocina*. It is always best to buy coach tickets a day ahead (tickets for Fridays are scarce) and to travel in mid-week. During holidays (when the Nuevo Circo is a thieves' den), it is imperative to buy a ticket at least three days in advance, and you will still have to battle for a seat. My best advice is to travel when the holidays or 3-day weekends are half over, if you must. Coaches are listed in the telephone book under *Expresos, Líneas de Autobuses*, or *Uniones*.

Buses to La Guaira and the coast or *Litoral* leave frequently from the west sector of the Nuevo Circo; they cost very little. Buses for El Junquito and Colonia Tovar now queue at Esquina San Roque off Av. Lecuna; they leave hourly from 5.00. The fare at present is equivalent to a dollar.

Note: Never travel without passport, student card, ID papers. Bus passengers are open to hassle from police or army checks searching for drug carriers and illegal immigrants. Mask your anger; flattery is more effective.

Por puestos Long distance *carritos* or taxis for which you pay by the seat leave from the bus terminal as soon as they fill up. The cost is triple the bus fare but they save time and may be more comfortable for long-legged men. Also *por puestos* will stop to let you go to the toilet, often an urgent traveller's need. Ask specifically about your route. You can take a local *por puesto* for short hops, but if you are going long distance, it is better to take the through *carro*, to avoid getting marooned in a village. In cities, owner-operated *por puestos* have grown into small buses providing most of the public transport. They have a *'por puesto'* number plate; taxis are identified as *'libres'*. Any other car picking up passengers is a *pirata*. Routes have set fares. You can hire all the seats of a *por puesto* for a journey; this is called a *viaje expreso*.

Taxis   The other word for a taxi in Venezuela is *libre*. Fix the cost before setting out even if the taxi has a meter or *medidor*. Inflation has cut down the number of taxis which are now scarcer. However, they are still not expensive and tipping is optional. Every district has its *línea de taxi* (see telephone book), operating during the day. Several radio-taxis provide reliable service day and night; phone early to reserve a car for the airport. Some Caracas numbers are: Teletaxi (02) 7519021, Taxis Gran Ciudad (02) 744522, Gran Línea Venezuela (02) 7815254. In view of high rental car rates, travellers report that combining taxi service with buses/metro is flexible, fun, even economical. No parking, no car theft.

Car hire   Half a dozen small and large rental companies compete at every airport. Almost all require credit cards. Prices are very high. Some local outfits in Margarita or Ciudad Bolívar may offer better rates than the large companies so check when you arrive. The advantage of working with Hertz, Avis and the like is a larger supply of cars so that you can make immediate pick-up. National Car Rental, with some 50 agencies around the country, requires drivers to be over 21, or 25 for jeeps. Their smallest car with gears costs $42 a day, plus insurance and Bs.14/km after 150km daily. The tag is over double for a 4WD *vehículo rústico* such as a Jeep or Toyota and these are scarce. Reserving a hired car from abroad has the advantage that if the model you reserved proves to be unavailable, the company must assign you a better model at no extra cost.

Drivers should be over 21 (in some cases 24) and have a credit card.

Chris Stolley adds this warning concerning the frequent rental car breakdowns: 'You will have signed a blank credit card chit or left a hefty deposit to rent the car. As security and service in general you cannot just leave it in the middle of nowhere. Consider well before hiring a car.' Also some drivers have been made to pay for cars stolen while rented, so read the fine print.

ARRIVING AND LEAVING — BY BOAT

Caribbean Ferry Service

A correspondent, Mr Barney Gibbs, reveals a well-kept secret: 'There is a new ferry service taking passengers (and cargo) through the southern Caribbean islands and on to Venezuela. The trip is scenic and cheap, and Caribbean islands such as Barbados and St Lucia have international airports and lots of charter flights throughout the year making them very accessible.

'I reached Barbados stand-by for under US$200 then stumbled onto the service offered by Windward. I went to Trinidad for Carnival (far better in my experience than New Orleans or Brazil) via St Lucia and St Vincent. We stopped for a day in these beautiful islands, and a week in Trinidad. From there I caught the ferry on its following week's circuit and continued on to Venezuela. The total fare (round trip from Barbados) was US$148.'

The ferry carries 250 passengers and 40 cars. The fare does not include meals and cabins cost US$10 per night extra. The current (1993) schedule departs from Barbados on Sundays, (St Vincent Monday, Trinidad Tuesday) arriving at Güiria (at the tip of the Paria Peninsula), Venezuela on Tuesday evening. The Venezuelan itinerary now includes one sailing per month from Pampatar, Margarita Island. There is a weekend service between St Lucia and Barbados. More information from: Windward Lines Ltd, #7, James Fort, Hincks St, Bridgetown, Barbados Tel: 809 431 0449. Fax: 809 431 0452.

COMMUNICATIONS

Post   An address with the word '*apartado*' is a post box, not a street. Outsiders have a hard time realising that letters take a fortnight or longer to Venezuela. Allow a *month* for an exchange of correspondence and be pleased if it takes less. No one uses letter boxes, except in large hotels. Important letters are sent by registered post, or *correo certificado*, although postcards are faster and just as safe. Post offices are open during lunch, 8.00 to 18.30, but not on weekends. The exception is the central post office at Carmelitas on Av. Universidad, open until 16.00 on Saturdays. For stamp collectors there is a Departamento de Filatelia, open Mon.-Fri. 8.30-16.00. The central post office also has a poste restante service, care of 'Lista de Correos', IPOSTEL, Carmelitas, Caracas 1010.

Private mail and courier services fill the gap for quick delivery both in and out of the country. Aerocav has many reception points in Caracas (ring the HQ at 225511, 223711) for 46 towns around the country. Competitor Domesa also delivers around Venezuela; they have offices in the Chacaito and Altamira Metro stations. DHL has desks at the Tamanaco and Caracas Hilton hotels, (02) 2087293, 5712322. P.O.Box Air will post your letters in 24 hours from Miami for a small fee plus postage, (02) 923505; mezzanine, Torre Las Mercedes, Chuao (same building as the British Embassy).

The San Martín and Chacao post offices are offering FAX service (national only), at Bs.250 the first page, Bs.170 additional pages.

Note: Unless sending a book, do not mail packages to Venezuela.

The stamps cost as much as the contents and the receiver not only pays duty but must make one or more trips downtown to claim the package if it arrives.

Telegrams   There is little urgency about delivering telegrams, losing the point of sending them. However, in Caracas some people send telegrams because they are faster than letters. They are used to request audiences with officials, for example.

Telephones   These will drive you crazy. (A friend here says, 'If anything drives me back to the First World, it will be the telephones.') Once you leave your hotel, the best place to find a working pay phone is in a Metro station, as half Caracas knows. Dial 103 for information, with luck. Numbers transferred to new exchanges may be checked by ringing 510144. Looking in the telephone directory can be frustrating because many changed numbers are not updated, and people in rented flats have phones listed by landlords.

Remember that CH is a letter which comes after the Cs, like LL after the Ls, and Ñ after the Ns. Subscribers are listed by their first surname (father's) and initial of the second surname (mother's). Government offices are listed at the front of the Caracas directory (but I once spent a fruitless hour searching for the Jardín Botánico). At the back are coastal communities (the *Litoral*), Colonia Tovar and towns in Miranda State. The final pages have an extremely useful map of Caracas (in sequence, NW to SE). The publisher of the directory also puts out volumes covering the rest of Venezuela; these may be consulted at Caveguias, Edificio Provincial, Ibarras a Maturín, (02) 5638611.

When ringing from abroad, omit the '0' in the area code. For overseas calls dial 122, *Larga Distancia Internacional*. Direct dialling is available in large cities, even from card phones in the Metro. All cities and major airports have an *Oficina Pública de CANTV* where operators place your international call while you wait. In Caracas, open 24 hours: CANTV, Edificio Sur, Centro Simón Bolívar, ground floor facing onto Plaza Caracas, (02) 418644; in the east, CANTV, mezzanine, Centro Plaza, Av. Miranda, a block east of the Altamira Metro station. Phone cards are sold here.

When there are long queues for coin phones, a card phone is a blessing (they are good for international calls). Cards may be sold at some CANTV offices (try airports), or at the check-in desk of large hotels. As CANTV has installed new public phones, there are now new *tarjetas magnéticas* as well as old ones; they are not interchangeable.

Chris Stolley adds his telephone warning: 'Do not count on being able to communicate by phone. Distances between working telephones are often great, the person who answers your call will probably speak Spanish only, or perhaps some English, and shouting is often necessary to be heard over a pay phone. As an added quirk, due to inflation it is almost impossible to insert coins into the box fast enough so that the call does not cut off; you need a second person to feed the coins. New phones are currently being installed in Caracas and Margarita that will accept larger coins and that use a new type of magnetic card (NOT compatible with the older phones). In rural areas card phones are rare (and rarely working), so forget it.'

Telex   Public service is available in Caracas at the CANTV office in the Centro Simón Bolívar, and in the Centro Ciudad Comercial Tamanaco, nivel C-1.

BANKS

Banks are open Mon. to Fri. 8.30-11.30 and 14.00-16.30. Except for regular clients, banks do not like to exchange cash pounds or dollars, and some make life difficult for holders of travellers cheques, refusing to change more than $200 and demanding proof of purchase. The Banco Unión handles Visa and Banco Consolidado American Express. However, there are many exchange houses in Caracas. Thomas Cook is represented by Turismo Maso, Edif. Seguros Adriatico, Plaza Altamira Norte.

'Whereas other banks told me it takes hours, days, to clear credit cards, confirmation was fast at the Banco Union, Av.Este 2, Caracas (NE of Bellas Artes station). They clear Visa, Master, Access.' (P.Ireland) Many banks such as the Union have cash points. 'In Mérida, just down the road from Plaza Bolívar, the Banco Unión has a cashpoint machine which accepts Visa and gives bolívars.' (A. Vickers)

ACCOMMODATION AND FOOD

Lodging

Visitors from abroad are required to pay a 10% surcharge on tourist-class hotel rooms. The government classifies hotels by the star system. Should you have a complaint, you must make it in writing to Corpoturismo, Depto. de Hoteles, piso 35, Torre Oeste, Parque Central. To secure a reservation, put down a deposit 4 to 6 weeks ahead. There is a prepaid reservation service for some 200 of the country's best hotels: Fairmont Reserv-Hotel, ground floor, Torre Capriles, Plaza Venezuela, (02) 7817091/8277), open Mon.-Fri. 8.00 to 18.00, Sat. 9.00 to 15.00. In any event, even paid vouchers should be reconfirmed at peak times such as summer holidays, New Year's and Carnival.

At the other end of the market, there are plenty of cheap hotels and *pensiones* for $8. This will buy you a room with dim lighting, an indifferent mattress and bathroom with shower. $15 usually secures a double room with private bath. In Venezuela *una habitación doble* means twin beds, while a *matrimonial* is a double bed. Some places may turn out to be *hoteles de cita*, also known as *mataderos* or slaughterhouses, where guests by the hour are preferred.

Camping is reasonably safe away from main roads, in the Gran Sabana, the Llanos, Andes and parks. Exceptions are beaches near towns. When possible, ask a local dweller for camping permission; this will usually give you protection. However, do not leave your tent unattended.

Local dishes

'Buen provecho' means *bon appetit* and in Venezuela many satisfying popular foods are almost made to order for travellers. *Arepas* are a national staple. These hot maize buns make a great meal-in-a-snack when stuffed with cheese, meat, avocado, chicken or any of a dozen other fillings. Another good snack is a *cachapa* which is a fresh maize pancake, usually served with white cheese. Such cheese is called *queso de mano* in the Guayana and *queso guayanés* in Caracas, and when it is fresh *queso guayanés* is truly excellent. *Hallacas* are a savory Christmas speciality of maize flour, chicken, olives and pork, all steamed, wrapped and tied in banana leaves, ready to travel. *Empanadas* (fried turnovers) are the cheapest of popular snacks, a bit greasy.

Discover the dozens of fresh juices called *batidos* (with sugar and water depending on fruit) liquefied on the spot — pineapple, mango, tangerine, guava, grape, even 3-in-1 made of carrot, orange and beetroot. Bakeries sell processed juices, chocolate milk and, also in a carton, *chicha*, a rice/milk drink which is sweet, soothing and custardy. Also nutritious traveller's food are guava bars, sold in supermarkets as *bocadillos de guayaba*. They are pure fruit and sugar. You can find tins of delicious guava shells in syrup, *cascos de guayaba*, a treat when accompanied by cream cheese.

Venezuelan cooking is simple and tasty, relying on seasonings such as bay, coriander leaf and garlic rather than hot peppers. Choose the 'national dish' called *pabellón* which combines *carne mechada*, appetising shredded beef, tasty fried *tajadas* or cooking bananas (*plátanos*) and black beans, the *caraotas negras* so cherished by Venezuelans. On the coast, sample excellent fish such as *pargo* (red snapper), *mero* (grouper) or *carite* (kingfish). Trout from the Andes, shipped frozen to Caracas, is very good. Generous grilled steak and sausages are served as *parrillada* accompanied by fried yuca (avoid *bistek* which is tough fried meat, not to be compared with beef steak.) Most towns have chicken rotisseries preparing succulent *pollo a la brasa*. Variety is added by many reliable Italian, Spanish and Chinese restaurants.

In small towns the rib-sticker is a bowl of *hervido*, a stew of hen, beef or fish with chunks of onions, yuca (manioc), yam and other roots such as *apio, mapuey* and *ocumo* (dasheen) or pumpkin. Although these roots are called *verduras*, there is little green in most Venezuelans' diet which relies heavily on rice and spaghetti. Traditional staples are regional: in the centre, maize; in the Andes, potatoes; in the east and south, yuca (manioc). *Casabe* is made of bitter yuca, grated, pressed and dried (the poisonous juices become harmless when cooked). Casabe, although nearly tasteless, qualifies as the early Indian invention of preserved food. Justine Freeth said, 'In England we were vegetarians, but after spending months in Paria, we were ready to eat anything except roots!'

Coffee

Coffee-drinking is an art mastered by Venezuelans. And Venezuelan coffee compares well with the best in the world. In the shops a pound of coffee costs the equivalent of a dollar.

The owner of the remotest farm or mining camp is proud to share hospitality, often a tiny cup of coffee. Over a wood fire the cook makes *café de olla*, bringing the coffee, sugar and water to a boil and letting the grounds settle to make a basic, rewarding brew. In the towns or *pueblos* drip coffee or *café colado* is traditional for its smoothness. The stronger Italian-style coffee is called *café de maquina* and is popular in cities where espresso machines are installed in every coffee bar.

A Caraqueño when ordering coffee does not just ask for *un café* but a certain kind or colour. Black can be *negro, negrito*; long or short — *largo* or *corto*; strong — *fuerte, cargado*; bitter — *amango, cerrero*; weak — *suave, claro*; thin — *guayoyo*; weak and sweet — *guarapo*. Plain coffee with milk is *café con leche*, but it can also be a darker brown — *marrón*, or *marrón claro*, or topped with cream like a rich *capuchino*.

HOLIDAYS

Venezuelans are serious about holidays. Families migrate to the coast during the best beach vacations (January-May). Traffic in Caracas is frantic, roads are clogged, bus and plane terminals are swamped. If you are travelling during these periods, wait for people to leave the city and then you *may* find transportation. On New Year's Day, even petrol stations close.

If a red-letter day falls on a Thursday or Tuesday, many people make a *puente* to take a 4-day weekend. This makes it difficult to keep appointments. In December, government offices close early, working from about 7.30 to 15.30. From Dec.18 on, rule out all ideas of business. The same applies to the day or two before Carnival weekend and to Easter week when many shops are shut. At such times, banks open normally until the legal holiday. However, if you should find banks mysteriously closed on a Monday, this is because they observe religious feast days (not listed below) by taking off the following Monday.

January 1:	New Year's Day
Carnival:	Monday and Tuesday before Lent
Easter:	Holy Thursday and Friday
April 19:	Proclamation of Independence
May 1:	Labour Day
June 24:	Battle of Carabobo
July 5:	Independence
July 24:	Bolívar's Birth
October 12:	Columbus' Day (Día de la Raza)
December 25:	Christmas Day

Chapter 3

National Parks and special interests

National Parks

Venezuela has an impressive 39 National Parks (four new ones were created in June 1991) and over 50 Natural Monuments, including 25 table mountains. All told, these cover 147,198 km² — representing 16% of the country. They are administered by the Ministerio del Ambiente y Recursos Naturales Renovables (MARNR), through the Instituto Nacional de Parques, known as Inparques. Enquiries should be addressed to the office in charge which is called the Dirección de Parques Nacionales, Av. Rómulo Gallegos, (02) 2854106/4360, by the north exit of the Parque del Este Metro station. They have a list of parks and monuments with the name and address of the regional director of each park. Parques Nacionales have an Avila map for sale; also some T-shirts.

Permits

Parques Nacionales' headquarters are open 8.30-12.30, 13.30-17.00 (in December no lunch hour, but early closing). In parks such as the Avila and Guatopo where rangers (*guardaparques*) are on duty, permits are issued at the park itself. If you are just hiking, permits may not be required. If you are camping, request a *permiso de pernoctar* (Bs.100 daily per tent). For hiking, a free *permiso de excursionismo* is issued on the spot in Caracas; you need only present passports for your group. This permit may cover several weeks and various parks (for instance, specify Sierra Nevada, Canaima). Backpackers have found the *excursionismo* permit useful when booking the Avensa flight to Canaima. Until park regulations are published, no permits are being issued for 'tepui' expeditions, so don't ask. In the meantime, people still fly to Canaima/Angel Falls and bus/trek to Roraima without formal permits.

People planning a scientific, filming, caving or diving

(*submarinismo*) expedition in a national park should request permission 60 days in advance from the Director, Arq. Mario Gabaldón, Parques Nacionales. List your objectives, group members including passport numbers, and Venezuelan affiliations.

Travel in Amazonas State, south of La Esmeralda, is restricted. Direct all enquiries to a new office called SADA in the same Parques Nacionales building: Servicio Autónomo para el Desarrollo Ambiental de Amazonas, (02) 4081822/1026; Dr W.Frank.

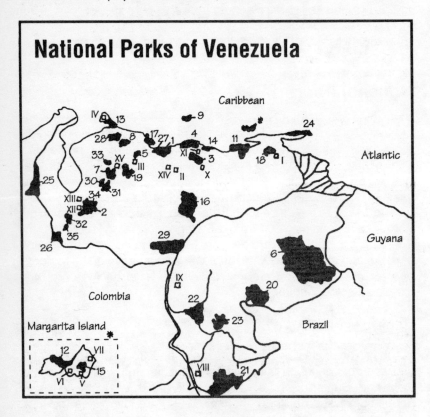

National Parks of Venezuela

NATIONAL PARKS

1. Henri Pittier	7. Yacambú
2. Sierra Nevada	8. Cueva de la Quebrada del
3. Guatopo	Toro
4. El Avila	9. Archipiélago Los Roques
5. Yurubí	10. Macarao
6. Canaima	11. Mochima

12.	Laguna de la Restinga	26.	El Táma
13.	Médanos de Coro	27.	San Esteban
14.	Laguna de Tacarigua	28.	Sierra de San Luis
15.	Cerro El Copey	29.	Cinaruco-Capanaparo
16.	Aguaro Guariquito	30.	Guaramacal
17.	Morrocoy	31.	Dinira
18.	El Guácharo	32.	Páramos Batallón La Negra
19.	Terepaima	33.	Saroche
20.	Jaua-Sarisariñama	34.	Sierra La Culata
21.	Serranía de la Neblina	35.	Chorro El Indio
22.	Yapacana	36.	Turuépano
23.	Duida-Marahuaca	37.	Mariusa
24.	Península de Paria	38.	Ciénaga del Catatumbo
25.	Perijá	39.	Parima-Tapirapeco

NATURAL MONUMENTS

I	Cueva del Guácharo	IX	Cerro Autana
II	Morros de San Juan	X	Morros de Macaira
III	Maria Lionza	XI	Cueva Alfredo Jahn
IV	Cerro Santa Ana	XII	Laguna de Urao
V	Laguna de las Marites	XIII	La Chorrera de las
VI	Las Tetas de María		González
	Guevara	XIV	Platillón
VII	Cerros Matasiete y	XV	Loma de León
	Guayamurí	XVI-XL	Tepuis (25)
VIII	Piedra del Cocuy	XLI	Pico Codazzi

Fishing permits

Seasonal permits for *pesca deportiva* are to be issued by local parks offices in Morrocoy, Mochima, Tacarigua and Los Roques. The permit specifies each species' limit and minimum size. For information about fees, by boat and by permit, enquire at Parques Nacionales, attention Midiam Biscochea. Allow 48 hours for this permit. For rivers and lakes outside of parks, permits are issued by Pesca Deportiva, Ministerio de Agricultura y Cría, Torre Este, Parque Central, 10th floor; (02) 5090276.

Maps

Cartografía Nacional is a bureau of MARNR, the Environment Ministry. They sell 1:100,000 and 1:50,000 maps and if the supply is out they will make photocopies. Cost, about $4. Downtown Caracas address is Edificio Camejo, Av. Este 6 opp. Esquina Colón, (02) 5452122. Metroguía sells the same maps from an outlet in the SW

corridor of La California metro station, (02) 2391622, fax 362437.
Hours: 9.00-13.00, 14.00-18.00; Sat. 9.00-13.00.

NATURE, CONSERVATION GROUPS

Bioma, Edif. Cámara de Comercio de Caracas-piso 4, Av. Este 2,
Los Caobos, (02) 5718831, 5713120; fax 5711412. The Venezuelan
Foundation for the Conservation of Biological Diversity has a good
specialised library and a data bank open to environmental
researchers. Biological stations in Páramo Piedras Blancas (Mérida)
and Monte Cano (Falcón). Regional offices in Mérida: Quinta Irma,
Calle 41 Esquina Avenida 2; tel/fax (074) 638633. Falcón: No. 10 Av.
Arevalo Gonzáles con Calle Páez, Pueblo Nuevo, (069) 81048. Lara:
Edif. Torre Centro, Oficina 4- C, Barquisimeto, (051) 313932, fax
314132.

Pro Vita, Oficina 106, Nivel 0f-1, Edif. Catuche (entrance by way of
USB-Edif. Tajamar), Parque Central, Caracas, (02) 5762828, fax
5761579. Hours: Mon. to Fri. 8.30-12, 14.30-18.00. The group,
headed by Jon Paul Rodríguez, includes many university students
dedicated to protecting endangered species such as the manatee,
spectacled bear, Margarita parrot. Pro Vita will serve as liaison for
scientific expeditions from abroad; write Apartado 47552, Caracas
1041A. Wildlife T-shirts. Quarterly bulletin in Spanish.

Sociedad Conservacionista Audubon de Venezuela, Centro
Comercial Paseo Las Mercedes, opp. Tamanaco Hotel, Caracas, (02)
9932525. In far right corner of La Cuadra mall; Mon. to Fri. 9.00-
12.30, 14.30-18.00. Non-members may buy books in English and
Spanish on Venezuela, biology, neotropics; some maps too.
Lectures/audiovisuals on nature (not only birds) are open without
charge; ring SCAV for place and time, usually third Thursday of the
month. Members organise camping or hiking trips (these are not
free) to mountains, caves, parks. These friendly people are usually
willing to give advice; you can help their finances by making some
purchases.

Sociedad Conservacionista de Aragua, Vereda 6 Sector 2, Urb.
Caña de Azúcar, Via El Limón, Maracay, (043) 831734; hours 8.30-
17.00. Information about area's parks, forests, nature walks; also
library.

Another active group is the **Sociedad Amigos del Parque Nacional
Henri Pittier**, Apartado Correos 4626, Maracay, Estado Aragua. Ring

director Dr Ernesto Fernández Badillo at (043) 544454, 453470 or fax
25204, for information on Rancho Grande biological station.

SPECIAL INTERESTS, SPORTS

Biking

Cycling in the Andes is made possible by Montaña Tours, Edif. Las
Américas, Av. Las Américas, Mérida; tel/fax (074) 661448. With a
vehicle to carry camping gear, bikers are spared some of the high
altitude grind among the páramos, even crossing to Los Nevados.

   For facts on motorcycling, ask Werner Glöde, Residencia Los
Sauces A-8-1, Valencia 2001, Carabobo; (041) 213007. For many
years Glöde led bikers on 'Venezuela en Motocicleta' tours. Although
high maintenance costs have dampened his enthusiasm, he says
motorcycling is ideal for seeing Venezuela and meeting good
people. If you bring a motorcycle customs agents give less hassle
in Margarita (avoid Puerto Cabello); no problems were reported by
a tourist who rolled in from Curaçao via the Coro ferry.

Birding

Read *Birding in Venezuela* (available from SCAV — see above) and
Mary Lou Goodwin's checklists for various national parks, and head
for the *monte* on your own. If needed, Audubon will make an
itinerary based on interests and season. The society charges a 10%
fee for arranging hotels, guides, car rental. Write Apartado Postal
80450, Caracas 1080A; fax (58 2) 910716.

Caving

Venezuela has over 1,500 caves. The Grupo Espeleológico of the
Venezuelan Society of Natural Sciences is the senior scientific
organisation. Contact: Eugenio De Bellard, SVCN, Edif. Sociedad de
Ciencias Naturales, Calle Cumaco, El Marqués, Caracas, (02)
217579, 217653.

   An active group of young cavers forms the Sociedad Venezolana
de Espeleología which meets every other week at Edif. Vorako
(sótano LE), Av. Caurimare, Colinas de Bello Monte, Caracas. For
information write Apartado 47334, Caracas 1041A, or ring Francisco
Herrera, (02) 9868630.

On April 1877, *The Spectator* printed the following under the heading
"Will no one explore Roraima?"

"...But if on exploration Roraima proves to be that which one dreams
it may, a question may arise whether it would not be worthy of modern
civilisation to secure its preservation... by international treaty, in [its]
privemal condition. If only the vegetation of the tertiary age subsists on
those weird summits, its trees have a right not to have their trunks
defaced with civilised "posters", nor their feet strewn with the remains
of civilised picnics - bottled-beer bottles and sardine tins."

Diving

Mike Osborn, Submatur, Calle Ayacucho No. 6, Tucacas, Estado Falcón; (042) 84082. Osborn, a three-star NAUI instructor, gives courses in open water and advanced diving, as well as underwater photography. Submatur, his small dive shop on Tucacas' main street, offers professional equipment and tank fills. He can take divers to the best reefs in Morrocoy National Park or on week-long expeditions to Las Aves Archipelago. Write to Apartado 68512, Caracas 1062A; fax (02) 9414939.

In Caracas, members of the Caraquáticos Scuba Diving Club meet regularly to plan dives (see *The Daily Journal* community page). Certified instruction, equipment and tank fills are offered by Marina Divers, Quinta 1408, Avenida 6 entre Transversales 3 y 5, Altamira, Caracas; (02) 2615229.

Hiking

In its five decades, the Centro Excursionista Caracas has trekked most of Venezuela's best trails. The walkers — of many nationalities — go out on Sundays, often to the Avila. For details of monthly programme ring Sr. Enrique Herrera, (02) 292-3747.

In Mérida, learn about high Andes hiking through the Grupo Andino de Rescate, Facultad de Ciencias Forestales, Universidad de Los Andes, Mérida. Or, on arrival, ask for similar organisations listed at tourism information booths in bus and air terminals.

Paragliding

Instructor Jimmy Marull, (02) 7526028, is the country's top ultra-light pilot and paraglider. Flights are scaled according to experience; advanced groups travel distances to catch thermals. Basic paragliding or ultra-light flying in a 2-week course with theory; also in Puerto La Cruz.

Sailing, water sports

A mine of information on regattas, fishing tournaments, kayaking, anything on water including the annual 1000-mile river rally *'Nuestros ríos son navegables'*, is available through a bimonthly magazine in Spanish: *Caza y Pesca, Naútica*, Edif. Continental, Oficina 8-A, Av. Los Jabillos at Boulevard Sabana Grande, Caracas; (02) 729489.

Shell collecting

The Venezuelan Society of Malacology unites professionals and amateurs. They meet in Caracas on the 15th of every month. Ring Dr Rafael Martínez, president, (02) 7527141; or Dr Santiago Rodolfo, secretary, (02) 414936.

SECTION TWO

CARACAS AND REGION

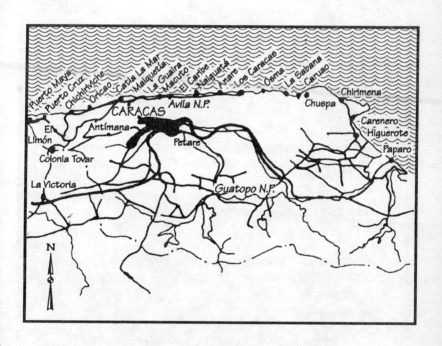

Cumbre de La Silla, Avila, climbed by Humboldt in 1800.

Chapter 4

Caracas

THE CAPITAL

Some people say Caracas is a horrible sprawl, others admire its air of sophistication; some say it's not a city at all but a once-fertile valley ringed by *ranchitos*, while others swear by its sunny climate and superb mountains. Like most big cities — and the metropolitan area is heading for 5,000,000 inhabitants — Caracas has its good and bad points. A passing acquaintance is necessary as most people will arrive in Venezuela via the capital, and it is the starting point of many air and road routes and the hub for tours to beaches, plains, the Andes, even nature reserves and southern jungles.

Not a place for walkers, Caracas is an inconvenient city. Its topography goes from long and narrow to high and twisty, with bottlenecks everywhere, and its traffic jams are infamous. Mail is slow (never rely on letters within the city), telephones fail to communicate three times out of five, and bureaucracy prevents you from getting anything done in a single visit. On weekends all banks and travel agencies, and most post offices are closed; if you want an air ticket, you must go to the airport. (The airport, by the way, is one of the few places with public toilets; travellers are otherwise hard pressed.)

Finding your way

In Caracas north is always where the big mountain is, so your compass points are never out of order if you can see the Avila. The telephone company publishes a map section at the back of the Caracas directory.

The city's heart is the old sector around Plaza Bolívar. All streets started at this central square in colonial times when Caracas was laid out in *cuadras*. A fifth part of a block was called a *quinta*, a name used today to mean a house with garden. Above Plaza Bolívar

Metro system in the year 2000

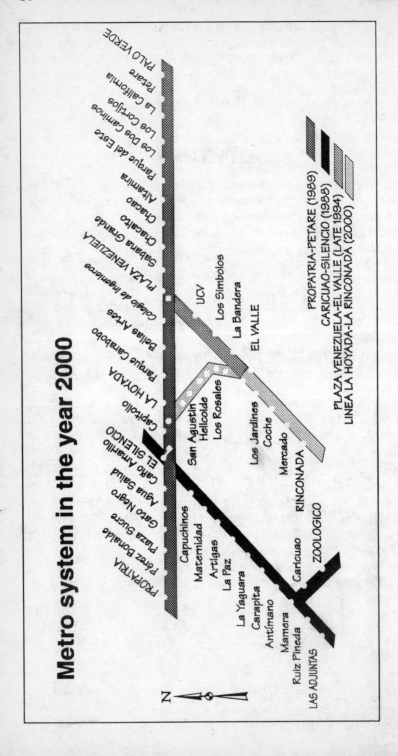

N

PALO VERDE
Petare
La California
Los Cortijos
Los Dos Caminos
Parque del Este
Altamira
Chacao
Chacaíto
Sabana Grande
PLAZA VENEZUELA
Colegio de Ingenieros
Bellas Artes
Parque Carabobo
LA HOYADA
Capitolio
EL SILENCIO
Caño Amarillo
Agua Salud
Gato Negro
Plaza Sucre
Pérez Bonalde
PROPATRIA

Capuchinos
Maternidad
Artigas
La Paz
La Yaguara
Carapita
Antímano
Mamera
Ruiz Pineda
LAS ADJUNTAS

San Agustín
Hellcolde
Los Rosales

UCV
Los Símbolos
La Bandera
EL VALLE

Los Jardines
Coche
Mercado
RINCONADA

Caricuao
ZOOLOGICO

PROPATRIA-PETARE (1989)
CARICUAO-SILENCIO (1988)
PLAZA VENEZUELA-EL VALLE (LATE 1994)
LINEA LA HOYADA-LA RINCONADA (2000)

all east-west *calles* are named Este (or Oeste) 1, 3, 5, 7, while below they are called Este (or Oeste) 2, 4, 6, 8, with 0 street being Calle Este-Oeste along the top of Plaza Bolívar. Avenida Norte-Sur runs up past the cathedral; to the west are Avenidas 2, 4, 6, and to the east are Avenidas 1, 3, 5, 7. Avenida Norte-Sur turns into the fancy new Simón Bolívar Boulevard at the top by the Pantheon.

Downtown locations, however, are commonly given by the nearest corner. Every corner has a name and a story. The Central Post Office is at Esquina Carmelitas, named after a Carmelite convent; El Conde Hotel is on the corner of the same name where the counts of La Granja once lived; and the National Library is between the corners of La Bolsa (the Exchange) and San Francisco (a church). If you cannot find El Silencio on your map although posted as the destination of many buses, it is because the corner was demolished in the 1940s to make way for the city's first urban renewal, the four-storey apartment buildings and shops with white colonnades. Today, renewal by the Metro has restored El Silencio's pride, the dolphin fountains by Francisco Narváez in Plaza O'Leary.

The Metro

A sparkling underground system, already the longest in South America and still abuilding, the Metro is the saviour of Caracas, making up for chaos above ground (no smoking, please, and — officially — no suitcases). It's beautiful, it makes people smile, it restores Venezuelans' faith that something works. And it makes crossing the city, 40km from Propatria in the west to Palo Verde in the east, fun, fast and cheap. Line 3 from Plaza Venezuela to El Valle is being added to Line 1 Propatria-Petare and Line 2 Caricuao-El Silencio.

Transfer tickets (*boletos integrados*) allow you to travel on surface Metrobuses. These lines link the subway with northern districts such as San Bernardino, Altamira and El Marqués, and southern areas such as Cafetal, La Trinidad and Colinas de Bello Monte. Area and route maps are posted in stations.

The Metro operates between 5.30 and 23.00 hours. A 3-station ticket costs Bs.10 ($0.15). If you have a fistful of coins, you can avoid queuing. Better still, buy a *multiviaje* ticket for Bs.130 which is good for 10 rides anywhere. Keep your ticket after going through the turnstile because you need it to get out. For cultural events and other information, write to CAMETRO, Edif. Miranda B-7, Multicentro Empresarial del Este, Chacao, Caracas 1060 (public relations — 2082740).

Warning: People riding Metro escalators have had necklaces and wallets taken. A frequent ruse involves two men, one ahead who trips or bends down in front of the victim, the other snatching the valuables.

EXPLORING CARACAS BY METRO

Colonial history, museums, theatres, cafés, shops and parks crowd along Line 1 of the Metro. This is the best way to see the city's points of interest. Except where noted, museums are open Tue. to Sat. 9.00-12.00, 14.30-17.00; Sun. 10.00-17.00. The only museums open at lunchtime are the Contemporary Arts and the Boulton History Museum. On Mondays public places are closed for maintenance, except for the Boulton History Museum and the Botanical Gardens.

History

I offer no apologies for the large dose of Simón Bolívar here. The places where this intense, passionate young man lived reveal an era whose traces have all but vanished in Caracas. Moreover, he means so much to Venezuelans. A town is not a town until it has a Plaza Bolívar — as you will inevitably see.

Start downtown at the **Capitolio** station. If you have time, walk a couple of blocks west for a hilltop view from **El Calvario**, once the town limit. From the top of its steep steps you can see how Caracas has grown eastwards. The Cathedral and the colonial grid around Plaza Bolívar were laid out in 1567 by Spanish founder Diego de Losada. In the north is the 19th Century **Miraflores Palace,** now office of the President of the Republic. The eastern skyline is dominated by office blocks, notably the **Centro Simón Bolívar**. Its twin towers, symbol of Caracas in the 1950s-70s, have been outstripped by the 56-storey octagonal towers of **Parque Central**, also government built. Fifty years ago Caracas ended at the coffee hacienda of Los Caobos, today a park. San Bernardino, another hacienda at the foot of the Avila, was just being built up. Sabana Grande was a plain popular for horse racing. Beyond, trains linked Caracas with the villages of Chacao and Petare in Miranda State.

From **Capitolio** station, walk to the Cathedral, town hall and places famous as settings of Simón Bolívar's birth, boyhood and burial. **Plaza Bolívar** makes a perfect meeting place with its spreading shade, its pigeons, squirrels and sloths. The martial band plays here on Sunday mornings. As old as Caracas itself, the square has had many guises; it was the Plaza de Armas where rebels were hanged, later a marketplace, a bullfight plaza, and in republican times the Plaza La Constitución. It became Plaza Bolívar on the centennial of the Liberator's birth. That was in 1883, when the famous equestrian statue by Adam Tadolini was ordered. A copy of one in Lima, the statue was cast in Munich and shipped in pieces; but the brig foundered on Los Roques and the boxes had to be fished out of the sea. It was finally unveiled in November 1874 by President A. Guzmán Blanco who had a 'time box' containing coins, documents and a map sealed into its base.

Anticlockwise around the Plaza are: north, **Federal District Government House**, where occasional exhibits are open to the public; west, the **Casa Amarilla**, seat of the Foreign Ministry, once infamous as a 17th Century royal prison and later a presidential residence; SW corner, **Edificio La Francia** — nine floors of gold and jewellery dealers, both wholesale and retail; south, the **Concejo Municipal** or Town Council which has a Caracas Museum of miniatures of 1920s daily scenes. Ask to see the council's handsomely restored Santa Rosa Chapel, known as the 'cradle of Independence' because congress declared Independence here on July 5 1811. The chapel served as a seminary in the 17th Century and the University of Caracas in the 18th Century.

The **Caracas Cathedral** has had many lives since the city was founded in 1567. It began as a mud-walled chapel dedicated to St. James of Santiago, patron of Caracas. The church which replaced it was destroyed by the 1641 earthquake. It was rebuilt with a belltower in 1674 and has been remodelled since. The cathedral holds many treasures, not the least being an altar gilded with 300oz of Mexican gold, paintings by Rubens (Resurrection), Murillo (Presentation of the Virgin) and Michelena, whose 'Last Supper' was his last, unfinished work. The Bolívar family chapel holds the tombs of Bolívar's Spanish wife, who died when Simón was 18, his father who died when Simón was 2½, and his mother who died when he was 9. Open daily 6.30-11.30 (Sun. to 14.00); and 15.00-20.00.

Bolívar's remains, brought from Colombia where he died penniless in 1830, were buried in the Cathedral until their removal in 1876 to the **National Pantheon**, six blocks north. Every 25 years the President of the Republic opens the casket below the monument by Pietro Tenerani to verify that the Liberator's remains are undisturbed. One of the five people buried with Bolívar in the central nave is his Irish aide-de-camp, Daniel O'Leary. Ceiling paintings are by Tito Salas.

In all, 130 founding fathers and national figures have tombs in the Pantheon. Two empty tombs await the remains of Francisco de Miranda who died in a Spanish prison and Antonio José de Sucre, assassinated in Colombia. Tradition has it that when the original church (completed the year of Bolívar's birth) was destroyed in the 1812 earthquake, part of a pillar rolled downhill to the Plaza where, in smashing the gallows, it gave the revolutionaries a moral boost.

The **Casa Natal** on Plaza San Jacinto is the house where Simón Bolívar was born on July 24 1783, fourth child of a patrician couple. Reconstructed after neglect by several owners, the Casa Natal is a tourist 'must', a block east and south of Plaza Bolívar. Here, and next door at the **Museo Bolivariano**, are housed Bolívar's uniform and documents, Independence memorabilia, period weapons and furniture.

(More charming in its authenticity, walled gardens, patios and stables, is the Bolívar family's summer home known as the **Cuadra Bolívar** at Esquina Bárcenas. This is a highly recommended detour, 8 long blocks due south of Plaza Bolívar. Near the erstwhile Guaire River, farmlands and riding paths once offered young Simón and his friends room for conspiracy.)

San Francisco Church, a block SW of Plaza Bolívar on Av. Universidad, also figures in Bolívar's career. Founded as a monastery in 1575 and rebuilt after the 1641 earthquake, the church was the setting for the proclamation of Bolívar, aged 30, as Liberator.

Today it seems miraculous that so young and slight a man should have been instrumental in freeing **Venezuela, Colombia, Ecuador, Peru** and **Bolivia**, a new state named for him. Fighting with ragged patriots, from the Caribbean to the Chilean border and from the Pacific to the boundary of Brazil, Bolívar sacrificed his health, dying of TB in Colombia in 1830. When his remains were repatriated in 1842, the streets, houses and churches of Caracas were draped in black for the biggest ceremony ever held: the Liberator's funeral at San Francisco Church.

To visit the gilt-domed **Capitol**, its cool gardens and the ceremonial oval hall called the Salón Elíptico, show your passport to guards at the west gate. The oval hall, where the Declaration of Independence is kept, is noted for Tovar y Tovar's ceiling murals of the Battle of Carabobo. The Capitol's ironwork was brought from England and the dome from Belgium. You may also visit the bicameral Legislative Palace at the southern end when Congress is in session; it was built in 1874 in a record 114 days.

From the Capitol it is two blocks up to the Post Office at Esquina Carmelitas on Urdaneta Avenue (daily 7.00-18.30; Sat. 7.00-16.30). Bureaucracy has left little of the former 18th Century mansion, once home of the Count of Tovar. Opposite, you may want to see the Banco Central's display of coins on the mezzanine, also Bolívar's sword and jewels. Or you can walk from the BCV three blocks west to **Miraflores Palace**, built in the 1880s, now the President's offices; but you may not photograph the building or the guards.

Near the Metro's **La Hoyada** station is a museum worth visiting before you leave downtown. The Fundación John Boulton, (02) 5631838/4829, runs an excellent **Museo de Historia** and library on the 11th floor of Torre El Chorro at the SW corner of Esquina El Chorro, Av. Universidad. Collected by the family of British merchant John Boulton (1805 to 1875) are rare china, portraits, and

Venezuelan documents. Don't miss engravings of Liberator-inspired fashions in Europe — double-tiered cape, *pantalon americaine* tights, the 'Bolívar hat'. Daily 8.30-16.00; weekends 9.30 to 13.30 with guided tours.

Art, music and museums

Many of Venezuela's leading artists have made pieces for the Metro. You can combine culture and communications along Line 1 where murals, stained glass windows and sculptures of many schools enliven the stations. Some stations even stage exhibitions and concerts.

If you are travelling west from the centre, note Marisol Escobar's bronze tribute to the hero of tangos in her 'Monument to Gardel' outside the **Caño Amarillo** station. A giant steel serpent and hummingbird by a team of artists, Sanabria/Silvestro/Zamalloa, grabs attention outside the **Gato Negro**. *Por puestos* run from this station to Maquetía. Striking an apparently impossible balance near the **Plaza Sucre** station in Catia is Rafael Barrios' 'Levitation', a tower of five iron cubes. The Catia Boulevard and Plaza Sucre, like the Sabana Grande Boulevard, are urban renewal gifts from the Metro to the pedestrians of Caracas.

Downtown, **La Hoyada** station has an exhibition hall for art and orchid shows. Among works commissioned for this station is a four-part stained glass window by Mercedes Pardo. On a lower plaza stands one of Francisco Narvaez' last works in Cumarebo stone blocks. This stop is linked to the Nuevo Circo bus terminal by a passage under Fuerzas Armadas Avenue. At the **Parque Carabobo** station, a ceramic bas relief by Rita Daini, portraying 'Caraqueños in the Metro', makes a gentle comment at the station's entrance. From this stop it is an easy walk north to **Plaza La Candelaria**, a district famous for small, crowded Spanish restaurants and tasca bars where beer flows freely. The parish has long been an enclave of Basques, Canary Islanders and Galicians. Among their most popular spots are La Cita, La Tertulia, Guernica, Don Quijote, the Bar Basque, La Carabela and the Club Cultural Candelaria. As lively as this area is by day, it has a reputation of being unsafe at night.

Get off at the **Bellas Artes** station for events at the Ateneo Theatre, Teresa Carreño concert hall, Fine Arts Museum, National Gallery, Los Caobos Park, Hilton Hotel, Contemporary Art Museum and Parque Central.

Parque Central is a concrete enclave where, it was advertised, 'nothing resembles the past'. You may not be attracted to the idea of seven 44-storey condominiums housing 10,000 people, but the development is undeniably conspicuous. In contrast, the hills directly

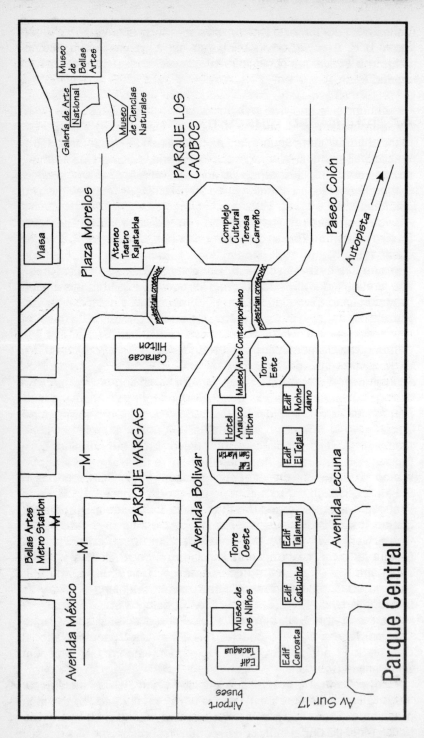

to the south are covered with *ranchitos* — huts, some rented, some better built than others. Nearly half of all Caraqueños live in precarious conditions of hygiene and security in such districts called *barrios*. The government-built complex, started in 1970 and finished in 1986, has schools, supermarkets, swimming pool, cinema, convention halls and five museums, of which the **Museo de Arte Contemporaneo** and **Museo del Niño** (see below) are of real importance. Other museums include: **Museo del Teclado** (5720713), a recital hall and collection of keyboard instruments in Edif. Tacagua, mezz., west of the Children's Museum; **Museo Audiovisual**, mainly a video library with auditoriums and booths for projections in Edif. Catuche, Nivel Bolívar; **Museo Criminologico** (5719001), a small showcase of weapons, forgeries, run by the Centre of Criminological Studies of Simón Bolívar University, Edif. Tajamar, Level Oficina 1, Room 118.

Parque Central's 56-storey towers are the tallest in the country. The penthouse of the East Tower is occupied by the Ministry of Transport and Communications. It is sometimes possible to get permission to go up to the top for a view. (The MTC has an information service, 5091711; road condition inquiries, 5091601.)

Among government offices in the East Tower are: **Aeropostal** on Nivel Lecuna, 5746511, for local and international flights; the Agriculture Ministry (MAC), 5090111, which issues permits for sport fishing, 10th floor, 5090276. In the West Tower are: the Mines and Energy Ministry with a library on 2nd floor, 5075080; and **Corpoturismo** where a Tourist Services desk receives written complaints, 35th floor, 5078611/2; also a library on 36th floor.

Museo de Arte Contemporaneo (Museum of Contemporary Art), 5634602, 5638289.   From its entrance on the NE corner of Parque Central beside the Anauco Hilton, down to its basement exit on Sótano 1, MACC displays some of the continent's finest exhibitions (Tue. to Sun. 10.00-18.00). Its permanent collection includes Botero's 2-metre fat cat in bronze, works by Maillol, Calder, Moore, Picasso, Leger and many top-notch Venezuelans including Gego, Marisol, Soto (whose kinetic pieces are also found in the nearby Estudio 1, Edif. Mohedano, Nivel Lecuna). MACC also offers an excellent reference library of art books and audiovisuals, and a classy gift shop on Sótano 1.

Museo de los Niños (Children's Museum), 5734112. Housed in a tri-colour building all its own, this is a very popular hands-on museum of fun & learning, often so full at holiday time you must buy tickets in advance. There is a small entrance charge (Wed. to Sun. 9.00-12.00, 14.00-17.00).

Other nearby museums

Cross the avenue east of Parque Central and head up towards the
Ateneo and Plaza Morelos. The **Museo de Bellas Artes**, 5737035,
is actually in Los Caobos Park; in the rear is a pleasant sculpture
garden. Major shows are held in the four-storey building designed
by Carlos Raul Villanueva, Venezuelan architect whose career began
in the 1930s with the neoclassical columns of the **Galeria de Arte
Nacional**, 5713519, facing the circular plaza. Opposite the National
Gallery is its lookalike, the **Museo de Ciencias Naturales** or Natural
History Museum, 5711265.

Museo de Arte Colonial (Colonial Art Museum), 518517. Known also
as **Quinta Anauco**, this house dating from 1797 is located on Av.
Panteón in San Bernardino. Of all museums in Caracas, it is likely to
be the most enjoyable. Set aside two hours to explore the former
country residence of the Marquis of Toro where lovely gardens and
gracious rooms shut out 20th Century chaos. Its kitchen, stables and
even a bath fed by a stream are a short taxi ride 1½km north of the
Bellas Artes station (ask about Metrobus service). There is a library
of colonial art and history. Evening recitals, folklore music and
Christmas carols are presented free. Tue. to Sat. 9.00-11.30, 14.00-
16.30; Sun. 10.00-16.30.

Theatres, cinemas and concert halls

In the **Bellas Artes** vicinity, opposite the Caracas Hilton, there is a
splendid new performing arts centre, the **Teresa Carreño Concert
Hall**, box office 5749122. The Sala Rios Reyna seats 2,500. Over the
lobby hangs a huge Jesús Soto work in tubes. Next door, the
Ateneo de Caracas, 5734622/32, houses a complete cultural centre
with a concert hall, Rajatabla Theatre, art gallery, cinema, library,
bookshop and cafeteria.

   The area's two low-priced art cinemas are: the **Sala Margot
Benacerraf** at the Ateneo, screenings at 17.00, 19.00 and 21.00; the
Cinemateca Nacional, 5710176, in the Galería de Arte Nacional, Tue.-
Sun. at 18.30 and 21.00, and children's films on Sunday at 11.00.

Midtown: university, cafés, shops

Still by way of the Metro, you arrive at the **Colegio de Ingenieros**
station where Lya Bermúdez' scarlet 'bat wings' loom over the
platform. At the north exit on Av. Libertador, the telephone company,
CANTV, has an art gallery and theatre open to the public. Around
the corner and up to Avenida Andrés Bello, the large **Guaicaipuro**

market spills into the street on Tuesday, Thursday and Saturday mornings. Fresh fruit, vegetables, fish...Chinese slippers, shirts.

Plaza Venezuela station is a block east of the circular plaza and fountain which mark midtown. Artist Carlos Cruz Diez was happy to use the plaza's large ventilation duct for one of his striped 'Fisicromías'. You can't miss Alejandro Otero's 16-metre rig of steel windsails, or the blue and white bars of a big Jesús Soto suspended from Torre Capriles.

Cross over the *autopista* bridge to the **Jardín Botánico**; its entrance is on the right just before the university gate. Like the university, the 150-acre gardens, now planted with palms, lilies, cacti and orchids, once belonged to Hacienda Ibarra. Although one of the few parks open on Mondays, and every day, from 8.00-17.00 (free), the gardens have few visitors. There is a Botanical Institute, 6629254, with a large herbarium.

The **Universidad Central de Venezuela** occupies a large campus. Saunter with some of the 52,000 students, or go to a concert at the 3,000-seat Aula Magna. Its ceiling has acoustic clouds by Alexander Calder, great friend of Carlos Raul Villanueva who designed the university city (1953-55). There are sculptures by Laurens, Arp and Pevsner, murals and stained glass by Leger. Ironically, this bastion of radicals was made possible by dictator Marcos Pérez Jiménez, who also built the cablecar systems in Caracas and Mérida, the race track, the *autopista* to Maiquetía and the Barquisimeto railway.

On the **Boulevard de Sabana Grande** watch Caracas go by...the shoppers, salesmen, office girls, urchins, chess players, hookers...and motorcycle cops. Day and night this pedestrian haven (also called Av. Abraham Lincoln) is a stage to sidewalk café audiences. Open till 2am every night, the Gran Café is king of capuchino coffee. Its marquee (alongside several competitors) is near the old Cine Radio City at the east exit of **Plaza Venezuela** station. There's an excellent chocolate shop, the Savoy, on the next corner at Av. Los Jabillos.

This is the best district for medium-range hotels and good, reasonable restaurants. Italian pasta houses and Spanish tascas line Av. Solano López, north of the boulevard; several hotels are east near Chacaito and south on Avenida Casanova. **Sabana Grande** station is midway; ask about Metrobus lines to Colinas de Bello Monte and Las Mercedes.

The boulevard ends at **Chacaito**, a large paved area. Here the Centro Comercial Chacaito has almost everything: supermarket, nightclubs, theatres, underground cinemas, English books at Librería Lectura, French books at La France, music, art and computer supplies. Good, fast colour developing at Foto Print beside the Papagallo's tables. The Metro has embellished Plaza Chacaito (officially, Plaza Brión) with Soto's 'Vibrant Cubes' of suspended blue and black tubes, Teresa Casanova's steel boxes and, underground, Beatriz Blanco's lively 'Human Silhouettes'.

Within walking distance of Chacaito are the classier dining and clubbing districts of **El Rosal** and **Las Mercedes**. Turn right at the first traffic light on Avenida Miranda. Pricey restaurants line the first and second streets in El Rosal (Avenidas Tamanaco, Venezuela). For Las Mercedes, continue under the *autopista*; restaurants line most of the streets between Avenida Las Mercedes and the Rio Guaire (not a nice river but wild parrots roost in trees here). Paseo Las Mercedes shopping centre and the Tamanaco Hotel are at the end of Avenida Las Mercedes.

Wild and escaped parrots have adopted Caracas

If parrots like Caracas, all is not lost. Every time a band of large, loud yellow-headed parrots cross the eastern sky early in the morning, their squawks and trills send me straight back to the rivers and forests of Amazonas. That's where *Amazona* species belong, not in the capital where space is haggled over by some four million people.

But many parrots, including foreign species and other escapees from houses, have found their niche in Caracas. Watch for the Amazon parrots just before dusk when flocks of thirty or more settle for the night in Las Mercedes in trees lining the Guaire River, little more than a sewer. After all, the trees are not natives either; many are African tulip trees. During the day the parrots fly off to feed on the Avila range or in the Parque del Este where more parrots live. In season, mango trees and palms also provide them food in Caracas.

On a busy corner near a gasoline station in Las Mercedes, I saw a small, brilliant green cloud settle in a *mamón* tree: it was a flock of tiny parrotlets (*Forpus passerinus*). In San Bernardino, late every afternoon a pair of green macaws (*Ara severa*) flies behind an apartment block to roost in a pair of royal palms. Once, at midday, I heard a macaw's screech as I walked by a construction site. The big red bird was perched on a crane.

Not all the parrots are naturalized. Some are migratory, like the maroon-faced parakeets (*Pyrrhura emma*) which visit when palm nuts are ripe, and brown-throated parakeets (*Aratinga pertinax*) which occasionally flock by. These parakeets hollow out nests in large termite mounds on trees, cohabiting peacefully with the insects.

East Caracas — Parque del Este, Petare

The Caracas Country Club starts where Chacaito (and the federal district) ends; in the 1930s its huge trees and golf links really were in the country. Today, they provide some relief from East Caracas' office blocks. The Metro tunnels below Av. Miranda to **Chacao**. Walk north and east two blocks to the church and square where the former village of Chacao, named after an Indian warrior, was founded in 1768. The area's shops offer low-priced shoes, jeans, shirts, and on Thursday mornings the **Chacao market** comes to life on Calle Cecilio Acosta. Chacao is also the station for the Metro offices: 4th floor, Edificio Miranda-B, Centro Empresarial del Este, Avenida Miranda. From the **Altamira station**, south side, Metrobuses leave for Chuao and Cafetal, stopping at the pricey shopping complex called Centro Ciudad Comercial Tamanaco (the British Embassy is in Torre Las Mercedes nearby).

Parque del Este, at the station of the same name, is by far the city's greatest park (gates open 5.30 for joggers and 8.00 for the public, closing whistle 17.30). It's officially Parque Rómulo Betancourt after the president who in 1961 asked Brazilian landscape architect Roberto Burle Marx to transform this old coffee hacienda. The 200 acres of walks, lawns and woods brim with people on Sundays, but on Mondays they are closed for clean-up and by Tuesday the park is trim and watered, serene again. Storks, egrets and parrots breed freely here and some fly out during the day. There is a monkey island, an otter pool, a snake house, an anaconda moat, an aviary and a lagoon with scarlet ibis. There is a replica of Columbus' ship, the 'Santa María', an acoustic shell for outdoor shows, and a **Humboldt Planetarium**, 349188, which has programmes on Sat. at 17.00, Sun. hourly from 12.00-17.00.

The **Transport Museum**, 341621, is reached by a pedestrian bridge from the park's east parking lot. Its collection of railroad steam engines, old cars and planes opens Sat.& Sun. 10.00-17.00, and for kids only on Wed. 9.00-16.00. Adjoining this museum is the Instituto Nacional de Parques, 2843266. Inparques oversees all parks, and delegates national parks management to a separate office (see National Parks).

South of the Metro stop called **Los Dos Caminos** are the barracks and presidential residence called **La Casona**, at the end of Av. Principal de La Carlota. But high walls prevent you from seeing the 18th Century plantation house, chapel or gardens. There is a somewhat lengthy process for permission to tour La Casona: first, ring 2846322 and ask for Protocol; you will be requested to bring round the names and passport numbers of your group, and you may be given a date in a week.

After Los Dos Caminos, the Metro continues through drab industrial areas such as Los Ruices, **Los Cortijos** and Boleita. At **La California** there is a big shopping centre, Unicentro El Marqués.

Crowning a hill by the Metro's next-to-last stop is the colonial centre of **Petare**, founded 1621. Leave Caracas behind as you walk up the old Spanish road to the village square; for a change this is Plaza Sucre, not Bolívar. The Town Council is on the north side. A handsomely restored pink church is called Dulce Nombre de Jesús; the structure dates from 1760. Signs point you to a beautiful colonial house, once the home of patriot Lino de Clemente, Bolívar's uncle, and now the **Petare Museum of Popular Art**, 215363, on Calle Lino de Clemente; open 10.00-18.00 except Mondays. The museum's concerts and art exhibitions are well attended. On the same street are the small Cesar Rengifo Theatre and the Jermán U. Lira Cultural Centre.

I will finish this Metro tour with Z for zoo. The **Caricuao Zoo**, 4312045/9166, is at Caracas' western extreme, at the end of Line 2. In the zoo's 1,200 acres live many native animals and birds without bars, some in mixed groups. Deer wander through woods and overhead are spider and howler monkeys. Wading birds, free to come and go, enjoy ponds. There is an African section with giraffes and rhinos, too. Open Tue. to Sun. 9.00-16.30.

LODGING

Below is a selection of hotels in Caracas, organised by the star system.

***** The deluxe hotels in Caracas sometimes offer surprisingly attractive package prices during holidays such as Christmas and Easter when many Caraqueños leave town. These big hotels are good if you have enough cash left after your travels ($100-150 day) to give yourself a treat with drinks by the pool. The front-runners, Tamanaco Inter-Continental (east/south) and Caracas Hilton (midtown), have been joined by the Eurobuilding, not far from the Tamanaco, and the Melia Caracas on Avenida Casanova in Sabana Grande.

**** Better value is the older Avila Hotel with fewer rooms, more gardens and pool, though less conveniently located in San Bernardino. The Avila charges only $50 a day, double. The President Hotel is well situated near the **Plaza Venezuela** metro, and the Lincoln Suites is on the Boulevard of **Sabana Grande**. About $85. Two others in this group, with swimming pool but no gardens, are located in shopping centres: Hotel Paseo Las Américas near the Tamanaco, and Hotel CCT Venantur in the shopping centre called Ciudad Comercial Tamanaco in Chuao. Any travel agent can make these bookings.

*** For do-it-yourself travellers without expense accounts, the following sample is given with the nearest Metro station (printed in bold type). Currently $30-40 a double, three-star hotels are mostly in business/shopping areas. Near **Chacaito** are: Las Américas, Calle Los Cerritos at Av. Casanova, 9517133, with swimming pool; Montpark, also Calle Los Cerritos, 9515520; El Condor, 3rd Av. Las Delicias de Sabana Grande, 7629911; Karibik, 2nd Av. Las Delicias, 7626606; Plaza Palace, Av. Los Mangos, Las Delicias, 7624821; Savoy, 2nd Av. Las Delicias, 7621971. Near **Sabana Grande** are: the Kursaal, Av. Casanova at Calle Colegio, 7622922; Coliseo, Av. Casanova at Calle 1 de Bello Monte, 7627916/19. In the **Plaza Venezuela** vicinity: Bruno, Av. Sur Las Acacias, 7818444; Luna, Av. Casanova, 7625851; Atlántida, Av. La Salle, Los Caobos, 7933211; Tampa, Av. Solano López, 7623772 (its good service has earned it four stars); and the Odeon, Av. Las Acacias, 7931345. 'We can wholeheartedly recommend the Odeon which seems to be quite new; very important is a laundry facility about 300m south, and opposite, a very good restaurant, Estación de Pollo.' (P.Weinberger)
The Plaza Catedral, next to the Cathedral on Plaza Bolívar, 5642111, is a small hotel near the **Capitolio**. El Conde Hotel, Esq. El Conde, 8622007 is an old standby one block west of Plaza Bolivar. North of **Altamira** station, the Continental Altamira, Av. San Juan Bosco, 2620243/1139, has a pool.

** Two-star hotels charge $15-25 a double. Facing Sur Plaza **Altamira** on Av. Roche are the Hotel La Floresta, 2631955, fax 2621243, and a residential hotel, the Montserrat, 2633533, which has doubles and studio apartments. Both hotels are usually booked solid. The redecorated Hotel Altamira, diagonally south of the Cine Altamira, 314255, has turkish baths. There are many hotels in the **Plaza Venezuela-Sabana Grande** district: Hotel Plaza Venezuela, Av. La Salle, 7817811; City, Av. Bolivia next to the Previsora building, 7930753; King's Inn, Calle Olimpo opposite Pro-Venezuela, 7827033; Jolly Inn, Av. Solano López opposite the Tampa, 7623665. Bruno Cuatricentenario, Av. Este 2, Los Caobos, 7812266. The Escorial, Calle El Colegio, 719621, is near **Sabana Grande**. The Broadway, end of Av. Casanova, 9511922, is by **Chacaito**. The Grand Galaxie has modern, clean rooms on Av. Baralt, 839011, about six blocks north of **Capitolio** station.
'A good cheap hotel is the Hotel Crystal. Hot water, air

conditioning, around £12 double. It is opposite the Savoy chocolate shop on Sabana Grande. They are very helpful and Henri speaks English.' (J and K Whitehead)

*? Downtown commercial hotels near **La Hoyada** include: Caracol, Dr Díaz a Peinero, 5416931, and the Peral, Esq. Peinero a Coliseo, 5453111. The old Waldorf, Av. Sur 17, 5714733, is near **Bellas Artes**. In Las Mercedes, the small Nostrum, Av. Orinoco at Calle Paris towards the Tamanaco, 927646, is okay during the week. But like many hotels which don't advertise, it does a too-lively weekend trade, and travellers are turned down.

Popular small hotels and pensions ($12 double) are almost always full, but you can try: Hotel Myriam, Av. Las Acacias, 713311, near **Plaza Venezuela** station. Also, Pensión Ana, Av. Santiago de Chile, Los Caobos, 7816691, rooms by month, good restaurant. Near **Chacaito** are: Hotel Villa Verde, 2nd Av. Las Delicias de Sabana Grande, 7621092; Pension Rita, Quinta Lourdes, Av. Coromoto, Bello Monte, 7621451.

Several cheap hotels and *hospedajes* are found in La Candelaria district, north of **Parque Carabobo** (some accept by the month only). Others are in the rough Nuevo Circo-Parque-Central area. There is an association of small hotel and inn owners, Avehotur, with offices in Edif. Catuche, piso 2, Apt.2-M, Parque Central, 5754060.

WHERE TO EAT

Caraqueños often talk business over the dinner table, and restaurants in Las Mercedes are favoured by executives. A lunch or *almuerzo* may start well after 1pm and linger past 3pm. Dinner or *cena* does not get going until 9 or 10pm, and a private dinner invitation may mean that you eat at midnight. Be sure to check whether your invitation to have a meal *comida* is for midday or evening.

Between **Chacaito** and the Tamanaco Hotel, the districts of El Rosal and Las Mercedes are crammed with fashionable steak, seafood, crepe, vegetarian and pasta houses. Check the ads in *The Daily Journal* for French, Spanish, Argentine, Texan, Thai, and Venezuelan restaurants. Many are in the $10- 20 range, without drinks, which makes lunch at the Tamanaco's poolside La Cabana a bargain at $8.

The area between the Metro stations of **Chacaito** and **Plaza Venezuela** has a reputation for good food at less than $10. In particular, along Av. Solano López there are Spanish tasca halls where beer and seafood are consumed with noisy gusto, and Italian family style restaurants where the pasta is fresh. To name a few: the Urrutia, Mi Tasca, Piccolo Tasca, Rugantino, Camilo's, Al Vecchio Mulino, the Sorrento, Da Guido. A small French restaurant with a fine tradition, Le Coq D'Or, is around the corner from Solano López at Av. Los Mangos. Top off a meal with an espresso coffee at the sidewalk cafés on the Boulevard, or an icecream at the Crema Paraiso bar in the same block as the Gran Café, for about Bs.40.

$5 goes a long way

Lunch bars (some are called *loncherías*) serve excellent juices made to order, of orange, *parchita* (passionfruit). Specify *jugo natural*, as opposed to carton juice. All-fruit *batidos*, blended on the spot of seasonal fruits from *lechosa* (papaya) to blackberry, cost about $0.45-70. Very good to accompany the hot *arepas* made of cornmeal which cost from $0.50-85, according to the filling...perhaps chicken salad, *cazón* or shark, scrambled eggs *perico* style, or 'dominó' of white cheese and black beans. Some *areperas* are open all night.

To my taste the chicken-on-a-spit served up by umpteen *pollo a la brasa* restaurants is always good value at about $3. There are large *criollo* restaurants on Av. Pichincha, 2-3 blocks directly south of the Chacaito Metro: Los Pilones, El Portón and, more economical, Rancho Grande (chicken) and El Arepazo (cachapas and arepas). Common to all *comedores* or low-cost restaurants is the Venezuelan meal-in-a-bowl, *hervido*, a chunky soup of chicken or beef that costs $1.50 at the most.

Quiche and cakes   For snacks, French bread and fabulous pastries, try one of Caracas' excellent delicatessens and *pastelerías*. La Selva on Av. Principal del Bosque, three blocks up from Chacaito, has a small cafeteria for inexpensive lunch, besides baking some spectacular bread. The Danubio in Chacao is at the north end of Calle Guaicaipuro, five blocks up from Miranda Avenue; open 7.30 to 19.00 every day. They specialise in strudel and profiterole, but also have six lunch tables. Nearby on Av. San Marino is the Manhattan Plaza which has tables indoors and out for croissants, cakes, quiche and sandwiches; open 7.00 to 22.00 every day. North Americans nostalgic for muffins and hash browns go to Cafe L'Attico, a good 2nd storey spot for Sunday brunch; it is a block above Plaza Altamira on Av. Luis Roche. Around the corner on Transversal 2 is Weekends, said to be the height of 'New York' style in short-order restaurants.

WHERE TO BUY CAMPING SUPPLIES

Bread   The best staple for trips up to ten days (wrapped in paper, not plastic). **Panadería Amistad**, Av. Rómulo Gallegos, 352771, north of El Trébol shopping centre, Dos Caminos metro station; rye bread is called *pan sucre* (tops), brown is *integral*. **Panadería Steinbuch**, Calle Barrialito 28, Baruta; the small blue door seen from Baruta's high street south (Av. Guayabitos) is open Tue.-Sat. 9-12; the whole wheat *integral* is unbeatable; the *pan negro* lighter. In Caracas this 'pan Baruta' is sold at 3.30pm at **Supermercado Veracruz**, Las Mercedes, opp. Lagoven gasoline station below the Tamanaco Hotel. **Frisco**, Centro Com. El Bosque, Av. Libertador near Av. La Arboleda sell a variety of black and brown loaves including Frisco's good *pan negro*, plus *pan sucre*; best hour 3.30.

Camping goods   Many students use rucksacks for books and belt bags ('koalas') for money. A textile chain, Bazar Bolívar (Sabana Grande, Chacao, California Norte), sometimes stocks light, cheap sleeping bags. For mountain gear: Verotex, downstairs at Edif. Arta, Plaza Chacaito, 9792443, sell quality sleeping bags. **Tortuga Sport**, downstairs at Centro Com. Unico, Plaza Chacaito, 9520292; camping, scuba, fishing gear. **Marumen Store**, Transversal 3 between Av. Roche and San Juan Boxco, Altamira, 2618134; large selection of tents, stoves, tarps, Bluet Gaz, unleaded gasoline, rope, etc. Check the Yellow Pages under *Deportes* for hunting and fishing shops such as El Cador, Calle 3, Las Delicias de Sabana Grande; El Bagueno, downstairs at Beco's, Plaza Chacaito.

Hammocks, crafts   Moriche hammocks of palm fibre are masterpieces but quite heavy and must not be left damp; hand-knotted nylon *chinchorros* are lighter, cheaper and last forever. (See box on page 121.) Artisans from the Guajira, the Andes, Ecuador and Colombia have market stalls in the **Paseo Las Flores** off Plaza Chacaito west; look for steps down from the boulevard near Kuai Mare bookshop. Check prices of rugs, tapestries, bags; various chipchorros come in single or double width (matrimonial). **Pro-Venezuela** is a large souvenirs/crafts shop on the Gran Avenida, 7923638, west of Plaza Venezuela metro; open Mon.-Sat 8-7. **Von Dangel**, No.4, Av. I de El Dorado, 2565220, three blocks east of California Norte metro; some good Indian hammocks and stools in an unmarked pink house up from Avenida Miranda; open all day, just ring the bell.

   If you have time to explore **El Hatillo**, an old village (newly chic) on the southern outskirts of Caracas, save an hour for **Hannsi's** on Calle Bolívar up from the plaza. Occupying a pair of houses, it is the biggest craft centre of all. Open Tue.-Fri. 9-1, 2:30-7pm; Sat.-Sun. 9:30-7pm. El Hatillo buses stop near the Cine Broadway in Chacaito.

Photo developing Bring plenty of film; supplies in small towns may be old or sparse (no black and white, no slide film). A 36-roll of 35mm Kodacolor costs about $6.50; Fujichrome is quite good and cheaper than Kodak. Two of the many places that do colour negative developing are: **Foto Print**, Centro Comercial Chacaito facing the plaza, 7624398, same-day service; **Campo Color**, Edif. Helena, Plaza Altamira Norte, 2841465, 24-hour service and enlargements of colour and black-and-white (no b&w developing).

T-shirts Places to buy *franelas* with nature and local themes include Pro Vita, Audubon and the Dirección the Parques Nactionales. Also: Para Ti Diseños, Calle Unión south of Blvd. Sabana Grande, 717256; Alfred, Av. Principal Bello Campo, 321271, three blocks east of the Teatro Altamira; Punto 4, Calle Santa Ana, Bello Campo, near Alfred's, 2613334.

Moreouer the countrey is fo healthfull , as 100. perfons and more , which lay (without fhift moft fluttifhly, and were euery day almoft melted with heat in rowing & marching, and fuddenly wet againe with great fhowers, and did eate of all forts of corrupt fruits, & made meales of frefh fifh without feafoning, of *Tortugas*, of *Lagartos*, & of al forts good and bad, without either order or meafure , and befides lodged in the open ayre euery night) we loft not any one, nor had one ill difpofed to my knowledge, nor found anie *Callentura*, or other of thofe peftilent difeafes which dwell in all hote regions , and fo nere the Equinoctiall line.

Sir Walter Raleigh praises the "healthfull countrey" of Venezuela in *The Discoverie of the Large, Rich and Bewtiful Empyre of Guiana.*

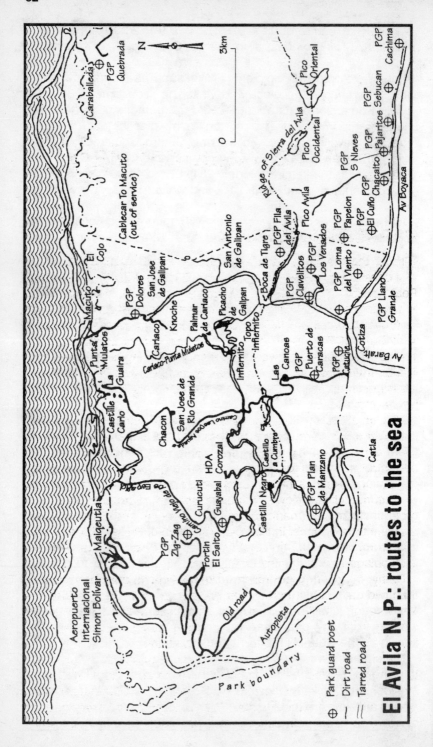

El Avila N.P.: routes to the sea

⊕ Park guard post
— Dirt road
〰 Tarred road

Chapter 5

El Avila National Park

CARACAS' MOUNTAIN

Without the *cordillera* Caracas would be as dull as its Guaire ditch. The coastal range soars to a sparkling 2,765m (9,071ft) at Naiguatá Peak. Much of the range comprises the Avila National Park, separating the capital from the Caribbean. The park stretches 86km from east to west and covers an area of 850km², a great part of it wild. Some 200 kinds of birds and 100 mammal and reptile species live here. Although most walkers can spot hummingbirds, hawks and lizards, there have also been cases of campers who have fled from terrifying roars, only to learn later that their 'jaguars' were in fact howler monkeys.

With its paths, shelters, ranger stations and spectacular *teleférico*, the Avila offers more visitor facilities than all other parks. There is even an ice skating rink in the cable car terminal. Sadly, the *teleférico* is closed for overhaul. More important, the Avila is an oxygen and weather maker. Caraqueños walk up for the crisp air as well as magnificent views. Naiguatá was first climbed in 1872 by a group including German painter Anton Goering and British traveller James Mudie Spence. In his book *The Land of Bolívar*, Spence said that from the peak he could see all the way to Los Roques Archipelago and the plains of Guárico.

Today, hikers in good training climb Naiguatá and return in less than two days. Most mortals find Avila Peak, at 2,159m (7,054ft), a day's tough challenge. However, there are many shorter walks starting from any one of a dozen points along Boyacá highway, known as the Cota Mil for its 1000m elevation.

The changes in climate and trees as you go up and the possibility of using the *teleférico* to come down are real attractions. Start early even for short walks because the sun gets hot by 9.00 and the lower slopes are almost without shade. The Avila's paths are steep enough to set your heart pounding so they are good preparation for any expedition. Most flatlanders will find walking down the mountain a worse strain than going up as rest stops do not restore weak knees and ankles. The dangers of falling are real.

Permits and maps

Park rangers at guard posts, *puestos de guardaparques* (PGP), issue hiking permits at no cost. Children under 12 need not have a permit but should be accompanied by an adult with one. A trail map is sometimes available at the guard post, or at the Dirección de Parques Nacionales located opposite Parque del Este by the Metro station of the same name. This map shows trails from PGP Puerta de Caracas in the west to Naiguatá Peak in the east; it does not cover trails to the coast.

If unavailable above, ask for a map or photocopy at the Audubon bookshop, 9932525, in Paseo Las Mercedes, at the far end of the shopping centre's ground floor; closed Sat-Sun.

A more complete Avila map showing the entire park, including trails on the Caribbean side, accompanies a useful book on the Avila National Park written in Spanish by Jesús Pereira and fellow hiker Pedro Aso. They outline 64 hikes, from ½ day to 2½ days. The book, *Guaraira Ripano Sierra Grande*, is being republished by Lagoven. Copies will be sold at the oil company's HQ on Avenida Leonardo da Vinci, Esquina Bonpland, Colinas de Bello Monte, Caracas.

Organised walks

A good way to explore the park safely and enjoyably is to join a walking party. There are various *centros excursionistas*, informal groups of usually mixed ages and nationalities who are only too pleased to show newcomers 'their mountain'. Jesús Pereira, whose home telephone is 7511974, is a pillar of the Centro Excursionista Caracas which meets to plot hikes, on Wednesdays at 20.30 at the Green Zone shelter, San Roman district, Las Mercedes near the Tamanaco Hotel. Jesús speaks English and will not be too surprised if strangers ring him.

Remember

The Avila is a big, bold mountain and careless walkers can come to grief when straying from paths, walking at dusk or in mist. The park guards' job is to bring you safely down in case of accident, but they cannot do this speedily if you are not on a trail. Do not attempt shortcuts; do not run downhill.

Campgrounds

Campgrounds, as listed below, are those with a sanitary facility (flush toilet). There are many places in the park flat and clear enough for use as a campsite. As the park is heavily used, it is very important that human waste be properly buried and other refuse packed out. The park is generally fairly clean considering its heavy use. The campgrounds that follow are listed in the west-to-east direction.

Los Venados: a large number of campsites available, many with kiosks which can be handy in case of rain. Caballeros (His) and Damas (Hers) sanitary facilities available. This area is very heavily used on weekends and in school holidays such as Christmas, Carnival, Easter, and summer.

Mirador La Zamurera: a number of campsites with a sanitary facility (in early 1989, two had been built but one was inoperable). This is reached by the start of the Traverse trail. The PGP La Zamurera area just above Mirador has considerable additional space. See *Traverse of the Park* for directions.

PGP Papelón: a number of campsites in the areas below the PGP. A sanitary facility (standup type but it flushes).

PGP Chacaíto: a relatively few sites but with new (and therefore clean) Caballeros and Damas facilities. Sabas Nieves, the next PGP to the east, is a frequent choice by trekkers overnighting in Caracas because the Metro's Altamira bus route passes the start of the trail. There is shelter and water above the PGP.

PGP Sebucán: relatively few sites and it is difficult to return to Caracas from here without a vehicle. The PGP can be reached from the Avenida Boyacá expressway going westbound just past the Sebucán entry. There is only space to park one vehicle.

The teleférico

The cableway provides a less strenuous method of seeing the park, but it is not currently working. The normal hours are 8.00 to 21.00 and, if your Spanish is adequate, you can telephone 7816324 to check status of operation.

Roads

Six roads and 4WD tracks to the coast cross the western half of the park. The first is used by buses, cars and heavy trucks.

1) The *autopista* or toll road.

2) Its predecessor, the Old Road or *Carretera Vieja*. (There used to be a parallel railway, but trains took two hours to reach La Guaira and were abandoned in the 1950s.) Little used today, the tortuous Old Road tends to get missed out on maps. In Caracas, it starts to the right of the autopista's Catia access, north of Avenida Sucre. Its 27km make an hour's exciting drive to Maiquetía, if you like hairpin curves. But walkers are warned of hold-ups and muggings near the *barrios*.

3) The *Camino de los Españoles*, historic Spanish road between Puerta de Caracas (La Pastora sector) and the coast, which provided the city's main access from 1632 to 1845 when a coach route was opened, is still drivable (just). Relatively low (1,500m) and 'civilised', this unpaved, 23.9km route to Maiquetía is interesting because of the remains of Spanish forts and cobblestones. The Spanish way is used by jeeps approaching from Puerta de Caracas and the Old Road via Plan de Manzano PGP, although its coast end is in very bad shape.

4) Splitting north from the Spanish road at Castillo Blanco is another colonial *camino*. Known as Las Dos Aguadas, the path crosses over the ridge to Gato Negro where it picks up a better road and descends through San José de Río Grande, coming down at Castillo San Carlos, 300m alt. This Spanish fort above La Guaira, built in 1768-69 by Conde Roncale, has been handsomely restored. It is a 20-minute walk from here to the sea by way of Calle El León.

5) From Las Dos Aguadas fork a rough road climbs east along the ridge to Infiernito, where pine woods stand by the ruined walls of a house (follow a trail behind the wall 5 minutes for water). From Infiernito a wooded mule track leads down to the abandoned groves of Hacienda Cariaco, an hour's walk and 780m elevation. A path from here continues to Punta Mulatos on the coast. Not for jeeps.

6) There is a park access road which starts in Cotiza at the top of Avenida Peñalver, San Bernardino district. People bound for Los Venados campsite and visitors' centre take this road and leave their cars at Los Clavelitos PGP, thankful to be spared the initial shadeless ascent. Unpaved, the main route continues climbing to the cablecar terminal and Humboldt Hotel. A jeep road forks north at Boca de Tigre, and descends to the sea by way of San Antonio de Galipán, San José de Galipán (starting point for route to 'Doctor Knoche's mausoleum') and PGP Dolores. This 15km walk takes most people all day.

As hikes, colonial ways make easier walking than park trails; they also pass the occasional farm or hacienda. Nevertheless, the distance from Caracas to the sea makes a good day's haul, knees are likely to turn rubbery half way, and the lower slopes are in full sun.

WALKS AND HIKES IN THE AVILA RANGE

The Spanish Road
by Paul Rouche

Not difficult, but long, so keep a good pace
The *Camino de los Españoles* is recommended for its 18th Century forts, the ruins of Hacienda Corozal with its elegant palm trees, the charming colonial house at Guayabal and the sea views from La Venta. This route crosses the park's western edge to Maiquetía, see map on page 58.

Access   Calle Norte 10 leads from Miraflores Palace to the old part of town known as La Pastora, specifically La Puerta de Caracas, starting point of the Spanish Road. *Por puestos* run from the Calle Real El Polvorín a kilometre further, and are worth the small price to get you up the stiff hill lined with *ranchos* or huts.

Rising from the last house, the road is asphalted in part only and is used by the occasional battered pick-up. The first 'fort' is a recent pastiche, home of a Spaniard. But near his 'castillo' is the first of 14 crosses built along the historic road as a Via Crucis. Each Easter, the faithful walk from La Pastora Church to Maiquetía Church, praying at each cross. The pilgrimage takes 12 hours.

Remains of the colonial cobbled surface are seen on the left just before the Puerta de Caracas guard post; altitude 1,370m; distance 2km. The road goes up at a steep incline for another ½km to Campo Alegre, passing Radio Tropical's tower and a chapel on the left; alt. 1,460m. The way continues north by small farms; it flattens briefly. Make no right turns, keep straight on. At 1,470m 'travellers are accustomed to halt near a fine spring known by the name of Fuente de Sanchorquiz,' reported Alexander Humboldt in 1799. He also noted that the Caracas-La Guaira road takes three hours by mule, or five on foot.

The road dips, you will see on the right a tree and shrine enclosed in a concrete wall and then on the left the entrance to Las Canoas, a house where you can beg water. Continue up; at 1,500m the road levels out and in 1km comes to a crossroads; go left. (The right fork

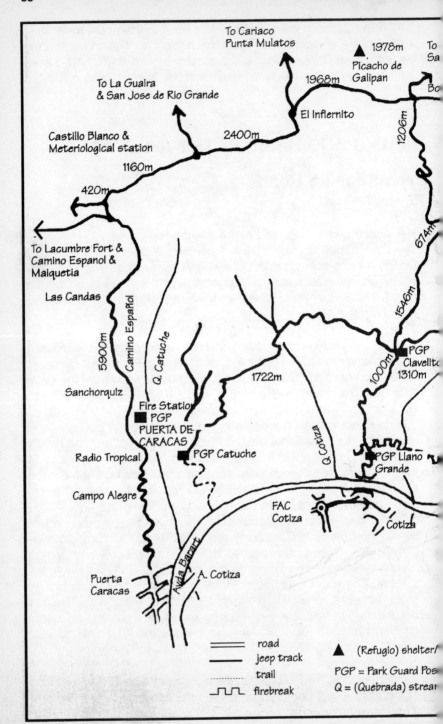

To Cariaco
Punta Mulatos

▲ 1978m
Picacho de
Galipan

1968m

El Infiernito

To La Guaira
& San Jose de Rio Grande

2400m

1206m

Castillo Blanco &
Meteriological station

1160m

420m

To Lacumbre Fort &
Camino Espanol &
Maiquetia

Las Candas

674m

1546m

5900m

Camino Espanol

Q. Catuche

1722m

PGP
Clavelit
1310m

Sanchorquiz

1000m

Fire Station
PGP
PUERTA DE
CARACAS

Radio Tropical

PGP Catuche

Q Cotiza

PGP Llano
Grande

Campo Alegre

FAC
Cotiza

Cotiza

Puerta
Caracas

Avda Barart

A. Cotiza

road
jeep track
trail
firebreak

▲ (Refugio) shelter/

PGP = Park Guard Pos

Q = (Quebrada) strear

...ulatos
...e Galipan

...gre 1875m
1023m

Lagunazo

2103m

To San Francisco
de Galipan

420m

Guayabo Mocho

661m

PGP Fila
Del Avila
2025m

Hotel Humboldt

Pico
El Avila 2250m

Teleferico

...nauco

Pica de los Pinabetes

225m 335m

546m

Est Teleferico
2150m

...450m

El
Vigia

Los Venados
1437m

Carricillo

2580m

Q Guayabal

PGP
La Zamurera
1580m

TV Antenna

Los Pinos

5362m

...ador
...Zumurera

Gamboa

Q Papelón

1560m

PGP
Papelon

Gamelotar

Q Gamboa

920m

1190m

Vivero
Loma del
Cuño

Q Avila

PGP Loma
Del Cuño

PGP Loma del
Viento 1160m

PGP
Chacaito

San
Bernadino

Est Teleferico
Mariperez

Alta
Florida

1km

Avila National Park: West

in turn divides into four ways, of which one heads up to Infiernito and Galipán Peak, and another, 0.8km, to the ruins of Castillo Blanco, a small fort built in 1770.) The toughest part of the road is now over.

You are on the downslope, with the cliff on the left. At the next two crossroads, 1½km, take the left both times, descending. (To the right in 100m is the way to La Cumbre Fort, also called Castillo San Joaquín or Castillo del Medio (1784). Look for the old well.) Continue west (left) 300m along the Loma del Viento, or windy hill, to a triple crossroads: the left is a jeep road to Caracas and PGP Plan de Manzano; centre is the Via del Medio to the nearby ruins of Castillo Negro and Castillo La Atalaya; and, on the right, the Spanish Road. Distance from Puerta de Caracas, 8.5km.

Very soon you will pass a path coming down on the right from La Cumbre Fort (a 5-minute hike). Keep left here and at the next fork (right for Hoyo de La Cumbre and Gato Negro communities). Shortly, a view of the sea opens up ahead; there are houses on the right. The altitude here is 1,330m. The remains of once-famous La Venta are at 1,190m elevation. Describing this colonial inn, Alexander Humboldt wrote that La Venta 'enjoys some celebrity in Europe and the United States for the beauty of its surrounding scenery... The spectator beholds at his feet Cabo Blanco, the village of Maiquetía with its cocoa-trees, La Guayra, and the vessels in port.' Humboldt spoke of the mists... 'trees and dwellings appeared at intervals through the openings which were left by the clouds.' Today it's a good spot for a campsite if you have water: breezy, some shade, no close neighbours. Distance to Maiquetía: 8.2km.

Twisting down, the colonial road passes an entrance way to Corozal, an interesting old coffee hacienda (right 1.4km) whose palm trees are seen from far above. Next reference point is Guayabal, 950m; 17km from Puerta de Caracas and 7km from Maiquetía. Another former inn, this simple, attractive colonial house is among the very few old structures still in use. From here down, the road has little shade. In less than 1km you reach the small, partly restored Fortín El Salto, ca. 1650, which used to have a drawbridge across a 10m crevasse (the 'salto' or leap), now filled in. The road continues steep and stony and in about 20 minutes you can see in the west the asphalted Old Road to La Guaira. At 630m elevation, the remains of walls on the right are all that is left of Torquemada, a colonial way station. (Just below, a path leads left to the Old Road, 30 minutes walk.)

The last open stretch drops fast to the community of Quenepe which clings to exposed flanks. From here it is 10 minutes walk to the coast. Or you can take a *por puesto* down. In Maiquetía the Caracas—Litoral buses go along the coast road.

Remember In dry weather, water and a hat are essential; in the rains, especially May to December, a hat and waterproof. For camping, a tent, hammock, or light sleeping bag. Biting insects are not likely to bother you at La Venta.

The Fila Maestra and Naiguata Peak
by Paul Rouche

Very strenuous
This is a rugged 2 day hike for backpackers who can carry rain gear, tent and cold-weather sleeping bag. Day temperatures may be hot. Distance is about 30km. Steep gradients are compensated by an aviator's view of cloudscapes, the Caribbean and Caracas, and by dramatic changes in vegetation from tall tropical forests to páramo flowers and shrubs.

Access In San Bernardino a wide paved road enters the park from the top of Avenida Peñalver where it is joined by Calle Forestal from Cotiza. Take the 'San Bernardino' bus, or the Cotiza *por puestos* which go from Avenida Baralt up to the police barracks (*cuartel de policía*) and the Luis Razzetti Hospital, stopping 200m from the park. If you have a jeep you can drive as far as Los Clavelitos PGP (see map 'West'), or, if you want to shorten the climb by several hours, take the cablecar up the Avila.
   The park road starts at 960m altitude, passes under Boyacá Avenue (the Cota Mil) and begins to ascend steeply after the Llano Grande guard post. There is parking space at Llano Grande as well as at the next ranger station, Los Clavelitos PGP; distance 2km; altitude 1,310m. Two ways lead up: the right via Los Venados campsite with its lawns and shelters, the left (faster) to Boca de Tigre and the ridge road. Hikers will find good signposts.

The trail The jeep track to Boca del Tigre on the ridge climbs steadily through woods to 1,880m elevation, about an hour's hike (not counting rests). Here one trail goes to the west (left) to El Infiernito and returns to Puerta de Caracas, one goes north to San Antonio and San José de Galipán, while the ridge road to the right brings you in about an hour to the teleférico terminal. No longer so steep but still climbing, the ridge road reaches 2,025m at PGP Fila del Avila, where the path from Los Venados joins up. The cablecar terminal is at 2,150m. Besides food and drink, gilded lilies and souvenirs are sold here. If you need water, there's a tap near the cable. If you need shelter, try the hotel lobby, a strange brass-and-glass intrusion among the mountain mists. It is very cold up here and the wind fierce, so go no further unless the day is still young. Without good visibility and footing, the trails are dangerous.

Leaving the concrete path (and the ridge) by some stone steps down to the left, about 100m before the Humboldt Hotel, take the trail east to Lagunazo and Pico Occidental. Ten minutes on, the way divides at a watertank. Go up to the left, a sharp incline with boulders giving way to gentler, moorlike gradients. The next choice is really one path: take the left for the shorter route; or take the right to the Lagunazo water collection tank if you need to fill up; alt. 2,200m; continue left of the cascade. Above here is a grassy spot suitable for a tent. It's another ten minutes' rocky ascent to the ridge itself where the panorama unfolds north and south.

From here to Pico Occidental the way is a series of short ascents followed by level ground. The path, which at times branches, takes about 40 minutes. 2,480m is the elevation of the western peak although it is more rounded than steep. The trail onward dips to the seat of the 'saddle' or Silla, 2,350m, which separates the west and east peaks: keep left where the paths fork. (A sign points right or down for shelter and water at a spot called 'No Te Apures', which means 'Don't hurry', because it's very steep, and below to Sabas Nieves PGP and Altamira in Caracas.) Before the trail rises again, there is a level clearing where people have camped, and a trail fork; go right.

Thick, low (and often wet) bamboo shades the climb to Pico Oriental. Several not-quite-so-steep variants of the path lead right, but all join up later. In about 50 minutes you reach the crown, 2,600m, where there is a possible campsite. To the right are the peak 'proper', another campsite, a cross and the trail down to Cachimbo PGP above Los Chorros in Caracas.

Alexander Humboldt, that supreme geographer, traveller and writer who spent 18 months in Venezuela, measuring everything, climbed Pico Oriental in 1800. He and his group, including slaves, were the first to do so. Standing by the enormous northern cliff, he warned that 'persons who are affected by looking downward from a considerable height' should stay on the small flat crowning the eastern summit. He described the summit as 'distinguished among all the mountains I have visited by an enormous precipice on the side next to the sea. The coast forms only a narrow border; and looking from the summit on the houses of Caravalleda, this wall of rocks seems ... nearly perpendicular ... A precipice of six or seven thousand feet, like that of the Silla of Caracas, is a phenomenon far more rare than is generally believed.' He measured the gradient at 53.28 degrees.

On a fine day, the long, narrow trail along the Fila Maestra or master ridge towards Naiguatá is superb and solitary. It seems to dip and rise forever between 2,300 to 2,500m, or at least for over 3 hours, through sub-páramo plants and copses of twisted shrubs. Before the evening's mist and clouds come up, the horizon is limitless. Half way to Topo Galindo is a pass among boulders called the Puerto de Hercules — Hercules' Gate. About 10 minutes west of Topo Galindo is a campsite, 2,550m. Beyond this grassy spot the ridge is rocky and exposed, rising to 2,600m at Galindo before dipping to a fork where a sign points east to Naiguatá (south to Pico Goering, Rancho Grande refuge and the way down to La Julia PGP, above Et Marques in Caracas).

The ridge path continues with more fine views and campsites. You skirt to the right of a 'topo' and come to La Pradera, 2,590m, where there is grass and water; a rock overhang offers some shelter. Another marked crossing points east to Naiguatá, south to Galindo PGP, above La Urbina in Caracas.

From La Pradera, the trail to Naiguatá is well trodden. It starts gently, passes rock formations with names such as the Devil's Plates and La Arepa, rises and comes to a seaview on the right. Two forks follow closely: stay left at the first and right at the second. In 10 minutes you reach the Amphitheatre, a protected vale at 2,630m where there is space for tents and rocks for shelter. Up the trail a path detours to the left to a spring called Manantial Stolk. The peak itself is only 10 minutes on, reached by a narrow, eroded path up an incline to 2,765m. A cross of metal pipe which can be seen from Caracas stands on the top.

At least four trails continue on from the peak: one to Naiguatá on the coast, others to Santa Rosa, Garate, Galindo. They are less trodden, however, and better crossed with a guide.

The descent from Pradera to La Urbina has two interesting stopping places. The first stage, rocky and wooded, comes down in an hour to a sign pointing east to Rancho Miguel Delgado where a shelter once stood by a creek. Good campsite (5 min. from the path, 2,000m). Return to the main path. Ten minutes on, a fork to the left diverges to the ruins known as Hacienda Mezteatis, 1,580m; the trail rejoins the main path half an hour downhill.

Count Mezteatis, famous in his day as a gambler, was born in Italy in 1860 and came to Venezuela with the job of settling Italian peasants: the story has it that he was booted out of Italy for leaving his bride at the altar in favour of a card game. When the immigration scheme failed, the count stayed, using his family allowance to buy the coffee hacienda — and gamble. He also cut down the coffee trees and planted onions which were so profitable that for years he was content to pay deforestation fines to the *jefe civil*.

The ruins are on the right (ignore tracks to the left leading to Quebrada Caurimare): the path crosses a creek, a low wall and the foundations of the house. Further on, there are steps down to the left. The way down continues to the right, passing through two small walls. The vegetation, now mostly bracken, offers no shade. Back at the main path (1,540m) the descent is a wearing series of zig-zags following a waterline down an exposed flank. Keep the electricity tower on your right: go right at the junction with a jeep road; almost immediately turn left for Galindo PGP, 970m. The path brings you out at La Urbina Norte by the Terrazas del Avila apartments.

Remember   Although the weather may appear dry, afternoons on the mountain often bring rain. Altitude and cold over 2,000m increase the hardship and risk of exposure. On the other hand, water sources are few and far in the dry season, (usually) January to April. Remember when climbing to look before using handholds: snakes live in woods up to 2,000m; others prefer to sun on hot rocks. The park guardposts are in theory equipped with snake serum; in case of snakebite do not drink coffee or alcohol which speed up blood circulation.

La Cueva de los Palmeros

Facing east, a 5m cross of aluminium stands atop a rock named 'Diamond' on the Pico Oriental. At sunrise, it reflects the rays and can be seen from east Caracas. At the foot of the cross is a sign placed by the Palmeros de Chacao. As explained by veteran hiker Eduardo Rosswaag, the *palmeros* are devotees of the Holy Cross. Their custom is to trek up before Palm Sunday to gather leaves of the wax palm (*Ceroxylon klopstockia*) in the headwaters of two streams, the Pajaritos and the Seca, under Pico Oriental. Among great ficus trees (strangler figs) at 1,620m elevation, the *palmeros* set up camp. The nearby Cueva de los Palmeros, a cave among the boulders of Quebrada Quintero, is the setting for an altar with crosses and rosaries, lighted by candles. On the Friday before Palm Sunday, the palm-bearers descend to Chacao in a procession greeted by crowds and fireworks.

The most direct route to reach the Cueva de los Palmeros, says Rosswaag, is from Transversal 10 in Altamira (by Tarzilandia Restaurant). At a fork above Sabas Nieves PGP you will find shelter and water. From the left enters the trail looping up from Chacaito PGP. Go up to the northeast over Loma Serrano. On the steep climb to No Te Apures, where there is another *refugio* or shelter, you go through cool forests with orchids, ferns, heliconias. A path leads west from No Te Apures (1,800m) to a water hole. But the east trail to Quebrada Quintero and, beyond, Pajaritos, is not marked and is easily lost. Walkers not familiar with the area should take a guide or get in touch with the Centro Excursionista de Caracas.

This route, which reaches the Silla, is in part that taken by Alexander Humboldt, the first to climb the Avila's Pico Oriental in 1800, the first to measure its altitude, and the first to calculate the height of Caracas.

Remember   Take a machete when walking through overgrown areas. You can avoid getting ticks by tucking your pants' legs inside your boots or socks and, before walking, spraying everything with repellent. Since the bites of even the microscopically small harvest mites or *chivacoa* (called chiggers by Americans and bêta rouge by Britons) can itch for weeks, this is a good practice. It doesn't work, however, if you sit down on the trail. Think of the cooler regions above 1,500m, where there are less pests, and keep moving.

Traverse of the Park
by Forest Leighty

There is a 'low level' route through the park, from Los Venados in the west to Los Polos Grandes Urbanisation in the east, which traverses the park without ever descending completely to Caracas. This traverse is 17km in length and has elevation gains estimated to equal a climb of 580m.

The trail goes from Los Venados (1,432m) to PGP Papelón (1,615m) to PGP Chacaito (1,310m) to PGP Sabas Nieves (1,360m) to near PGP Los Polos Grandes and then descends to Caracas in Altamira district. All of the park's guardposts (PGP) offer a possible entry or exit point to and from Caracas. Each section of the trail will be given a brief description in the west-to-east direction as described above with an indication of where an east-to-west traveller might have a problem.

The best route from Los Venados starts from the parking area headed from the museum and *cafetin*, passing alongside the museum. Follow the signed trail toward La Zamurera and immediately enter a pleasant forested area with a number of kiosks. Soon the trail takes a semi-natural staircase alongside a small cascading stream. After about 100m of elevation gain, a small waterfall is passed and the trail reaches a junction. To the right is the Mirador La Zamurera camping area and on a clear day one would want to make the brief detour down to the Mirador area as it has an exceptional view of Caracas. To the left, the traverse trail goes up a short stretch of jeep road for about 60m of elevation gain to where the jeep road makes a sharp left, the signed trail to Papelón goes to the right. From here to Papelón the trail is relatively

Avila National Park: Central

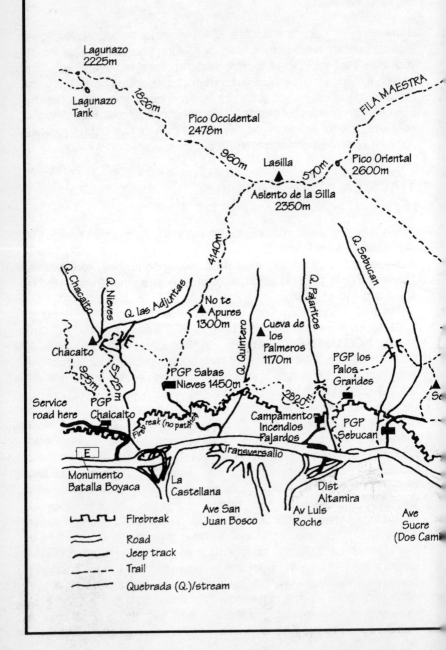

Lagunazo
2225m

Lagunazo
Tank

1826m

Pico Occidental
2478m

FILA MAESTRA

960m

Lasilla

570m

Pico Oriental
2600m

Asiento de la Silla
2350m

Q. Sebucan

Q. Chacaito

Q. Nieves

Q. las Adjuntas

4140m

Q. Pajaritos

No te
Apures
1300m

Cueva de
los
Palmeros
1170m

Q. Quintero

PGP los
Palos
Grandes

Chacaito

925m

5725 m

PGP Sabas
Nieves 1450m

2820m

Service
road here

PGP
Chaicaito

Firebreak (no path)

Campamento
Incendios
Pajardos

PGP
Sebucan

S

E

Transversalio

Monumento
Batalla Boyaca

La
Castellana

Dist
Altamira

Ave San
Juan Bosco

Av Luis
Roche

Ave
Sucre
(Dos Cami

Firebreak

Road

Jeep track

Trail

Quebrada (Q.)/stream

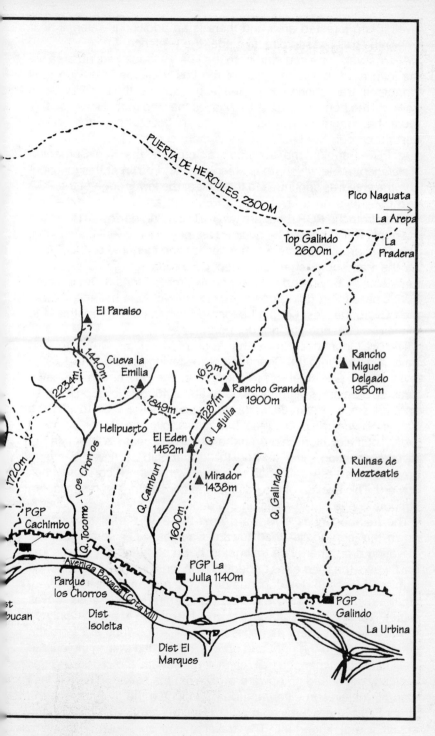

PUERTA DE HERCULES, 2300M

Pico Naguata

La Arepa

Top Galindo
2600m

La Pradera

El Paraiso

Pico Naguata

1440m

Cueva la
Emilia

2234m

165m

Rancho
Miguel
Delgado
1950m

Rancho Grande
1900m

1849m

1287m

Helipuerto

Q. Lajulla

El Eden
1452m

Ruinas de
Mezteatis

Mirador
1438m

Q. Cachimbo - Los Chorros

Q. Camburi

Q. Galindo

1600m

1720m

PGP
Cachimbo

Avenida Boyaca (Cota Mil)

Parque
los Chorros

PGP La
Julia 1140m

st
bucan

Dist
Isoleita

PGP
Galindo

La Urbina

Dist El
Marques

level. It is a forested area and there is an additional waterfall near where the trail passes directly under the teleférico.

Alternatively, one can start from the Los Venados parking area via the jeep road that is the start of the Los Venados-Teleférico (Los Pinabetes) trail, continuing on the jeep road past the Los Pinabetes trail until the bend where the trail leaves the jeep road. However, this route has more uphill stretches to negotiate and the above described route via La Zamurera is more scenic.

At PGP Papelón the traverse trail crosses the San Bernadino (Teleférico) route which goes steeply up and down at this junction. The traverse trail continues to the east at the lower edge of the PGP and continues on a level course for about a kilometre. In the first section from the PGP there are two trails leading downward from the main trail which should be avoided as they are not well maintained. This level area is forested with pines, hence its name of Los Finns. As the trail approaches the deep Quebrada (gorge) Chacaito, it turns steeply down and in less than two miles drops 300m to reach PGP Chacaito. In going down, a spur trail about a half mile before the PGP to the west should be ignored (when coming up, this is to the left — continue straight up, north).

The trail continues past the front of the PGP Chacaito and traverses back into the Chacaito gorge staying at about the 1,200m level. About a kilometre into the gorge, the trail enters a heavily forested area and switchbacks down about 45m of elevation to cross another small stream/cascade and bears to the east to join the Sabas Nieves (Pico Oriental) trail just above the upper camping area. Total elevation gain from the Chacaito stream is 213m. In the reverse direction, after leaving the upper Sabas Nieves camping area, the traverse trail goes to the left while the Pico route goes upward. This section of the trail with the dense forest and cascading streams is one of the nicest in the park.

The trail continues downward past the PGP Sabas Nieves and down the jeep-quality road toward Caracas. After some 150m of elevation drop, there is a trail going down off to the left (this is just past where the road goes under the high tension lines). If this cut-off is missed (easy to do), continue down the road until meeting a very small stream not far above the park exit (entrance on Sabas Nieves route). Take the trail upward to the left of the stream. Continue upward, in the stream as necessary, until an obvious exit from the stream course to the right and up to a very broad trail. In the east to west direction, when the trail reaches the stream, the continuing trail is clearly seen leading upward away from the stream. There is less than 35m elevation difference between where the trail crosses the stream and where the jeep road crosses the stream, so missing the cut-off is not important. The traverse trail continues, passing a cascade, up to an electricity tower. Here there is a trail leading off to the left which climbs 305m to a water source but no campsite. The traverse trail continues around below the tower and soon comes to a junction. Take the right hand, descending trail (the left, ascending, is a dead end). After a very short descent there is a trail leading horizontally to the left away from the descending trail). This next portion is little used and not in great condition (very narrow in spots). After less than a mile, a cascade is reached which is 30m or so high and just misses being a free waterfall. There is a small, not too smooth campsite at the cascade. The trail continues upward until a junction is reached where the descending trail is the exit to Caracas at Urb. Altamira. The continuing upward trail goes shortly to a campsite with piped water and thereafter to the abandoned PGP Los Polos Grandes.

You are now on Boyacá Expressway and there is no sidewalk. On a weekday, entry can be made via taxi to the road to the Campamento Incendios Pajaritos. (On Sunday the Boyacá Expressway is closed until 13.00 for pedestrian and recreational use).

If you are planning to hike the east-to-west direction, the entry trail leads to the right of the park guardpost (at the rear of the parking area), down, and across the stream and then up.

Miniature orchids in micro-habitats

Plants and insects compete for every habitat in the tropics, no matter how small. A single large tree may have a variety of microclimates: a sunny, windy canopy, branches with filtered sun and moisture, lower levels with little air circulation and light. Tiny orchids cling to twigs and leaves in treetops, or hide among mosses on a trunk kept damp by a waterfall's vapour.

These secretive plants have jewel-like flowers, some as small as a capital O. You can really appreciate their colours only under a microscope, each pinhead flower glowing. Wherever orchid species abound, the number of orchids with small flowers far outnumbers the large-flowering ones. (The larger extreme is a *Phragmipedium* with 2' petals.)

Microscopic orchids are in a class by themselves, say collectors who try to duplicate the micro-habitats. *Notylia norae*, pictured here*, was mentioned in the Guinness Book of Records as the world's smallest orchid plant, several fitting into a thimble. But its collectors, Nora and Stalky Dunsterville, found many smaller *flowers* in the rainforests of Guatopo, the cloud forests of Pittier Park, and even on Andean páramos.

Portrait of the rain forest by Carl Appun, a German 19th Century botanist and traveller.

Chapter 6

Guatopo

A RAIN FOREST SOUTH OF CARACAS

Few people stop to explore Guatopo's dense forests despite their amazing wealth of plant and animal life so close to Caracas. If you could glide like a swallow-tailed kite, Guatopo would be just 50km south of Caracas (instead of double by road). The highway to Altagracia curves through this national park in Miranda State. Drivers slow down, thankful for the cool green canopy and dapple of sun and shade. They may notice that as the elevation rises, great trees, philodendrons and orchids replace bamboos, but luckily most people explore no further. Much of Guatopo's 926km² is untouched wilderness.

Because this part of the Serranía del Interior (highest point 1,450m) is the first to catch storms sweeping over the plains, yearly rainfall may exceed 3,000mm. Its rivers and reservoirs are important to Caracas and nearby industries. Guatopo is bounded by the factories of Santa Teresa in the north and the burnt hills of Altagracia de Orituco in the south.

In July-August I have seen flocks of fifty kites from Guatopo on forays to the north, snatching insects from treetops and jostling branches to dislodge caterpillars. Birdlife in Guatopo is particularly varied. And noisy. You hear belligerent hummingbirds, chattering parrotlets, chachalacas in raucous chorus, and large colonies of oropendolas gossiping in hanging nests. Birder Mary Lou Goodwin's list includes the crested guan, macaw, toucanet, tinamou, collared trogon, jet antbird, golden-headed manakin, king vulture, as well as euphonias, tanagers, honeycreepers and many more. She reports that the restored Hacienda La Elvira is well worth a visit for birding and for its 'exceptional' beauty. It is a coffee plantation dating from the 1800s, located on the park's southeastern rim. To reach Hacienda La Elvira: take the Ipare road west of Altagracia, then turn north towards San Francisco de Macaira. The entrance to La Elvira

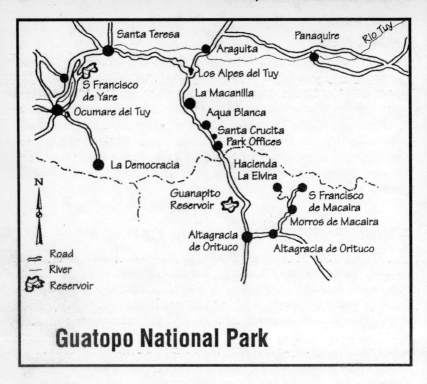

Guatopo National Park

is 13.6km up this road, on the left. The gate may be locked if there is no park guard on duty.

Guatopo is one of the country's few parks with visitor facilities. (But no restaurant.) Ranger stations and camping grounds are all next to the road. The guard at La Macanilla Information Centre, 10km from Los Alpes junction, will point out nature trails and explain camping regulations. (He lives there, so he's disposed to be chatty.) The first recreation area is called Agua Blanca (12km from La Macanilla), where there is an old *trapiche* or sugar mill by a river, fine for splashing, with changing rooms and weekend food kiosks. 1½km south is Santa Crucita; it has a lagoon, grounds for tents and caravans, bathrooms. The park's administration is housed 5.4km beyond Santa Crucita (ask here about visiting Hacienda La Elvira). And shortly after this is Quebrada Guatopo, near the south end of the park; it has a camping area, clear stream, and changing rooms.

At a small research station in the park HQ, visiting biologists have studied foxes, bats, rodents and monkeys. Seldom seen are large mammals such as deer, puma, anteaters and tapirs, but they are all here, as well as capuchin monkeys, tree porcupines and sloths. The same goes for snakes, both harmless and poisonous, so look where you put your hands and feet.

Getting there

If you are going by bus from Caracas, take the Altagracia de Orituco line from the Nuevo Circo. If you are driving, follow the Autopista de Valencia out of Caracas until the second exit, for Charallave, then head east to Santa Teresa. Shortly after this untidy town (about 200m elevation), the highway crosses a bridge over the Tuy River and winds into the park; a 30km climb leads to a fork called Los Alpes del Tuy where there is a cafeteria. Traffic for Caucagua and the east coast goes left; for the park, and Altagracia de Orituco (55km), right.

La Guzmanera Trail
By Paul Rouche

I highly recommend this easy 9km-trail for its beautiful, cool vegetation. The main part follows a cart track built 120 years ago; it parallels today's highway along the west side of the mountain. Start at La Macanilla Information Centre. Park guards request that you report in here, in case of accident. You can obtain a permit and check the map in the small museum.

Opposite La Macanilla (alt. 530m) steps ascend the bank leading to a water tank. Go left without passing the tank, along a path which rises, crossing La Macanilla creek several times. In about 45 minutes, the path reaches the ridge called Fila La Macanilla (650m). It continues along an old cart track, clear and wide, at times level, at times up and down. If you don't linger, you will emerge at the asphalt highway within an hour and a half, at a spot known as El Danto (tapir); alt. 400m. From there, it is 4km north to La Macanilla PGP, or some 8km south to Agua Blanca.

Remember Although the wettest months are said to be October-December, cloudbursts are common from June on. During the rains, frequent landslides make an already slow road precarious. Unless you plan to camp, make an early start.

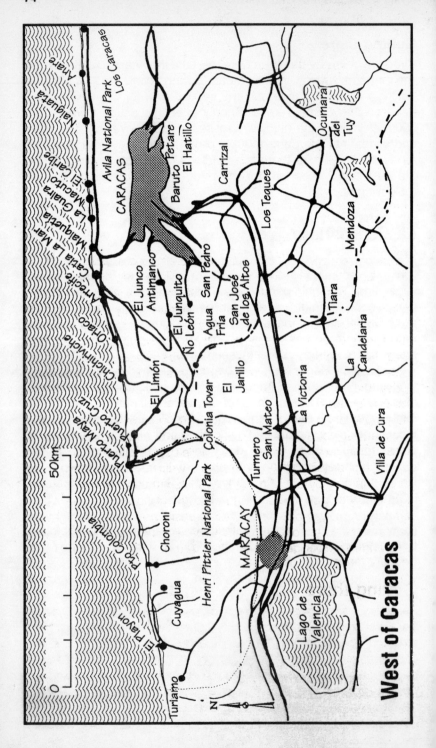

West of Caracas

Chapter 7

West of Caracas

COLONIA TOVAR

In the cool cordillera west of Caracas, trails wind among the cloud forests and German-style inns of Colonia Tovar (alt. 1,786m). To the north, side roads drop sharply to the sea; to the south, a road spirals down to La Victoria in the hot Aragua Valley. Except for the Avila National Park, no area has as many wooded paths as the environs of Colonia Tovar where Black Forest peasants settled in 1843. For a century, while the colony was almost totally isolated, settlers clung to the customs and language of the Schwarzwald. Today, the village prospers through tourism as well as horticulture and fruit growing.

Exploring beyond Tovar's markets, you will soon find bracken and blackberries, palm trees and pines, orchards and farms. The sea is about 35km away by three pretty, little-used roads. Once on the coast, jeep drivers can now continue west to Puerto Maya, long accessible only by sea. So Tovar, with its inns and hearty food (no night clubs or golf course), makes an ideal base for walkers and campers. Although day temperatures easily pass 22°C, at night the thermometer drops to around 4°C. Campers will need good sleeping bags and rainproof gear.

Getting there

Be sure to avoid weekends. Although the distance from western Caracas to Colonia Tovar is only 52km, the road winds up from industrial Antímano through *barrios* and ugly wreckers' yards and it can take an hour and a half. In fog or rain, holiday traffic crawls as day-trippers throng El Junquito, a half-way market town, in search of rural delights — increasingly scarce unless you count pork crackling (*chicharrón*) and sausages (*chorizos*).

Por puesto vans or small buses to Colonia Tovar leave Caracas daily from 5.00 through early afternoon; they park along Lecuna Avenue by the Nuevo Circo bus terminal, Esquina San Roque. The two-stage journey requires changing buses in El Junquito (033) 21419). *Por puesto* minibuses to El Junquito also leave from the Metro station of La Yaguara.

Once past El Junquito, traffic thins; the ridge road winds on for another 19km to arrive at an archway marking the Aragua State border. Colonia Tovar is 8km to the left. Before you get there, you'll pass Charcutería Tovar, makers of excellent knackwurst, smoked sausages and all kinds of picnic goodies. On weekends the narrow streets of Tovar itself are bumper-to-bumper with sightseers. Beyond Colonia Tovar, heading south from the village high street, is the paved road down to La Victoria, 34km. Served by *por puesto* jeeps, the route is very pretty, dramatically steep and never crowded.

During the week the restaurants and small hotels in Tovar really are worthwhile. The bread is German, the jam homemade, and the strawberries and vegetables garden fresh. If it's Carnival time, you'll see old-country revelry with masked *jokili* or jesters.

Lodging

Small hotels often work on a two-meals-plus-lodging basis, at about $30 a day. To phone, dial area code 033 (the Colonia Tovar numbers are listed at the back of the Caracas telephone directory). The Selva Negra, 51072, best known hotel, was built in 1938 with lots of woodwork by Carlos Breidenbach whose family settled in 1851. It now has 37 rooms, cabins. Others are: Alta Baviera, 51483, 11 rooms and cottages; Bergland, 51229, 10 rooms and cabins; Drei Tannen, 51246, 8 doubles and triples; Edelweiss, 51139, 11 rooms; Freiburg, 51313, 8 rooms and 7 cabins; Kaiserstuhl, 51132, 18 rooms. Cabañas Baden, 51151, offers doubles only (no children), without food but with equipped kitchen, at about $20 double.

Colonia Tovar on foot

In walking around the village I like to pause at the cemetery because it is on a central hill with a lovely view over the church and valley below. Among the graves you can trace the colony's growth: wooden crosses for early leaders such as mayor Alexander Benitz (d.1865) and botanist Karl Moritz (d.1866) who planted the cypress still growing here; and marble mausoleums for later richer residents. Graveyard tender Enrique Collin (also miller, baker and water wheel maker) knows all the local history. Relics of the past can also be seen in Nestor Rojas' private museum, on the same road slanting down as you enter Tovar. His display includes immigrants' contracts and belongings, farm tools, pieces of the original forge, printing press and mill, even a petroglyph. Rojas, who runs the Cabañas Baden, likes to track down petroglyphs.

Below is the belltower of the church named St. Martin for the colony's (and founder Martín Tovar's) patron saint. The *fiestas patronales* are on Nov.11. The church's black timbers, raised in 1862, make it unique in Venezuela. Inside, you will see the twin naves separating men from women. The timbered houses opposite are among Tovar's oldest: the Benitz House, now the Muuhstall Café, and the Jahn House where map-maker Agustín Codazzi lived. Alexander Benitz, guiding spirit of the colony, had a brewery (first in Venezuela), printshop and store in his house, largest in Tovar. In the late 19th century the Ruh family became important coffee growers and built two warehouses, one with a tavern. Look for their pitched roofs and porticos at the south end of the high street, near the petrol station.

To the petroglyphs, and other walks

During his field trips in 1844, naturalist Hermann Karsten found the way to a set of boulders known as the 'Piedras de Los Indios' or petroglyphs made by Indian artists long before the arrival of Europeans. Ask for Potrero Perdido; it's a good walk of some 16km round trip. Start downhill (east) from the church (if you continue left, this road will take you back to the asphalt highway in about 2km); at the first crossroads past the Humboldt-Tal Hotel, turn right, passing the Evangelist chapel. If you hear a grinding noise opposite, it is Enrique Collin's mill at work. Cross the bridge over the upper Tuy; continue along its banks a way. After climbing through coffee farms and gardens, the sandy path comes to a spring and bridge; go left at the junction (right goes back to Tovar). Views open over the valley as the road leads through woods and fields to a community called Potrero Perdido (6km from Tovar). The Piedras de los Indios are about 2km further. Follow a track leading uphill; at a spot with a fine open view, look for a pair of pine trees on the left. The trees help to locate the flat boulders on the right which may be hidden by long grass. Unfortunately, someone has painted the petroglyphs white, probably to photograph the incised designs.

Codazzi Peak

You have only to ask at the Edelweiss, Alta Baviera or Bergland for paths uphill: to strawberry fields near the INOS watertanks, to the chapel of the Virgen de los Dolores named for an image the settlers brought from the Black Forest, or to the woods by an area called

A hard life for pioneers

In the early 1840s Venezuela needed farmers to work the land after devastating Independence wars. Don Martín Tovar, a congressman and supporter of immigration, put up a 60,000 peso loan to back a colony of Germans. His nephew, Manuel Felipe Tovar (later president of the country) set aside a mountain tract west of Caracas. Two foreigners were key to the settlement's success: Agustín Codazzi, an Italian geographer, and his map maker Alexander Benitz, a young engraver from the Kaiserstuhl. They met in a Paris printshop and later visited sites in Venezuela at the government's request. Codazzi returned to France to hire the emigrants' ship and buy food and equipment such as a printing press and sawmill. Benitz signed up land-hungry peasants and craftsmen with their families; he also signed on as an immigrant. On January 11, 1843, both Benitz and Codazzi sailed aboard the *Clemence* from Le Havre with the emigrants, in all 392.

Things did not go well. On the 52-day sea crossing to La Guaira many lives were lost to smallpox. Then there was a 3-week quarantine on board — which luckily Codazzi was able to switch to a landing near Choroní. Next, the settlers shouldered their gear up the cordillera and down to Maracay. There they were welcomed with a big barbecue by the President of Venezuela, General José Antonio Páez. Páez also provided some wagons to take women and children to La Victoria, starting point for the trek up to Tovar. Skirting chasms and tripping over roots, the colonists, who now numbered 374, finally arrived on April 8 at a clearing where a few dismal huts stood among burnt stumps. Each settler was indebted for two hectares of this wilderness (children under one received one hectare), as well as for the voyage, food and gear.

The debt was interest-free, however, and could be paid off in work for the colony's promoters. There were typesetters, carpenters, a blacksmith, shoemaker, tailor, baker, brewer (who made the first beer in Venezuela), barrel-maker and teacher. Classes began on the fourth day for some 80 children; more than a third of the settlers were under the age of 14. As their leader and later mayor, Benitz helped the colonists tackle hardship, disease and isolation. He was named chief justice replacing Codazzi, an army colonel who had brought in soldiers to enforce the colonists' labours.

Desertions soon depleted the colony and among the first to go were the teacher, doctor and typesetter. The *Colonia Tovar Bulletin*, in German and Spanish, ceased publication. The priest from La Victoria came only once a year. Remote and unprotected, the colony was sacked during civil wars. A project to open a road to Caracas failed. And the colonists themselves worsened their isolation by banishing members who married Venezuelans and confiscating their lands. This led to inbreeding and cultural poverty. Illiteracy, once only 5 percent, grew to 40 percent.

However, new immigrants arrived and the colony still had leaders. One mother gave classes in reading and writing; her daughter helped a Swiss physician for two years, then treated the sick herself; botanist Karl Moritz led Bible studies and gave horticulture lessons. Coffee growing brought some degree of prosperity. But, even in the 20th century, teachers and priests sent from the outside world could not stick Tovar's rigidity. It was not until 1942, when Colonia Tovar became a township and Spanish became the official language, that land could be bought by anyone and colonists could marry freely. Finally, with the opening of an earth road to Caracas in 1950, Tovar's mulish isolation ended. From 700 inhabitants, the village grew to over 5,500 (1988). Caraqueños 'discovered' Tovar.

Los Lecheros. Codazzi Peak, at 2,425m, is the highest point of this part of the Cordillera de la Costa. It has a television relay tower on top. Take the road leading out of Tovar towards La Victoria (pass the Cruz Verde shops). In about 3.5km, where a cross stands by the road, go right (left for Capachal). Less than 10 minutes up, where the road goes over a brook, look on the left for a path leading through bamboos. The walk through woods and shrubs to the top takes half an hour. The view can be breathtaking, east to Naiguatá peak above Caracas, north to the sea, west as far as Lake Valencia.

The peak and surrounding 117km² were recently declared **Monumento Natural Pico Codazzi**. Its cloud forests feed the headwaters of the Chichiriviche, Limón, Tuy and other rivers. The protected area was designed as Venezuela's first 'ecological corridor', linking Pittier National Park in Aragua State with Macarao National Park in Miranda.

LONGER HIKES IN THE REGION

The Costa Maya

By Paul Rouche

A strenuous circuit with links to the sea

By following this rough jeep road used by farmers you can make a circle, returning to about a kilometre from the starting point. Descending the Caribbean slopes, locally known as the **Costa Maya**, the road drops from wonderfully cool cloud forest to coffee plantations and, lower, sunny banana and bean plots. With a very early start, it is possible to complete the circle in one day. However, the return is a stiff haul uphill from 680m to over 2,000m. The route is important because several stretches give access to longer hikes (2-3 days) down to the sea: Puerto Cruz, Puerto Maya, and even Chuao in Henri Pittier Park.

Getting there

The entrance to the road is by a farmhouse called La Pollera, on the paved road between Colonia Tovar and La Victoria. La Pollera is 7.5km southwest of Tovar and 1.1km north of a crossroads signposted 'Entrada de Costa Maya'. *Por puestos* leave Colonia Tovar at 6.30, then at 8.00 and hourly through 16.00. In La Victoria, the *por puestos* leave from Calle Sur Libertador, between Calles Páez and Rivas Dávila, hourly between 8.00 and 18.00.

The trail

Leading west, the asphalted entrance by La Pollera turns into a jeep road penetrating cloud forest at an altitude of 2,150m. After crossing the ridge at 2,250m, the trail begins a long NW descent. The way is superbly misty and green, with dripping tree ferns, epiphytes, palms and rushing brooks. Within half an hour you'll see a huge rock on the left (possible shelter); 15 min. further, a clearing (campsite). Keep straight on at a crossroads lower down (right for distant farm of La Llanada); alt. 1,650m.

For another hour and a half the road continues down, with fine views of coffee hills and planted valleys. Before Hacienda Buenos Aires, a trail comes in on the left from Portachuelo (this is a very long and complicated route). Buenos Aires is an old, tile-roofed house with a *patio de bolas*; alt. 1,060m. Take a left fork below. At Quebrada Las Minas — instead of entering Las Marías, a community on the east bank where the path to Puerto Cruz begins — take the left road, fording the river's 8m bed. There are no problems crossing except after a storm (rainy season, July-Sept.); alt. 680m.

Now begins the return climb. You may see the occasional jeep, and a few houses in small *caseríos*. Keep to the left (right, for Puerto Maya, another 4-5 hours north). The hamlet of Las Luisas, at 900m, has a small food shop and medical dispensary. The road continues up steeply, without branching, through coffee plantations. At 1,250m there is a *bodega* called Las Mercedes; at 1,360m, Portachuelo which also has a shop where you can buy tinned sardines, crackers or soft drinks. This part of the ascent is a hard walk of nearly 2 hours but the road is wide and the tree canopy ever thicker and cooler. The stage above Portachuelo is, if anything, more strenuous. However, there is a fine mountain brook in half an hour. The final ascent to the ridge takes 1½ hours (without stops). A wayside cross at a fork, La Cruz, marks the left turn to the east (right for Sta. Ana and a rutted jeep track down to La Victoria). The altitude is 2,100m.

The hike's last stage (1¾hr) is known as La Entrada, or the Entrance to Costa Maya (although you are leaving). This is a thickly wooded area often swathed in mist. After half an hour's walk, you come to a creek; the road from here on is asphalted. If you are short on time, you may be lucky enough to hitch a ride with a farmer to the main highway; from there it is 8.5km (left) to Colonia Tovar, or 24km (right) down to La Victoria.

Hiking to Puerto Cruz   From the previous circuit two main paths lead to the sea. The way to Puerto Cruz is possibly wilder and less frequented than the route to Puerto Maya. In either case, I doubt that you will meet another outsider. Although neither track is usable by jeep, I have been told that a new road to Puerto Maya has been made as a result of the laying of an electricity line (northwest of San Estéban). There is a dry-weather track, inland and hilly, between Puerto Cruz and Puerto Maya — for jeeps only.

Because from Puerto Cruz it is possible to hitch a ride to Colonia Tovar (there appears to be no public transportation), a summary of my walk may be useful. To simplify the 5 hour descent through beautifully shady woods: at the Quebrada Las Minas (do not cross the ravine), take the right hand road into Las Marías and look for the path (10 min.) to Topo El Paraiso, alt. 950. There follows a long stretch of fine rain forest; the trail nowhere divides. Magnificent old trees shade the fila or ridge of La Virginia before the trail dips to the huts of San José. Ask the campesinos here for the path to Rio Grande; this descends through a handsome, open deciduous forest to a left fork (right for Riitos and Hacienda El Limón). Reaching the Limón River (Rio Grande), the old trail comes to an eroded tunnel-like spot where mule drivers once rested before starting the way up; alt. 100m. Follow the river left. It is an hour's walk, crossing eight times the clear waters which tumble among huge boulders (good camping), before the track emerges at the main road. Less than 3km away is Puerto Cruz, set back from the sea. When fishermen haul their catch into the small, pretty bay there is good fried fish to be had in the village.

EXPLORING BY CAR AND BOAT

If you have a car, remember to fill up in Tovar because there are no services (or restaurants) on the paved roads to the sea, except in Carayaca. The descent begins at the arch of Colonia Tovar, winding through bracken and cool forests to coffee groves shaded by bucares, the coral trees whose bright orange flowers are so splendid in February/March. At the end of each road there is a bay and fishing boats, usually for hire.

El Limón-Puerto Cruz

Farthest west, this road has more twists than a snake so allow 4 hours round trip if you plan to return to Tovar. The distance is 43km to the tranquil little harbour of Puerto Cruz, crossing the coffee hacienda of El Limón half way.

Staying in El Limón

Retired archaeologist Luis Laffer and his wife Margarita have built a small house with guest rooms, on the right 2km before Hacienda El Limón. It is hidden among the coffee shade trees in an area littered with petroglyphs. There are two independent units, very basic (tin roof, shower, cooker). Bring enough food because there are few supplies to be had once you leave Colonia Tovar.

Alison Vickers and Tim Wainwright found their stay in El Limón 'by far our most interesting experience in Venezuela'. They drove in by way of the coast, warning that this should not be attempted without a 4-wheel-drive. 'We made it as far as Chichiriviche, at which point we got stuck. We eventually arrived at Puerto Cruz in the dark to find that there is nowhere to stay. Feeling tired and fed up we headed back towards Colonia Tovar and decided to investigate a sign we had seen earlier saying "Rooms-Zimmer & Museo de Petroglifos". Driving up a grassy track we were warmly greeted by Luis Laffer and thus began the richest part of our stay. A refugee from Hungary some 40 years earlier, he has spent much of his life recording, cataloguing and attempting to preserve the traditional culture of Venezuela. He is an incredible source of information. His simple house which is also a museum has a wealth of books, sound recordings and anthropological relics. He and Margarita support his archaeological work by growing coffee, renting out a couple of rooms for $20 a weekend — you pay the same whether you stay the whole weekend or not. He will also take you on jeep trips to visit remote petroglyphs for about $7.50 trip. A weekend simple in accommodation and food, but rich in company.'

Puerto Cruz

This offers a lovely intimate beach, trees for hammocks, fried fish (on weekends), beer. A very stony, tortuous jeep track crosses the sun-baked promontory to Chichiriviche and another track has been opened west to Puerto Maya, 7km, so you need no longer hire a fishing boat.

Puerto Maya

The village is on an even smaller cove marking the boundary of Henri Pittier National Park. Here, sheltered between the skirts of two mountains, 'the race with time seems to stop.' Outsiders, in this case C.J. Arteaga, reported spending hours in a small boat rounding the cape under cliffs sculpted by the surf into caves like open jaws. Behind Puerto Maya's sandy cove shaded by coconuts are the village huts and a chapel. Some 200 inhabitants live from fishing, maize, yuca, pigs and chickens. Descendants of African slaves, the people of Maya laugh, dance, play the big drums and drink quarts of rum at traditional fiestas. There's a deluxe new pension called the Hotel Guaka-Maya (reservations with Sun Chichi in Caracas on 02-315891). In Caracas, Sun Chichi offers a 3 day/2 night package at $100, including transportation from Puerto Cruz; (02) 312953, fax 320046.

Chichiriviche

Holy days such as the Feast of John the Baptist (June 24) are celebrated in Chichiriviche as in other villages along the central coast. Like Puerto Cruz, Chichiriviche (Vargas District) should not be confused with larger towns of the same name in Falcón and Anzoátegui. Start on the road towards Puerto Cruz and take the 2nd right turn, about 6km before El Limón (the first fork is the Carayaca road). You will want to go slowly over the next 22.5km to the sea to take in fine sea views and the richly varied plants. Ferns, flowers and heliconias proliferate at the roadside; vines, orchids and bromeliads drape trees in the cloud forest. Lower down, and hotter, are small farms. Because the last half is pot-holed and crosses a river many times, a car with ample clearance is a good idea. The clear Chichiriviche River and the road come out at a tidy village on a clean crescent bay enclosed by promontories. There is good fried fish, but no accommodation at the last report.

If you are camping, you can explore a track to the west which dips to pebbly shores such as Petariquito, before rejoining the road to **Oricao**. There is a private beach club in Oricao, so the bay is no longer primitive. Some 4km beyond, a turn-off heads back into the mountains, with another choice of routes. By taking the right hand, you twist up another wooded road to Colonia Tovar again; the left fork heads for the pueblos of **Tarma**, 2km, and **Carayaca**, 5km (gasoline here). From Carayaca, there is a return road to the sea, plus a road covering the 30km back up to the Junquito-Tovar road.

Sloths, the champion survivors

When on the ground sloths are completely helpless, rather like moth-eaten doormats. (It's true, their fur has moths; but the moths eat algae, not fur.) Their legs cannot hold their belly off the ground and they move by hooking themselves along. Yet when a sloth crosses the road, drivers stop, or even lend a hand. This is done safely from behind by grabbing the sloth under the armpits and holding the creature, often surprisingly light, with its long claws *away* from yourself. In Venezuela, many rescued *perezas* are put in town squares and if you look high in the canopy you can often see sloths in the Plaza Bolívar in Caracas and cities in the interior. They are not early risers and stay curled in a ball until the 9 o'clock sun warms them.

Sloths make almost no alarm cry, grunting or hissing in a whisper. They appear to see poorly, and locate each other with a thin, high whistle. If a baby is separated from its mother, or falls out of the tree, it stands a poor chance of finding her again. Mothers bear a single young, which rides around on her chest for several months. William Beebe observed that infant sloths walk upright on branches but soon learn to hang upside down. And their fur grows from the belly to the back.

Wet or dry, sloths keep an endearing half-smile, as if bemused. How do they survive? Very well, thank you. Leaves give them both food and water, and as their usual habitat is evergreen forest, one or another tree species in their territory will have tender leaves. They can swim across rivers. They are not so slow as believed and given a few moments will disappear into the canopy. Greenish algae grow in microscopic grooves on their fur, making splendid camouflage. Their feet, having no free toes, are adapted for hanging by hook-like claws (our sloth is the threetoed *Bradypus sp.*), and their grip is like iron. I have seen a male fight his rival to the death.

Best of all, people in Venezuela seldom eat sloths because they are more mat than meat. Boys think to kill so sluggish an animal is unsporting. Dogs pay them little heed, perhaps because sloths have almost no smell. Curiously, sloths cover over their faeces, coming down from their tree to do so. While clinging to the trunk they have been seen to open a hole at the base with their stumpy tail, and defecate in it. Even zoos don't want sloths because they do not adapt well to captivity. However, a clue to this mystery lies in the umbrella-leaved cecropia or *yagrumos* where sloths are most often found. These trees have hollow stems colonised by ants. Apparently it's not freedom that sloths pine for, but something in their diet akin to formic acid which is what ants contain.

Chapter 8

The coast: La Guaira to Barlovento

LA GUAIRA — THE OLD SEA PORT

The sea approach to La Guaira, Venezuela's main port lying about 36km (± 1hr) from Caracas, is striking. 'It seems as if the Pyrenees or the Alps, stripped of their snows, had risen from the bosom of the ocean, so much more stupendous do mountains appear when viewed for the first time from the sea.' It's as true now as when Alexander von Humboldt wrote these lines in 1799. Then, however, the landing was difficult and the anchorage bad. Today, docks handle a constant flow of freighters and cruise ships, at times the Cunard Countess on its Caribbean circle, the Queen Elizabeth in from New York, the C Line on weekly cruises, Holland America from Florida, and the Victoria which also touches at Margarita Island. But berths on freighters to/from Europe are as hard to find as hen's teeth.

Take almost any *Litoral* bus from Caracas to the coast, except those for Catia La Mar (west). From the Nuevo Circo Terminal buses leave constantly for the port and Macuto, Caraballeda, Naiguatá and Los Caracas. Also, from Avenida Sucre at the Gato Negro metro station, *por puestos* go to La Guaira and Maiquetía.

La Guaira's origins as a port date to 1567 when Diego de Losada founded Caracas in a valley some 24km over the mountains. But La Guaira never had an official founding and for over a century was exposed to attacks by pirates such as Amyas Preston, who actually sacked Caracas in 1595. The old coast town, a kilometre east of the present port, is nearly intact, built on the steep streets up to the forts. A look around the old sector's charming streets, some too narrow for cars, is fun. One alley is called Salsipuedes, meaning 'get out if you can', because the houses on either side are so close you can touch both at once.

The imposing Casa Guipuzcoana, perhaps the largest civil structure of the colonial era, stands on the coast road. Now the seat

of municipal offices, it dates from 1734 when it was built as
headquarters for the royal trading monopoly, the Guipuzcoana
Company, run by Basques who exported cacao and indigo and
brought back guns, tools, wine and cloth. Rife with corruption and
abuses, the Guipuzcoana was hated by the *criollos*. The three-storey
building was used as a customs house for 200 years. Restored in
the 1970s, the building's balconies, patios and tall rooms are open
to the public, Tue.-Sun. 8.00 to 18.00.

At No.18-13 Calle Bolívar behind the Guipuzcoana is the beautifully
kept Boulton house. Here British trader John Boulton, who arrived in
the late 1820s as a young man, began an import-export business
which is still going strong today. The Boulton family have restored
the house as a museum of La Guaira's history. The floor came from
Scotland as paving stones used for ship's ballast. The museum,
(031) 25921, is open Tue.-Fri. 9.30 to 13.00, 15.00 to 18.00; Sat.-Sun.
9.00 to 13.00. A few steps along this street of converted warehouses
is the tile-roofed home of José María Vargas, a doctor who became
Venezuela's second president in 1835. And, facing shady Plaza
Vargas, is a two-storey balconied house where the English La Guaira
Harbour Company managed income from all the country's major
ports, given as guarantee for an 1864 loan of 1.5 million pounds.
The concession was nationalised in 1936.

Another colonial house at No.9, Callejón San Francisco (go 3
blocks east and turn right 50m uphill), bears the name of rebel José
María España who was hanged by the Spaniards in 1799. Across
the arroyo here is the Iglesia San Pedro Apostol which dates from
1847. Continuing uphill, you find Callejón Salsipuedes, half a block
below (and west of) La Ermita Church built in 1863 to replace an
earlier church. Much of La Guaira had to be rebuilt after the 1812
earthquake. Today's square-towered La Ermita has been beautifully
restored, as has the 17th Century powderhouse or Polvorín about
250m further up the Camino Real. The steep royal road, which may
still be hiked to Caracas by way of Las Aguadas, passes El Vigía, a
fort also called Zamuro, or vulture (take a right fork above the
Polvorín). And, 2km up, with its own eagle's view over La Guaira, is
San Carlos Fortress, built in 1769 on the Spanish star plan, and
restored in 1980.

MACUTO AND THE CENTRAL *LITORAL*

The drive east to Los Caracas follows a dramatic coast of
overhanging cliffs, breakers and seaside towns, dotted with safe,
walled-in (and therefore less appealing) public beaches. If you can
rent a sturdy car by all means spend two days exploring beyond Los

Caracas where the coast is surprisingly untouched. The road is mostly unpaved, although with the great advantage of providing a circular route back to Caracas via Higuerote. You will do well to get a morning start from one of the modest hotels in Macuto, and to avoid Sundays and holidays when long queues of cars stream to clubs and beaches on the developed *Litoral Central*. Such beaches suffer from overcrowding, although recent clean-ups and improved sewage treatment have lessened water contamination to 'acceptable levels'.

Macuto, 5km from La Guaira, was the seaside spot favoured by Caraqueños in the 19th Century. The town has a pleasant nostalgic air, a plaza full of pigeons and a *Paseo* or shore promenade shaded by seagrape trees. Its overused *balneario* or public beach has changing rooms. Hotels and restaurants facing (but not on) the sea are modest. One such hotel-restaurant is El Alamo where tables are set under trees. Other better known hotels include the Riviera, (031) 44313; Macuto, (031) 461854; and Las Quince Letras, (031) 461011; plus smaller ones such as the Coral, (031) 46132, and the Diana, (031) 461553. Behind Las Quince Letras is the small studio dwelling built by home-grown impressionist painter Armando Reverón (1889-1954), the 'wild man' of art who made life-sized rag dolls for models.

'We booked in the Hotel Santiago, a new hotel on the seafront, with a pool on the roof; about £18 double, a/c, (031) 461433. Hotel Alamo is very good value at £8, but basic and no hot water. The restaurant is excellent, especially nice sitting under the seagrape trees; probably the best food on the coast. To return to the airport get a *por puesto* for Catia la Mar and ask for "Entrada Aeropuerto Nacional" (or "Internacional").' (J and K Whitehead)

Along the pedestrian seawalk leading eastward from Macuto to **Los Corales-Caraballeda** are more protected public *balnearios*: El Playón, Camurí Chico, Ali Baba, and Caribito. Respect the signs saying *PROHIBIDO* on unused beaches: these mean dangerous currents. In the posh resort area of Caraballeda, the 543-room Macuto Sheraton, (031) 944300, has a public beach, so is troubled by trash. On an adjacent beach the Melia Caribe, (031) 945555, has 300 deluxe rooms. Some smaller and medium hotels in the area, without private beaches, are: the Royal Atlantic, (031) 941350, Bahía by the Sea, (031) 942417, Costa Azul, (031) 943530, Fiore, (031) 941743, and Mar y Cel, (031) 942174. Canadian tourists first promoted the attractions of this 'sophisticated ocean playground' which they call simply Caribe. Besides the Melia Caribe, the Canadians use small modern aparthotels such as the Golf Caribe and Avila Caribe, not on the beach (apartments cost some $100 a day without meals).

The **Marina and Yacht Club**, (031) 940271, by the Sheraton are good places to charter vessels for deepsea fishing or cruises to Los Roques Archipelago — anywhere you want to go. If you have a party of at least four, and are sure of your sea legs, a holiday to tropical islands can be fantastic AND reasonable on a fully crewed motor-sailer: some $550 a day includes boat, crew, food and beer. One agency, Yachting Tours, operates in the Sheraton and another, Rentaboat, operates from the Melia. Gigi Charters have a 5-room house opposite the Sheraton; they charge $750 for a day's deepsea fishing. Enquire at Correa Travel, (02) 7625815, fax 7625952. This coast reputedly has some of the best white marlin fishing in the world. Also good for snapper, snook, tarpon, bonefish, kingfish, wahoo, barracuda, tuna.

Seaside restaurants in road stops such as Carmen de Uria, although bare of niceties, serve really fresh fish at modest prices. Worth the trip.

Beyond Caraballeda is a string of beach clubs such as the Tanaguarena and Puerto Azul, followed by the public beach (nice, but dubious sanitation) at **Naiguatá**. The streets of this old village throb to big drums on the Fiesta de San Juan, June 24, and Corpus Christi, an occasion for costumed devil dancers (usually a Thursday in early June). Continuing east, the coast is splendid as the road hugs a narrow shore between surf and cliffs.

The workers 'vacation city' of **Los Caracas** is at the end of the paved road (47km from La Guaira). By the entrance an INCRET office has a map of the aging and very large holiday complex built by dictator Pérez Jiménez in 1955. It's open to anyone, although give-away prices guarantee full occupancy during school holidays. In a green park of 125 acres, trees shade 170 bungalows which provide kitchen and beds for six at about $15. There are also 160 hotel rooms and apartments (with kitchen) in the same range, unadorned but clean. Salt water pool, cafeterias, supermarket, cinema, chapel.

To Chuspa

The last telephones and petrol are in Los Caracas. Beyond, the lush coast is miraculously undeveloped and beaches are solitary most of the year. With few services a rough road goes east about 80km (2½-3 hours) to join the Chirimena-Higuerote highway. A jeep is recommended if you go in the rainy season. A *por puesto* jeep line runs from Plaza del Consul in La Guaira as far as La Sabana. There are modest hostels in Todasana, La Sabana and Chuspa, and rooms can be rented in some villages. Small restaurants (*comedores*) will prepare fish and rice if you arrive in good time. Few shops sell fresh fruit although oranges, bananas and mangos seem to grow everywhere. Adventure Jeep Tours run 2-day packages, beaching along uninhabited coves, overnighting in Todasana; costs, all inclusive (pick-up from Caracas hotel), are about $120, 2 days/1 night; speak to Max Baena at (031) 20872, or leave him a message at 6619222 'clave 5344'. On this coast the big fiestas celebrate June 24, the Tambores de San Juan, and September 8, the day of the Virgen del Valle.

The first hamlet is Quebrada Seca, 2.5km, followed in 7.5km by **Osma**. A left turn at the creek leads to Osma beach (nothing special). A right turn follows the Osma River inland 3km to Granja Osman, a green spot with six thatched bamboo cottages for rent and facilities for snorkelling, windsurfing and fishing at a different beach every day. Owner Pedro Luis Paredes cooks by torchlight; no electricity, no telephone. For reservations contact the Audubon Society or Agencia Paisajes at (02) 321683, fax 322656; prices (without transportation) are about $30 a day with food, snorkelling, beaching.

Passing the picture postcard bay of Oritapo with its summer homes and small river, the next village is **Todasana**, 12km from Osma River. I arrived on a weekday at 4pm and found nowhere to eat: the fish restaurant near the sea was closed, even the cook at the Egua Hotel had gone home. Evidently travellers were expected only on weekends. The roadside Egua (trees but no view) has 29 simple rooms with bathroom, fan, at about $12 a double. Behind a high wall up the street is the Mini Hotel Simti, a good economical base with 10 comfortable rooms. Bring your own pasta and the Italian owner, Silvio Merletti, will cook it *al dente* (information (031) 23174 office hours). 1.5km beyond Todasana is Playa Grande, a long crescent beach where seagrape trees serve for slinging hammocks; the sea can be fairly rough from January to March. Another natural campsite, 7km eastward, is known as La Cascada where a brook cascades into a small pool on the right of the road behind a bamboo clump (if you reach a small bridge, you've gone too far); no houses nearby, yet.

La Sabana, off the main road (12km from Todasana), is on a bluff above the sea. Sparkling with flowers and fresh paint, it is one of the prettiest villages on the entire coast. It has a church, hospital, restaurant, police station. A Spanish couple runs a small hotel (no phone). Some villagers let pleasant rooms; try Juan Escobar, Calle 5 de Julio. To the east of La Sabana coconut-shaded sands extend towards a beach several kilometres long. The sea may be rough in windy weather, but the beach is deserted more often than not. Above this bay is a new house built by Andrés and Beatriz Berman who are making a spa in their aloe plantation. They have a good site where they plan to put cottages.

Karen and John Whitehead got to La Sabana by bus from La Guaira. They write: 'The bus (called Rosita!) is very slow but very cheap, Bs.100. It goes daily and is quite an experience, not dissimilar to a scene from *Romancing the Stone*, chickens and all. When in La Sabana we stopped in a room (around £5) above the large bar. We were there for the San Juan fiesta, June 24. Note — try not to get a room too close to the drums. A nice beach with a bar and fried fish shop, although it is difficult to get food at midweek; ask at the large bar. A few mosquitoes around, too.'

Caruao is close by, its entrance neatly cobbled. For the fine beach, turn left at the church. However, outsiders have been prey to thieves despite a conspicuous police station. Rooms to rent vary: at the top end is Posada Turística Caruao Mar on Plaza Bolívar. The house has 6 doubles with bath, at Bs.900 a person with breakfast. For information or transportation ring (02) 818069, 812491. Ask the way to the shady Aguas Calientes River with its five falls and deep pools, one called **El Pozo del Cura**. The earth road there is a pleasant walk of 2.5km; a left fork half way goes to the experimental garden planted with fruit trees and palms by Capt. Harry Gibson. He advises drivers not to leave vehicles by the road, but to park at the caretaker's, Sr. Romulito, in the village.

Chuspa is the last seaside village (7km from Caruao, good shade) before the road cuts across the headland. The old fishing village is at the beach's east end at the mouth of the small river. Unusually well cared for, it has clean streets and a tree-lined paseo with a statue of Francisco Fajardo who founded a settlement here in 1555. Many inhabitants are descendants of plantation slaves. Their catch is sold at the Venta de Hielo or icehouse by the river's outlet where small boats are hauled in. On work days (remember that Friday is called '*pequeño sábado*') and on Saturday until noon, you can buy fish at half the Caracas price. A restaurant by the sea serves fried fish. In the village ask about rooms to rent.

Cool and green, although at times very muddy, the road winds on through tall forest. It passes the river and community of Aricagua to arrive at a tiny village, Pueblo Seco, 16km from Chuspa. From here it is 6.8km to the paved highway. At the junction turn left for **Chirimena**, 3km. Houses crowd Chirimena's best beach but a small cove opens to the sea at the east end. Or, turn right on the highway, and in 6km take a left fork for **Puerto Francés** on Cape Codera, 8km. Dry and hot, this good road passes access to Buche beach (unkempt and sometimes tarry) and Lagoven's oil storage tanks at Los Totumos. Keep straight for the cape's north side and the lovely bay of Puerto Francés, erstwhile anchorage of French pirates. Weekend stalls sell fried fish; during the week the beach is yours.

Carenero means a place for careening, to haul boats on land for scraping the hull. Near the Puerto Francés fork, the old port today has several marinas and yacht clubs (bar and restaurant with tablecloths). Ask about hiring a boat to Los Roques... Continue 6km to the unappealing seaside town of Higuerote where the bay is shallow and boring and the beach is brown (not very clean water). There are several hotels. Buses and *por puestos* go frequently to Caracas, about 130km.

Barlovento   You won't find it on road maps but Barlovento is important as the region inland from Higuerote which is renowned for lush cacao and fruit plantations and for its traditional black culture. Many inhabitants are descendants of Nigeria's Yoruba tribe. There are old songs about Barlovento: *Tierra ardiente y del tambor/ tierra de las fulías y negras finas/ que llevan de fiesta su cintura prieta/ al son de las curvetas/ qui-ta qui-ta qui de las minas...*

   The *curveta* and *mina* drums of Barlovento call visitors to the pueblos of **Curiepe, Chuspa and Caruao** on the Fiesta de San Juan, June 23-24, and San Pedro, June 27-28. The street dances are nonstop, the rum also. It's quite an experience. Curiepe is 8km west of Higuerote (there's a new access road north of Carenero, too). **Birongo**, another 10km further along the same road through shady cacao hills, is an apparently uneventful village of slave descendants. But it has a lively reputation for *santería* rituals; people come long distances to consult famous *brujos* or witchdoctors.

   On another track, shortly before Birongo there is a sign for Marasmita; take this for the Cueva Alfredo Jahn, second largest of Venezuela's caves with 4km of galleries. It is above the left bank of the Birongo River, alt. 210m. Although declared a national monument, it is little visited. (More information: see *SPECIAL INTERESTS — Caving*.)

---

   they are called *Ewaipanoma:* they are reported to haue their eyes in their ſhoulders, and their mouths in the middle of their breaſts, & that a long train of haire groweth backward betwen their ſhoulders.

Sir Walter Raleigh describes an "ethnic group" in *The Discoverie of the Large, Rich and Bewtiful Empyre of Guiana.*

SECTION THREE

THE CARIBBEAN RESORTS

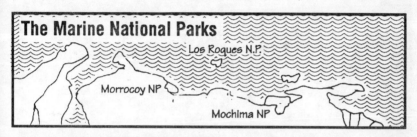

The Marine National Parks

Margarita & West Sucre

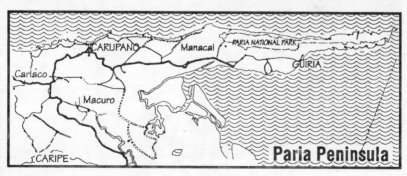

Paria Peninsula

Chapter 9

The marine national parks

The Robinson Crusoe experience

There are three island groups where you may stay on uninhabited beaches: Los Roques (see page 96, 97), Morrocoy (offshore Tucacas and Chichiriviche in Falcón State) (see page 100, 102), and Mochima, west of Cumaná (see page 105). All have been declared national parks in view of their fragile ecosystems of coral, salt flats, mangrove swamps and marine communities.

In all cases you must be self-sufficient with enough food to last your stay (you may be able to supplement your food with sea produce). Water will be the main problem; you should bring a supply with you and a large sheet of plastic for collecting rain water. Or use your tent rain fly for the purpose. You will also need your tent for shade (hammocks are a possibility on the few islands that have palm trees or mangroves but otherwise you are better off with a tent).

The keys are popular with holidaying Venezuelans on long weekends and school vacations. Avoid windless months such as November-December when tiny biting midges make camping miserable, not to say impossible, after sundown!

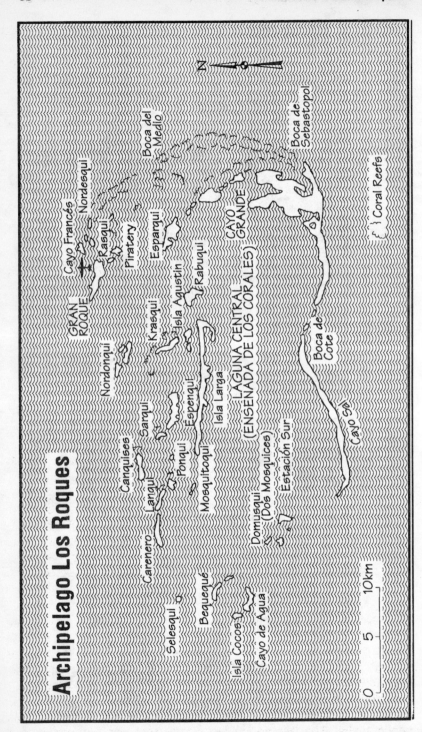

Archipelago Los Roques

PARQUE NACIONAL ARCHIPIÉLAGO LOS ROQUES

The park comprises about 50 named islands and a further 200 or so banks, islets and coral reefs. The archipelago is 36km east to west, 24km north to south, and lies 160km north of La Guaira. Its odd names come from old English navigators (who turned the Indian *cayo* into 'key'): Spanish Key - *Espenquí*, Salt Key - *Sarquí*, Northeast Key - *Nordisquí*, Sail Key - *Selesquí*, Little Spar Key - *Esparquí*, Robert's Key - *Rabusquí*, West Point - *Uespén*. *Cayo Mosquito* was once Musket and *Domusquí* was Domain Key. The shallow central lagoon is crystal clear and wonderful for snorkelling where there is coral. Barrier reefs in the east and south drop off into deep ocean water. All islands, except Gran Roque which is part of the continental shelf, have fine coral-sand beaches.

The archipelago is home to 80 species of birds — petrels, pelicans, frigate birds, flamingoes, down to canaries. **Selesqui, Bequevé, Canquises** and **Cayo Bobo Negro** are noted for birds. There are lizards but no snakes, and no native mammals except for a fishing bat. Four turtle species are all on the endangered list, the most persecuted being the green turtle (*Chelonia mydas*). During laying season the females are easily captured on beaches by fishermen who also steal the eggs. Many fishermen come from Margarita, 300km east, for the lucrative lobster season (November to April). Their temporary shelters are called *rancherías*.

The beautiful queen conch (*Strombus gigas*) is also protected. It is now illegal to sell or eat conches (*botutos*) because they have been overfished. Empty shells form huge mounds as high as 10m. Valued as high protein food, conches have been eaten by islanders since pre-history. Archaeologists Marlena and Andrzej Antczak have found tools, spoons and ornaments made of shell, the remains of a 'conch culture' a thousand years old. Their excavations show that groups which came from the mainland used empty conches to gather rainwater. Piles of conch shells left by such Indians at the water's edge are today well inland, measuring the islands' growth.

Gran Roque

The main island has a fishing village of about 600 people. Gran Roque is the park headquarters. There is a Guardia Nacional post, fishing inspector's office, primary school, desalination plant, telephone service and town generator. However, water and electricity are erratic; the rubbish truck (one of the island's few vehicles) dumps all garbage into a bay NW of the village and there are no septic tanks. The airstrip shows clearly that Los Roques is a playground of the rich.

Once on Gran Roque you can negotiate with local fishermen for transport to an uninhabited island. Nearby inhabited islands are Madrizquí, occupied by vacation houses of the wealthy, and Isla Fernando and Crasquí, fishing settlements. Check with the locals which of the islands has the best snorkelling — not all are fringed with coral. At present it seems that scuba diving and non-commercial fishing are covered by permits from Inparques. Check out the situation when you arrive, or get a permit beforehand from Parques Nacionales (see *Chapter 3, Permits*). You can easily arrange for the crew who drop you at the island of your choice to stop by from time to time with fish — and to pick you up when it's time to return to the mainland.

Getting there

You may with perseverance find a small fishing boat to Los Roques. Ask at the Muelle de Pescadores in La Guaira who is the next *capitán* due to leave (most skippers pull out at midnight). CAVE, (02) 9521947 and (031) 551054, flies daily to Gran Roque from Porlamar and Maiquetía, $30, as well as conducting day tours from Caracas for $140. CAVE's agency is Diadema Tours, (02) 9521840. Aereotuy also has daily flights from Porlamar and Maiquetía, specify *traslado unicamente*. For day trips with fresh fish lunch, boat ride, watersports, insurance, bilingual guide, ring Aereotuy, (02) 7616231, 761247, fax 7625254. Charter companies such as Chapi Tours, (02) 7812108, lay on excursions using a glass-bottom catamaran; lodging at the Villa Chapi (2 days' fishing, $290). Scuba diving is offered by Sesto Continente for about $130 a day including flight, pension on Gran Roque, all food and equipment; reservations (02) 5637244, fax 5627432.

All kinds of crewed yachts and sailing craft can be hired in Caracas or Puerto La Cruz. Linda Sonderman who runs Alpi Tours offers cruises and fishing/diving trips in 35' to 52' sailboats to Los Roques, or a luxury 76' sailboat with 4 cabins, a/c. Such cruises, with captain and sailor, include all food, national drinks and sports such as snorkelling, windsurfing, fishing, waterskiing and diving. Write Alpi Tour, Torre Centro, Centro Parque Boyacá, Los Dos Caminos, Caracas; call (02) 2831433, or fax 2847098.

Where to stay

On Gran Roque there are some informal restaurants and lodgings as well as air-conditioned pensions in remodelled cottages. The expensive pensions arrange packages including flight and tour of keys. For example, the 9-bed Posada de Los Roques charges $100 for a day tour plus $100 a night; reservations through Correa, (02) 7625815, fax 7625952. The Villa Turística, 7 doubles, offers 3 days/2 nights for $400, extra night $135; reservations through Majestic, (02) 210356, fax 211135.

Marine Biological Station

On Dos Mosquises, an island in the southern archipelago, the Fundación Científica Los Roques runs a biological station. There are breeding tanks where green turtles and other endangered species are raised for later release in the archipelago. The station's biologists were the first to raise queen conch larvae in captivity. Visitors are welcome on Saturdays, Sundays and holidays. The station has T-shirts, maps and books for sale. Dos Mosquises is the only island with an airstrip aside from Gran Roque, but prior permission to land should be requested the Foundation in Caracas, (02) 2613461.

Chipichipis and guacucos

Chipichipis are small and you need about half a bucketful to make a good broth, but *guacucos* can be eaten directly like a small oyster.

In eastern Venezuela and Margarita, people on the coast go to the seaside early in the morning to dig for the *chipichipis*. Yellow, cream or pink, these wedge-shaped bivalves (*Donax sp.*) leave air-holes in the sand as waves recede. Wash them well and boil in water, adding chopped onion, garlic, sweet pepper and salt. The pot should have a close-fitting lid to keep in the aroma. Done when the *chipichipis* open up, about 30 minutes.

In La Restinga Park on Margarita, the wide beach lining La Guardia Bay is made of broken shells and *guacucos*. You just need a knife to open them.' (Luis Armas) This mollusc, an inch or so long, is a kind of venus shell (*Tivela mactroides*).

PARQUE NACIONAL MORROCOY

The mangroves, canals, coral keys and headland which make up this national park of 320km² were saved from runaway development in 1974 by a government determined to preserve the fragile ecosystem. Home to frigate birds (they nest on Isla de Pájaros in December-January), spoonbills, flamingoes, ibis and a host of marvellous coral-dwelling creatures, here is a region easily accessible for the backpacking Robinson Crusoe. However, when the trade winds die (Nov.-Dec.), tiny biting gnats can make camping a torture. Look for a hotel!

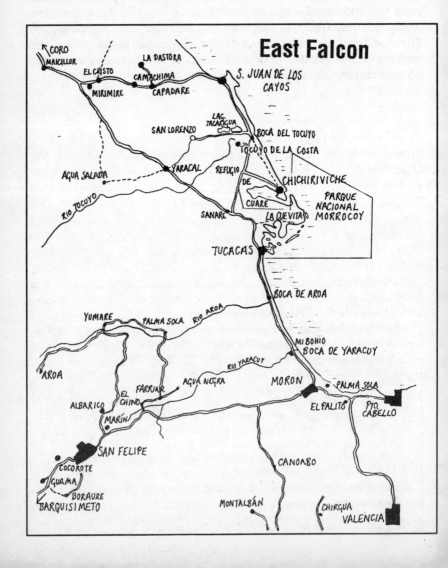

Tucacas

The town is scruffy but right on the coastal highway of Falcón State. Nearby an airstrip has been reconditioned, and plush new resorts have opened. Tucacas has marinas, a diving centre, bank, food and liquor shops (plenty of the latter), ice and restaurants.

Getting there

A car can cover the 250km from Caracas in 3 hours; *por puestos* will take 4. As reported by Mark Dutton in 1991: 'Bus service from the Nuevo Circo to Valencia seems to be very regular; we got straight on a bus that left five minutes later. At the Valencia terminal (2hr 3min), you pay Bs.2 to enter the departure area. The *por puesto* to Tucacas took an hour and a quarter and dropped us on the highway. Some Morrocoy packages include flight from Caracas (plus hotel, 2 meals, boat to the keys; enquire at Parnass, (02) 2614618, fax 9590787.

Where to stay

Waterfront hotels range from a 600-suite condominium resort, the Morrocoy Conjunto Náutico, to family-run inns. Providing all food and launch services, inns such as Chalets Morrocoy, (042) 84858, and Posada Balijú on Calle Libertad, (042) 84603, charge about $70 day; ask at Colorama, (02) 2617732, fax 2621828, for arrangements including car and driver from Caracas. Town hotels such as the Manaure, 45 rooms and restaurant on Avenida Silva, (042) 84286, and the Gaeta on Calle Ayacucho are convenient and fill up quickly on weekends. If you can overlook its excruciating taste, the Complejo Turístico Said offers motel accommodation on the highway with 30 cabins for 6 people; reasonable.

Karen and John Whitehead reported recently, 'the Hotel Manaure looks good from the outside but this is misleading. The rooms smell of mildew, the electricity supply at best is irrational and at worst dangerous. The staff are very unhelpful. The rooms are very expensive. Also the restaurant is expensive, offering poor quality and unappetising meals.' They recommend trying the cheap small local hotels near the waterfront.

Morrocoy's keys

You don't have to take a boat to reach the park — just walk down the main street and over the bridge to Punta Brava. This fairly large island with huge parking lots is very crowded on weekends.

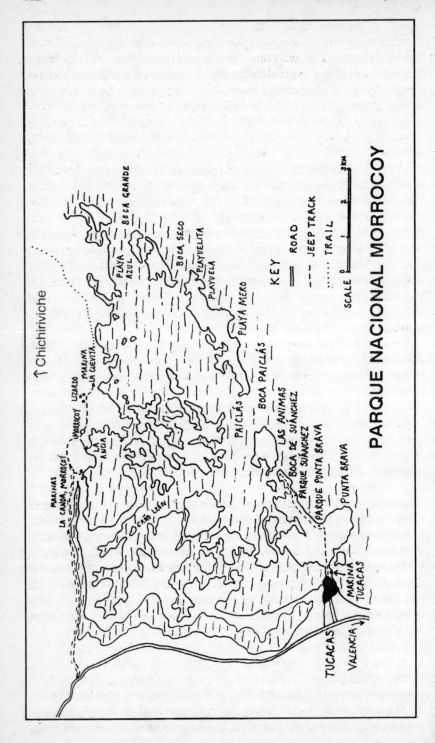

PARQUE NACIONAL MORROCOY

Camping is permitted and there are some palm trees. For an uninhabited island, however, go to the Puerto and hire a boat there to one of the *cayos* with fine beaches such as Paicla, Playa Mero, Playuelita and Sombrero. Monday to Wednesday is the best time. No camping fires permitted.

Mark Dutton and James Mead provided the following information. 'The cost of a small open boat or *lancha* to Cayo Sombrero, one of the farthest, is about $20 return, but this covers as many passengers and gear as will fit, 4 to 8 people. El Sombrero island reputedly has the best and breeziest beach. We loaded up with a wheelbarrow from a local supermarket, including two large containers of water. There are many palms to sling a hammock from. We preferred the far side as there was a stronger wind to blow away insects.

'The windward beach is protected by a coral reef. The sea inside, named La Piscina or pool, is ideal for swimming and snorkelling; we were rarely out of our depth. We arranged for our boatman to pick us up on Friday morning, but changed our minds and were able to hitch a lift with another couple. Boatmen are always happy to bring you more food or water if you stay on. There are regular visits by a fish and chips man and icecream vendor (the coconut icecream is luscious but expensive at Bs.70). The beach is cleaned every day and has many toilets.'

Steve Whitaker called it 'Paradise — all palm trees and white beaches and clear sea. Some of the islands are fabulous for birds and all along the coast towards Chichiriviche are flocks of flamingoes.

'Diving in the area was good and we saw superb coral, spotted rays and barracuda. Excellent diving facilities and trips can be arranged through Mike Osborn, at Submatur.

Scuba diving   Mike Osborn's small dive shop, Submatur, is at No.6 Calle Ayacucho, the end of Tucacas' main street near the port; (042) 84028, 84679 (night). A NAUI licensed instructor, Mike takes divers to the best reefs and provides all equipment for about $55 a person; snorkelling about $15 (less, if you bring your own gear). Write to his Caracas address: Apartado 68512, Caracas 1062-A; fax (58 2) 9414939. Ask him about organising a week-long trip to the uninhabited **Archipiélago de Las Aves** 160km north. This is formed by windward and leeward islands, *barlovento* in the east and *sotavento* in the west.

Punta Tucacas   An earth road borders the Morrocoy headland. It leaves the Falcón highway at Km 71 and continues to Tucacas Point and Mayorquines, a hot area of thorny scrub where wildlife includes crab foxes, ocelots and monkeys. There are few facilities apart from private marinas such as La Canoa, Morrocoy, La Cuevita; with luck you can find a boatman with a *lancha* for hire. One or two rather exclusive guest houses operate near Lizardo. No beaches.

Chichiriviche

On the park's northern rim are decent hotels in a town which is pot-holed and rubbish-ringed. However, the road to Chichiriviche crosses 12km of lagoons where wading birds are spectacular. At dusk scarlet ibis, roseate spoonbills, parrots and egrets fly in to roost in mangrove swamps. In the rainy season, flocks of flamingoes come to feed. Nearby is the Gulf of Cuare, a wildlife refuge. Launches take beach-goers to nearby keys such as Pelón, Peraza, Los Pescadores, Cayo Sal and Cayo Sombrero which is closer to Chichiriviche than to Tucacas. The price of the boat ride corresponds to distance, not to how many passengers; you pay when you return. You can be shuttled to the closest keys, Sal or Muerto, for about $5, or the farthest, Pescador or Sombrero, for $20. Boatmen add an extra $2.50 for following day pick-up. Or hire a boat at about $50 to explore beaches for the day.

Getting there

Chichiriviche can be easily reached from Puerto Cabello or from Barquisimeto. From the latter get a bus (terminal on Carrera 24 and Calle 42) to San Felipe, and cross the road to catch the bus for Morón and from Morón to Tucacas.

Where to stay

Among the hotels, the Mario (042) 86814, and La Garza (042) 86711, are pricier, about $30; the Parador Manaure (042) 86452, and the Capri (042) 86025, quite reasonable. The Garza and Manaure's prices include breakfast and supper. They are not on the beach but most have pools. There are two new hotels on the shore road to the Fábrica de Cemento: La Puerta (042) 86621, and Vaya Vaya (042) 86304, popular for its disco and ice cream parlour. Especially good value is the small Hotel Náutico, with two good meals and launch service for about $20 a day. The only hotel on the sea, it is a rather old structure patronised by birders and foreigners. In Caracas, ring Sun Chichi, (02) 312953, fax 320016.

Andrea Bullock writes: 'If your group is large enough (4-6) stay at the Villa Marina Apart-Hotel which provides self-catering apartments by the day or week. The address is Via Fábrica de Cemento, Sector Sur Chichiriviche, (042) 86205, 86441.

'There is a small snack bar that sells beer and hamburgers (no coffee) and a swimming pool. I met several Venezuelan families on holiday here. It's a hundred yard walk to the boat launch where you can get rides to the islands. The ride to the furthest island, Cayo Sombrero, costs £14. The rest are less than that. You can book diving tours at the boat launch. And the boats will pick you up again. You just tell them when you want to return. There is a guide who speaks French, Marcel Longon, at the Hotel Náutico (200 yards down the beach from the boat launch) who has his own boat and does specialised tours to the islands.'

Diving Scuba and snorkelling equipment may be rented from the Chichiriviche Diving Centre (043) 86150, and Varadero Tours (042) 86754, on the main street.

PARQUE NACIONAL MOCHIMA

Just before the beautiful coastal highway reaches Cumaná, a fork on the left goes to Mochima National Park, 5km. Every turn gives a lovelier view of headlands and fjord-like bays. The wilderness park covers 949km^2 of the Gulf of Santa Fe and Caribbean coast and islands, some opposite Puerto La Cruz.

The sea, clear and gentle in narrow bays, is rough at the headlands. From the clean village of Mochima, fishermen do ferry services to isolated beaches such as Playa Blanca. You just jump off the boat onto the sand with your tent or hammock and cooler. Except for cold drinks and fried fish sold by local women, there are few facilities. But if you need extra ice or food, your ferryman may oblige by bringing it on his next round.

In Mochima village, the fishermen's cooperative is called Asotumo, and you may call to contract a launch, (093) 653663, or just show up in the morning. Arrange the cost per boat, round trip (to Playa Blanca about Bs.300). The same telephone (it's the village public phone) may be rung for rental of simple rooms with fan, or cottage with kitchen; ask for Iraida, or Eucaris, Lía, Milagros ...

Scuba diving In Mochima this can be arranged through Lolo's diving centre, (02) 2831715, (081) 682885.

Margarita Island

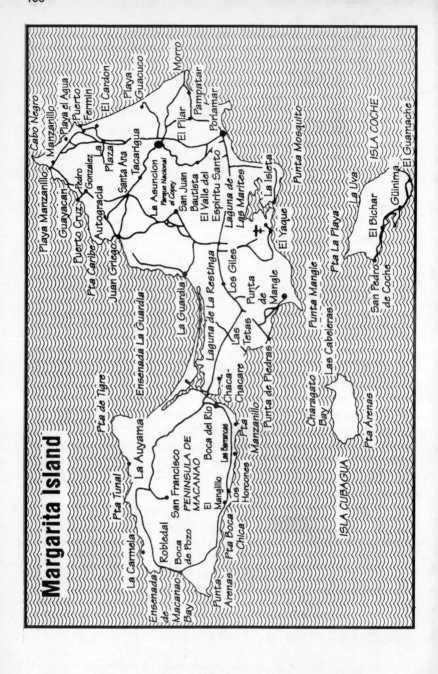

Chapter 10

Margarita

by Chris Stolley

CARIBBEAN ISLAND

The island of Margarita is Venezuela's 'Caribbean paradise island' and is the traditional destination for Venezuelan honeymoon couples. It is probably the country's most important centre for tourism, both national and international. During the high seasons (Nov.-Apr. international and July-Sept. national), especially at Christmas, Carnival and Easter (*Semana Santa*), the island is a hive of activity with beaches, hotels and roads thronged with visitors. Crowds of package tourists may repel some travellers, but '*Margarita sí vale la pena*' ('Margarita is worthwhile'). It is compact and varied. Its beaches are many and beautiful. Its towns and villages are generally clean and well cared for, notably more so than the rest of the country. Plazas are filled with trees and houses overflow with plants. Margarita is mostly arid and people have learned to appreciate greenery. (Elsewhere in Venezuela you can recognise a Margariteño's house by its plants.) It is a centre of crafts — pottery, hammocks and straw hats. There are colonial forts and churches to explore. It has a busy night life and good restaurants.

But of utmost importance to the long-term traveller, and especially first timers in Latin America, Margarita is an ideal 'transition zone'. Several British companies offer inexpensive flights direct from London. You will find many people who can communicate with you in English. Services have been honed by experience with foreign tourists in general more demanding than Venezuelans. It is a good place to acclimatise, get your initial suntan and prepare for the continent.

As you arrive at the airport look for the tourist information booths. They are well supplied with folders and maps of the island and main town, Porlamar, listing numerous hotels, travel agents, car rentals, restaurants, sights — really just about everything. As this information is so abundant in Margarita, I will only touch on some highlights and pass on friendly suggestions.

History

Margarita and the smaller islands of Coche and Cubagua make up Nueva Esparta State, named for the valiant local freedom fighters (the New Spartans) in the wars for independence from Spain. Before a water line was laid from the mainland in 1956, life was indeed Spartan. The *tinajones*, large earthenware water vessels, are a legacy from the time when everyone carried water from the closest well or spring, often miles away. It is only below the mountains of Cerro El Copey that there is enough rainfall to sustain a limited agriculture.

European intervention in Margarita began in 1499 when Spaniards found the source of pearls adorning the natives — the oyster beds off Cubagua. Margarita means 'pearl' in Greek, but the pearl that named Margarita was Margaret of Austria, Princess of Castile, and the namer was Columbus (who did not land on the island). The first shipment of 80 pounds of pearls to the Spanish court opened the fortune hunters' eyes, and the rush was on. The wealth was immense and represented 40% of all New World riches transported to Spain between 1500 and 1530. The ruthless exploitation soon told, however, and pearling diminished from 1513 onward. Enslaved native divers were fed only on oysters and forced to work until they died from exhaustion, blood gushing from mouth and nose. The only alternative to this ugly death were the sharks attracted in ever increasing numbers. Added to such production problems were constant pirate attacks as well as retaliation by mainland natives enraged by Spanish raids to replace the dead slaves. The last straw for Cubagua and its town of Nueva Cádiz was a devastating earthquake and tidal wave in 1541. The pearl fishery moved to Coche and Margarita. Pearling continued sporadically until 1962 when it was banned. It is not clear whether the beds are recovering.

During the colonial era a string of seven forts were built to protect Spanish wealth from pirates. Worth a visit today are San Carlos Borromeo in Pampatar, Santa Rosa in Asunción and, especially at sunset, La Galera in Juangriego.

Margarita and neighbouring Cumaná on the mainland were strong supporters of the move to separate from Spain. Simón Bolívar landed on Margarita in 1816 to begin his third campaign. Margariteños will still speak with pride of their part in the eventual victory and of their heroine Luisa Cáceres de Arismendi. Imprisoned in the Castillo Santa Rosa, this 16-year-old patriot gave birth — her baby died — was sent to Spain, escaped, and later returned to a free Venezuela.

In the 1970s Margarita was declared a free port and became the 'shopping capital' of Venezuela. The bargains are now gone, eliminated by the bolivar's devaluation and a more open market policy. Today the business of Margarita is tourism, although fishing and wooden boat building continue strongly on Macanao Peninsula.

Getting there

International flights   Margarita is a point of direct entry into Venezuela (and the entire continent), a boon to those wishing to bypass hectic Caracas. Viasa goes to Porlamar from New York. A new airline, Air Margarita, is offering flights at competitive prices to and from two US points: Miami, (800) 6971247, and Newark, NJ. Their office in Margarita is at the Margarita Concorde, Local 14, (095) 331229.

National flights   There are some 20 scheduled flights a day between Caracas and Margarita. Avensa, Aeropostal, Aereotuy and Cave link Margarita by at least as many more flights from major points in Venezuela (except Mérida). Aereotuy and Cave also fly from Margarita to Canaima and Los Roques. The fare from Caracas is about $30, from Valencia $34, from Canaima $60.

Allow at least an hour before national flight time, 2 hours before international flights. Even reconfirmation of bookings may be of no avail if you arrive late for a crowded flight (lines overbook sometimes). The Aeropuerto Internacional del Caribe is 20km west of Porlamar. Taxis are expensive; check the Cámara de Turismo leaflet for rates. There is an economic **airbus service** to town. The minibuses leave from the airport entrance and go when full. To return from Porlamar, look around Plaza Bolívar for the *carritos por puesto*.

Ferries   Conferry runs ferries between Punta de Piedras on the south coast of Margarita (about 15km west of the airport) and two mainland ports: Puerto La Cruz and Cumaná, about a 5-hour trip. The Puerto La Cruz service is best with large and comfortable car-carrying vessels, adequate food, comfortable seating both inside and out. Passenger fare is Bs.450 1st class, Bs.225 2nd class to Puerto La Cruz, and Bs.270 to Cumaná. There are eight sailings daily to and from Puerto La Cruz. Conferry: Porlamar, opp. Bella Vista Hotel (095) 619235, 626780; Punta de Piedras, (095) 98148; Cumaná, Ferry Terminal (093) 661462; Puerto La Cruz, Terminal Los Cocos (081) 668767; Caracas, Edif. Banhorient, Av. Las Acacias at Casanova (02) 7828544, 7819711, fax (02) 818739.

The car ferry to and from Cumaná is often out of service and vehicle traffic must suffer with a *chalana* or open-decked ferry. It is uncomfortable on deck because of spray and sooty motor exhaust;

passenger accommodation is in the rumbling cave below the car deck. Sailings are roughly morning and evening, whenever they complete a load. Operated by Naviarca, this *chalana* is to be avoided. It is better to take the extra time and go by way of Puerto La Cruz. Naviarca: Punta de Piedras, (095) 98072; Cumaná, (093) 661209, 210230.

For passengers without cars there are *lanchas* operated by Turismo Margarita between Punta de Piedras and Puerto La Cruz-Cumaná. The *lancha* is another rumbling cavern filled with cigarette smoke and blaring TVs. Sometimes passengers are allowed on deck to enjoy the sea air. The advantage is that it is faster, about 2½ hours depending on sea and mechanical conditions. This is strictly for transport. Two sailings from all terminals at 07.30 and 13.30 daily, except on Fridays when there are three: 07.00, 13.00 and 18.00. You will have to show your passport and may have your luggage looked at. Note well: all luggage on the *lancha* must be checked as there is no space for it in the passenger area. This presents a possible security problem. You will be able to carry on only a small bag; this rule is rigidly enforced. 1st class fare to Puerto La Cruz Bs.450, Cumaná Bs.300; 2nd class to Puerto La Cruz Bs.315, Cumaná Bs.170. Turismo Margarita: Punta de Piedras, (095) 98128; Cumaná, (093) 26868; Puerto La Cruz, (081) 692301-06.

'It was worth paying the small amount extra to travel first-class as this meant that you could stroll around on deck enjoying the scenery rather than being cooped up at the stern of the ship directly over two engines in something that resembled the Black Hole of Calcutta.' — Paul and Tracey Weatherstone.

Getting around

Car hire   Renting a car is a good way to see Margarita and if you can afford it, try to rent it for a day. One day's exploration can help you to identify places that you wish to revisit by public transport. Many companies make their offers through hotels, travel agents and at the airport. Rentals are expensive in all of Venezuela and Margarita is no exception. There are two general plans, one without *kilometraje* or mileage and one with 150km included in a higher price. Cost per km is high, starting at roughly $0.18/km for the smallest most basic car and going up to $0.60/km for a luxury seven passenger minivan. One mile is equivalent to 1.6km (multiply the km price by 1.6 to get price per mile). As 150km is only two hours of highway driving, it is easy to quickly find yourself with a bill of frightening size for what seemed like a small journey.

As well as being costly rental cars are generally poorly maintained — I have reports from people who had to change cars three times in one day on Margarita because of breakdowns.

In response to her frustration and that of her clients, Helga Pfeifer, owner of the Oasis bed and breakfast, has started her own car rental company with all new vehicles and her own maintenance and repair shop. Prices are no higher than others. Contact Baveca Rent a Car, (095) 48194.

Public transportation   Porlamar's large *Terminal de Autobuses* is a dozen blocks north of the bay (and a block west of Calle Narváez). It is in the Centro Comercial Bella Vista (shopping centre). Many Caracas-Porlamar lines run at night. The ticket does not include the ferry ride to/from Puerto La Cruz. The Unión de Conductores Margarita bus leaves Caracas at 17.00, arriving 22.00 at Puerto La Cruz; the ferry leaves (with the bus) at 24.00. Cost is about Bs.500.

Carros por puesto and minibuses traverse the island. They are inexpensive and go almost everywhere, but at their own speed and schedule, not yours. Service diminishes considerably after 9pm. Taxis can be arranged by the trip, hour or day; get the price clear before setting off. The Cámara de Turismo distributes at the airport a general information brochure which includes taxi rates. The scale goes from Bs.300 an hour in Porlamar to Bs.400 outside the city, adding a night surcharge of Bs.30 hourly in Porlamar and Bs.50 outside.

Where to stay

Every kind of accommodation is available on Margarita from luxury hotel on down. Here are a few suggestions and personal preferences for the budget traveller.

Porlamar   On Av. Raul Leoni there are several comfortable hotels in the $15-$20 range. They are centrally located but off the main drag and right above the Playa Bella Vista. Imperial, (095) 614823; Hotel Evdama and Chez David, (095) 610075; Tama, (095) 615935. Close by on Calle Fermín at Calle Cedeño is Daisy Suites, (095) 619922, single/double Bs.1,500.

For those on a watch-every-penny budget, there are numerous *hoteluchos* (holes-in-the-wall). The best located of these is on Paseo Guaraguao, a small deadend street below the Bella Vista Hotel, right on the beach. For the small price difference I recommend something with a little more class. On your ventures in the interior you will probably stay at more than one hotel of this type, as many places offer nothing more. Hotel Miramar, no phone, single Bs.700, double Bs.800.

Paul Weatherstone writes: 'We made the mistake of not booking a hotel and ended up, in desperation, taking the last available room in the 4 star hotel Bella Vista at about £15.00 per night each. There are cheaper hotels but obviously this was a busy time of year (August/September) and all of these were full. I would advise anyone going to Porlamar to book.'

Elsewhere   Assuming that anyone who comes to Margarita wants to spend a lot of time on the beach, try the northeastern area for accommodation close to Playa El Agua, Playa Cardón and Playa El Tirano. My favourite is Los Tinajones, located on the Aricagua road above Playa El Tirano. It is well apart, far enough up the mountainside to have a cool breeze, privacy and a good sea view. This is the home of Peruvian Enrique Doberti and his Chilean wife María Julia (both speak English), and the atmosphere is friendly. They offer single and double rooms and two larger rooms with stove and fridge. There is a bar, small pool, common eating area, hammocks for everyone and mountain bikes to rent. Price includes breakfast and guests can arrange for other meals daily with María Julia. The Dobertis can help you with excursions on Margarita and to other parts of Venezuela. Contact is through Isla Azul, Calle Fermín between Marcano and Cedeño, Porlamar, (095) 613755, fax 615521. Prices per person are $195 for 7 days, $324 for 14 days.

Residencias Vacacionales Don Miguel is on the Aricagua road between Los Tinajones and the highway. Don Miguel is a retired gentleman who learned his English in Trinidad. He offers three bedroom suites with equipped kitchen, comfortable for six people, at Bs.1,500 per unit. There is an outdoor common area with roof, tables and grills. Each unit has an enclosed patio with *batea* for hand-washing clothes. Margarita phone, (095) 48296; Caracas, (02) 615266.

Oasis, on the main road at the Aricagua junction, offers continental-style bed and breakfast. It is pricier but very comfortable. Owner Helga Pfeifer speaks German and her clientele is generally, but not exclusively, German. She provides such niceties as refrigerators and strongboxes in every room. There is a bar and small pool, and Helga also rents reliable cars. Tel/fax (095) 48194. See *Car Hire*.

Casa Trudel in La Mira above Playa El Agua is run by Canadian Dan O'Brien and his Dutch wife Trudy; they speak English, Spanish, Dutch and German. They offer king-sized beds with breakfast; $40 per room. Trudy serves supper Wednesday and Saturday and is reputed to be an excellent cook. Other meals can be arranged. Fax (095) 613169.

This is a small representation of the vast accommodation (16,000 beds) available in Margarita. During the high season rooms will be hard to come by, so plan in advance. More information can be had from the airport booths and the island's numerous travel agents. A good one is Isla Azul, Calle Fermín between Cedeño and Marcano, (095) 613755, fax 615521. They speak English, Portuguese, Italian, Dutch and German. They can help you with travel in Margarita, the mainland and the rest of Latin America.

Where to eat

Margarita, tourist mecca that it is, abounds in restaurants. Prices range from the sky on down, with appearances a good indicator of price. Menus are often posted at the door. Look for signs that offer *comida criolla* for local style affordable eats. I recommend the following.

Porlamar   La Cueva del Pescador on Calle Fermín between Cedeño and Marcano is a quiet *tasca*. Good food at good prices, about Bs.300 a person. Pida Pasta on Calle Malave at Calle J.M. Patiño makes good pasta and brick-oven baked pizza. The Heladería Italiana 4D, opposite Pida Pasta, is tops in icecream and coffee. Not to be missed. For typical dishes, Sven Berge recommends La Churuata de Goyo in the Centro Artesanal, Los Robles, by the big new roundabout on the autopista.

Elsewhere   Many beaches have fried fish establishments. A favourite is El Caballito del Mar (The Sea Horse) at the south end of Playa El Tirano by the bridge. It is run by Mama María and her well-fed family. Bs.300 per person.

Night life

Aside from window shopping and people-watching, Porlamar offers the night person a variety of bars and discotheques. These range from the flashy glass and chrome Gran Pirámide on Calle Malavé at Calle J.M. Patiño, to the currently most popular Mosquito Coast on Av. Santiago Mariño, a block from the Bella Vista Hotel. Mosquito Coast has a casual bamboo and rattan atmosphere, plays a mix of old and new Latin and American popular music and serves American style hamburgers and Texas style Mexican food.

Things to see

The Virgin of the Valley

Of particular interest may be the chapel that shelters the image of La Virgen del Valle, Margarita's *patrona*. People come from all over Venezuela to visit her shrine and image, both highly ornate and quite beautiful. The obvious devotion paid to her is a delight to see and feel, especially on September 8, her feast day. To Margariteños this is the year's most important date. An 8-day festival attracts as many faithful as will fit into the town called El Valle del Espíritu Santo near Porlamar. The Virgin's famous image was probably sent from Spain to Peru but was delivered to Margarita instead. Since the 16th century she has been elaborately dressed and paraded through the town on her day.

The town's history began in 1529. For the lifetime of the founder's family, it was the capital of Margarita and when the last member died, Asunción became the capital, and so it is today.

Margarita has some of the earliest churches surviving in Venezuela. A good example of the strong, plain architecture is the Cathedral in La Asunción dating from 1570.

Hammocks and pots

Margarita is known for its crafts. The Margarita *chinchorro*, an open weave hammock that is a development of fish net technique, is known throughout Venezuela (see box on page 119). La Vecindad, between Santa Ana and Juangriego, and Tacarigua, the other side of Santa Ana, are centres of this art. The village of El Cercado, somewhat off the track near Santa Ana, is almost completely dedicated to making pottery that ranges from the ordinary to the exotic. Here you can find earthenware plates and coffee sets, as well as fantastic dolls and gaudily painted religious figures. To find this village, you must ask directions in Santa Ana.

Beaches

Margarita's beaches in general can be divided between sandy and rocky, and with or without surf. This is NE tradewind country, so that the beaches on the exposed NE side will be surfy and those in the lee of the prevailing wind more tranquil. The northern point of the island makes a sharp demarcation. One map lists 41 beaches. This is stretching it a bit and includes beaches at which you would not want to swim. Remember when choosing a beach that those with shorefront development will be affected by the universally inadequate sewage systems. If you rent a car you can easily see all the island's beaches in a day.

Of the windward beaches the most popular are El Agua, El Tirano and Guacuco. These are easily reached by public transport and have prepared food for sale. El Agua is the most developed, a 4km stretch of beautiful white sand and palms. This is where the exclusive hotels are, the tour buses stop, the big bellies swing and the sunburn per square inch is the highest. There is a wide variety of eating places, sunshade rentals and souvenir sellers.

El Tirano, by the fishing village of Puerto Fermín, is less crowded and developed. The village has some character with an attractive shady plaza and fishing boats with all their attendant paraphernalia. There is neither shade nor sunshade rental on this beach. Guacuco is long and slightly developed, away from any village but with various eating establishments. It is rougher than either El Agua or El Tirano.

Beaches on the NW side have quieter water, and for the moment are less developed. There is much construction underway, however. For those seeking secluded sands and rocky points for snorkelling, this is the best part of the island. With your own transport you can explore these beaches, a number of which you will see from the highway and have to walk into. Remember that their seclusion makes them less safe, and leave your Rolex in the hotel vault. Do not leave anything of value in an unattended car. Playa Manzanillo (not the pueblo of Manzanillo) is a quiet fishing village with a good fried fish stand. Playa Puerto Cruz has a nice beach a bit off the highway, quiet and sandy, but with a tremendous Las Vegas looking hotel under construction.

For those who want to be in the centre of everything, the Bella Vista and Margarita Concorde hotels have beaches with all services, nice sand and quiet water.

Sven Berge reports: 'To my view, there are too many tourists on Playa El Agua and Playa Parquito and Playa Caribe is located close to a rubbish dump. But one of the nicest beaches we discovered was Playa Guayacán by the little fishing village of Guayacán on the north side of the island. There was hardly a living soul except for a handful of local children playing in the lovely great waves. A tiny "bar" serves beer and *refrescos*. In the same area we explored Playa de Escondidos, also a lovely beach. It is possible to stay overnight; just bring food and drink and, of course, a hammock (do not forget mosquito net). The way to Escondidos goes down from Punta Ausente where you can leave the main road at the same place as for Guayacán; instead of driving down, you turn to the right into a tiny path. Park your car if it's not a jeep (but do not leave it overnight) and walk down for 10 to 15 minutes. You come out to a dry river bed; continue left for another ten minutes to the playa, simply a paradise which very few people know about. Another possibility is to hire a fisherman to take you there from Guayacán.'

Warning — Some of these secluded coves are shaded by twisted trees including the poisonous manchineel, called *manzanillo* after its toxic green 'apples'. Its stiff leaves, milky sap, and even smoke from burning wood, can cause skin and eye irritation.

Parque Nacional Cerro El Copey

A cool and moist retreat from the arid heat and bustle below, this mountain park is reached from La Sierra road between La Asunción and El Valle del Espíritu Santo. Take the *por puesto* from either town and get off at the high point of the road in front of the Guardia Nacional post. It is a short walk past the gate to the *mirador* or lookout, complete with picnic shelters and grills. There are some attractive trails, and the park warden, *guardaparques* Isidro Salazar, is happy to talk (in Spanish) about his domain. Named for the broad-leafed copey tree (Clusia family), the park is home to the *mono mandarín*, a capuchin monkey whose mysterious presence on the island has never been accounted for. This is dense forest with few trails and hard going, but a good place to see cloud forest with its tree ferns, bromeliads (air plants), orchids, mosses, vines and elegant mountain palms. The paved road (closed to traffic) is a walk of about 1½ hour from the lookout up to the peak, site of a number of communications repeater stations.

'From Fuentidueno it is possible to take a footpath. Drive to the end of the valley, and then walk further up toward La Sierra. There is a nice little river coming down the mountain, with places for a good picnic.' (Sven Berge)

Parque Nacional la Restinga

La Restinga is a mangrove lagoon that makes up the isthmus connecting Macanao (see below) with the island's eastern part. It is a national park and is well organised and popular. Take a *por puesto* of the Línea La Restinga from the Avenida Mercado along the waterfront between Calle Arismendi and Calle Mariño. Behind the park buildings, boats leave from the *embarcadero* for a 45 minute tour through mangrove canals. On the ocean side is another dock where you can arrange to be left and picked up later by your boatman. Cost of the tour for up to 5 people is Bs.500. The ocean side of La Guardia Bay has a long solitary beach made of *guacuco* (clam) shells, and cold rough water. There are several restaurants selling simple but high priced food. La Restinga was once known for its throngs of flamingoes, scarlet ibis, roseate spoonbills and other water birds, but the onslaught of tourism has apparently encouraged them to seek happier hunting grounds. Nevertheless, this is a worthwhile excursion.

Macanao

Macanao is the 'other side' of Margarita, a rugged desert peninsula separated by a narrow isthmus. It has only scattered fishing villages. Although at first glance Macanao is a wasteland of cactus, it supports a tremendous amount of life. Look carefully at the tops of the cacti and you will see numerous birds roosting. You may see flocks of the green Margarita parrots, a species that mates for life and nests in the same hollow cactus year after year. A closer look will reveal snakes, lizards, scorpions, foxes, rabbits, the occasional deer and, of course, feral goats.

Macanao is served by the Línea La Restinga *por puestos* (see above). The principal town is Boca de Rio at the mouth of the 'river' outlet of La Restinga Lagoon. This is a boat-building, fishing and fisherman's supply town that is seemingly in a different world from the bustling and flashy eastern half of the island. Margarita has been, and still is, an important centre of wooden boat building. Its boats are known throughout the Caribbean and northern Atlantic coast of South America. Boca de Rio is a good place to see boats under construction and repair. Also visit the Museo del Mar with its collections of fish, shells, corals and marine mammal bits and pieces.

There are big plans in the works (aren't there always) to 'transform' Macanao into a sort of Las Vegas of Venezuela with casinos and luxury hotels. But at present there is no accommodation for the traveller. An adventurous and self-sufficient person with good Spanish (dialects are strong and villagers are unaccustomed to modifying their form of speaking for foreigners) might ask to sling a hammock in one of the numerous boat shelters found along the beach in every coastal community. Every village has its *abasto* selling canned fish and basics, or you can find someone to prepare you fried fish or *hervida* and *sopa de pescado*, the staples of coastal Venezuela. Remember to carry a water container, good shoes, a hat and sunscreen (the thing here is protection). The beaches of Macanao are without shade and generally rocky. But the scenery is rugged and the people friendly.

COCHE AND CUBAGUA

These two desert islands lie to the south of Margarita. Coche is the more developed and has piped water and a small permanent population. There is a hotel under construction and possibly operating by the time this edition reaches the public. Ask at travel agents in Porlamar. Ferry service is from the Conferry terminal in Punta de Piedras to San Pedro on Coche. Check at the terminal or Conferry office in Porlamar for current schedules.

On Coche 'time nearly stands still; the island appears to be almost like Margarita 30 years ago.' From Sven Berge's notes: 'There are two ways of getting there. The daily ferry from Pta. Piedras leaves at 16.00 and returns at 5.30 the next morning from Coche; on Sat.-Sun. there may be two sailings daily, leaving Punta de Piedras at 8.00 and 17.30, and returning at 5.30 and 15.30. Or take a *por puesto* from Calle La Marina in Porlamar to La Isleta. The local fishing boats to Coche sail from here at 23.00, taking passengers for Bs.80 and returning the next morning. This trip is specially recommendable, quite an experience crossing with the natives and all their belongings and supplies. On the island is a tiny inn, (095) 99141, run by Daniel Mosco, my friend. I do recommend to phone before going. The only restaurant in San Pedro de Coche is absolutely the place for a good meal as well as cheap. It is run by very friendly people and the food is excellent.'

Cubagua is the site of the ruins of Nueva Cádiz (see *History*), the first city in the Americas, built on the pearl trade. The excavated ruins on the east side are worth a visit but one must make special arrangements to get there. This can be done by prowling the Punta de Piedras waterfront to find a fisherman willing to make the trip. You should expect to pay no less than Bs.3,000, depending on the size of the boat, the desperation of fishermen and your bargaining ability. It will be an all-day trip there and back in an open peñero, wet and cold returning in the afternoon chop. Take a polyethylene sheet or poncho to keep cameras and yourself dry. Carry water and food as there is none on the island, as well as full sun protection. There is no shade and lots of wind and reflected sun. The island's only inhabitants are transient fishermen who live in ramshackle huts, and occasional visitors to a university research station on the west side. Tour boats visit Cubagua but do not go to the ruins as the water is too shallow to bring their boats in close. These are comfortable tours with food and drink provided, and perhaps some fishing along the way. Boats leave from the marina at the Hotel Margarita Concorde. Price is about $60 per person.

Hammocks: travellers' and sailors' boon

by Hilary Branch and Chris Stolley

The first navigators to the New World brought back a great native invention used all over the tropics: hammocks. English ships soon saw the advantages of hammocks below decks and sailors have been swinging ever since. Hammocks are the only traditional furnishings of Warao houses (see chapter on *The Delta*). In their language *hanoko* means the "hammock's place" or house and in all probability it is the origin of our word. In Venezuela two basic kinds are distinguished: the *hamaca* made of woven cloth and the *chinchorro* which, like the fishnet it is named after, is usually knotted. Most hardware stores sell pre-cut lengths of *mecate* or rope for slinging hammocks.

The open weave of the *chinchorro* makes a very cool and soft bed, but if you are looking for a hammock to take travelling, remember that bugs and cold air pass easily through the holes. What is a delight in the daytime on the beach may be a misery at night. Less elegant, but more rough and ready and less costly (most *chinchorros* are handmade), is the normal hammock of solid cloth. These too are very comfortable if you remember to get one wide enough to allow you to sleep on the diagonal with a relatively straight back. A warmer hammock that you can partially wrap around you will allow you to carry a lighter bedroll.

A hammock is almost a must for the overland traveller in Latin America. They are used in all the warm areas and allow you to sling your bed up off the (wet, buggy, crawly) ground, and sleep anywhere there are two points to hang it from. You will see them everywhere. Every trucker carries his to sling under the chassis to wait out the inevitable delays of Latin American travel.

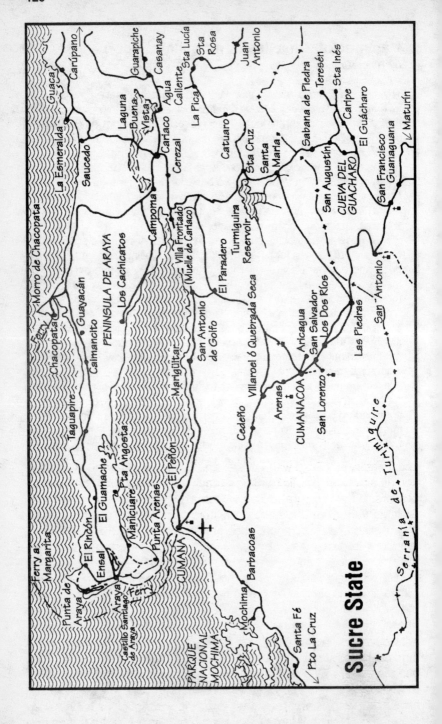

Sucre State

Chapter 11

The 'Oriente' coast

by Chris Stolley

SUCRE STATE

To most Venezuelans, the 'Oriente' stands for Sucre's long Caribbean shore. Beaches are popular on peak holidays although farther from towns there are many less visited coves. Araya Peninsula is more like a desert island, it is so arid and little inhabited. Sucre's daily life revolves around fishing and farming; inland beyond Carúpano huge trees shade lush cacao plantations. Further east is the Peninsula of Paria, little inhabited. Sucre has plans for resort hotels and an airport enlargement to bring jets from Europe and the USA direct to Cumaná — an excellent base for travel to Margarita, or points east and south such as the Guácharo Cave, Monagas State and the Orinoco Delta.

What 'Underdevelopment' means in terms of the independent explorer is quiet beaches, lush forests, mountains, meandering rivers known as *caños* filled with wildlife, and towns where people will treat you as a person. Public transport reaches to all but the most remote corners. A visit to rural Sucre will challenge your ear and tongue. Dialects vary from the staccato accents of Cumaná's fishermen to the English and French influence of patois in Güiria. For a whirlwind tour or a leisurely stay (my recommendation), Sucre has much to offer.

Sucre State is considered by most Venezuelans to be a backward part of the country and in terms of industry it is. What does not please the fast-lane developers, however, does offer to the slower paced traveller opportunities for some relaxed exploration in a relatively, but probably not for long, unspoiled backwater. On the tourism side, development is steady with one of Paria's nicer beaches, Playa Medina and 15km of adjacent shoreline, slated to go to Club Med. A number of smaller hotels with bars and restaurants have sprung up along the coast, catering mostly to the local trade.

The people still live largely by farming and fishing. Centred on the

Sugar, a bitter-sweet industry

by Chris Stolley

Sucre (which does not mean sugar) has two large sugar producing areas, the wide valleys around Cumanacoa and Cariaco. In these towns are located big sugar refineries or *centrales azucareros*. Sugar cane has been planted on a large scale here for several hundred years, and remains of old water operated mills with their adjacent rum distilleries can still be seen. Sugar production is a difficult business as world price is low. Even with Venezuela's inexpensive labour (legal minimum rural wage is less than $120 per month and workers are often paid less), competition is stiff. Cumanacoa's *Central* is government owned but due to be privatised. Cariaco's *Central* is privately owned and its owners have not found it profitable to buy all the local cane, a situation which has caused much distress and many confrontations.

Sugar production is an environmental disaster in all its aspects. A monoculture, cane is chemically fertilised and pesticided: a soil destroyer. Land retired from cane production is so exhausted as to be good for little else. Fertiliser and pesticide residues are washed into local water systems. The Manzanares River passing through Cumanacoa is heavily polluted and all ground water is affected as well. Prior to harvest the fields are burned to clear off the sharp edged leaves and drive away snakes and insects. In the refineries, the dried remains of pressed cane stalks are burned to provide heat for reduction of the juice. Smoke and ash from these processes produces an intense respiratory irritation known locally as 'Cumanacoaitis'. It is a vicious cycle, difficult to break because of massive dependence on this one crop. Alternatives are being sought, including small scale industrialisation.

Raw sugar called *papelón* is made on a small scale at numerous operations dotted around the countryside. The cane is pressed in a *trapiche* or heavy mill powered by a large displacement 'one lunger' diesel engine. The cane residue or *bagazo* (locally corrupted to 'gabazo') is laid in the road to dry to provide fuel for the reducing kettle. This is generally a series of 3 deep iron basins set atop a stone base, mouth at one end to receive dry *bagazo*, chimney at the other. The raw juice called *guarapo* is poured into the first kettle. When the master stirrer and mixer decides it has reached the proper consistency, he dips it into the next kettle, usually with an aluminium hard-hat attached to the end of a long pole. In each succeeding kettle it is reduced a little bit more. After the final consistency is reached, he dips the concentrated syrup into a wooden chute that leads to a cooling trough hollowed out of a solid log. It is then ladled into conical moulds made of fired clay. The sugar cools rapidly and is shaken out of the mould and wrapped in dry cane leaves for shipment and sale. The entire operation resembles scurrying slaves attending a dragon breathing fire at one end, expelling smoke at the other, steam rolling off its back, all accompanied by the roar of the mill and motor. The final product has a rich brown colour and, freshly made, the better quality *papelón* will have a flavour not unlike maple sugar.

rich valleys of Cariaco and Cumanacoa and their *centrales* or refineries are large sugar plantings. The Peninsula of Paria has cacao and coconut plantations, and the mountains are planted with coffee. Cashews are abundant, but their processing is complicated and most of the harvest is not used. Mangoes are so numerous that in season they cover the ground in their many varieties. In fact, harvests of many fruits and vegetables are lost because of poor roads and low prices. The Cariaco Deep is an important fish breeding ground and Cumaná is a major tuna port and canning centre.

CUMANÁ

Cumaná, state capital, is at the outlet of the Manzanares River which divides the city roughly east and west. This is the tuna fishing capital of Venezuela and reputedly one of the world's largest tuna ports. Activity has been curtailed over the past two years by a US led embargo against Venezuelan caught tuna, because of an unacceptable level of dolphins caught along with the tuna. The embargo has been a blow to Cumaná.

A walk through Cumaná's small centre will not lead you to believe that this city is home to 350,000 or more people. Most inhabitants live in outlying *barrios* and their daily comings and goings have produced a serious transportation crisis. For the traveller, however, the small city centre and large population makes a concentration of activity that offers unlimited opportunities for people-watching.

History

Cumaná is the continent's oldest city. Before it was a Spanish settlement it was the most important native community on the coast, home to the Cumanagoto Indians. Although the official founding date is 1521, Franciscan missionaries came here to convert the natives in 1506. The discovery of pearl beds off Margarita made Cumaná an important centre of supply for water and slaves to support the pearling. In 1569 Cumaná received its first group of settlers and in the 1660s two forts, San Antonio de la Eminencia and Santa María de la Cabeza, were constructed. These forts, and the whole city, have been destroyed several times by earthquakes, in 1684, 1797, 1853 and 1929. San Antonio has been partially restored, but of Santa María there remains little. Cumaná joined the Captaincy-General of Venezuela in 1777, and during the wars for independence from Spain in the early 1800s played an important part, being taken and retaken a number of times. (Sucre State is named after Grand

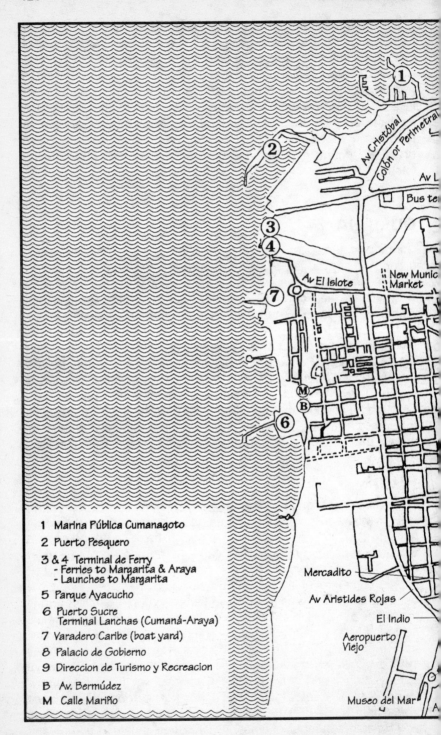

1 Marina Pública Cumanagoto

2 Puerto Pesquero

3 & 4 Terminal de Ferry
   - Ferries to Margarita & Araya
   - Launches to Margarita

5 Parque Ayacucho

6 Puerto Sucre
   Terminal Lanchas (Cumaná-Araya)

7 Varadero Caribe (boat yard)

8 Palacio de Gobierno

9 Direccion de Turismo y Recreacion

B Av. Bermúdez
M Calle Mariño

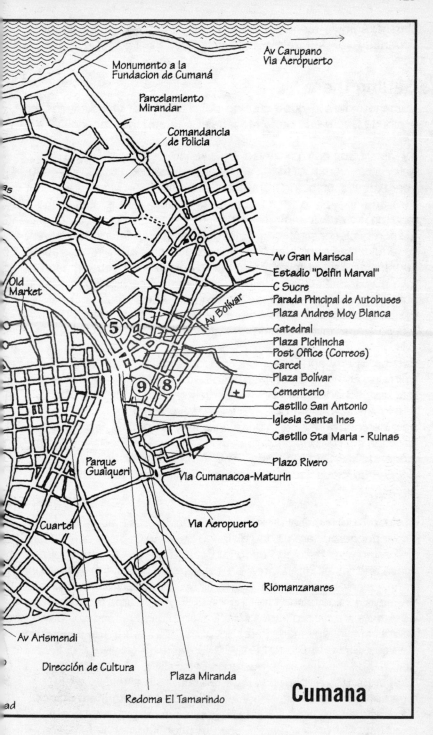

Av Carupano
Via Aeropuerto

Monumento a la
Fundacion de Cumaná

Parcelamiento
Mirandar

Comandancia
de Policia

Old
Market

Av Gran Mariscal

Estadio "Delfin Marval"

C Sucre

Parada Principal de Autobuses

Plaza Andres Moy Blanca

Av Bolívar

Catedral

Plaza Pichincha

Post Office (Correos)

Carcel

Plaza Bolívar

Cementerio

Castillo San Antonio

Iglesia Santa Ines

Castillo Sta Maria - Ruinas

Parque
Guaiqueri

Plazo Rivero

Via Cumanacoa-Maturin

Via Aeropuerto

Cuartel

Riomanzanares

Av Arismendi

Dirección de Cultura

Plaza Miranda

Redoma El Tamarindo

Cumana

Marshal Antonio José de Sucre who fought with Bolívar and liberated Ecuador, Peru and Bolivia — he was Bolivia's first president.)

Getting there

Cumaná makes a good starting point and base of operations for exploring Sucre and on to Monagas State and the Orinoco Delta.

By air   Cumaná is served by Avensa, (093) 312484, 315289, Aeropostal, (093) 671429, and Aereotuy, (093) 661130, 671030. There are flights to and from Caracas (about $30), Margarita (about $15) and Carúpano (don't bother, as waiting time is usually more than the *por puesto* trip). Air service to Cumaná is notoriously erratic, a source of constant complaint by residents. Check for current schedules, but don't plan any tight connections. The airport is about 10 minutes east of town. From the airport to town you will need to take a taxi, Bs.250-350. Do NOT walk out to the highway to flag a ride. To get to the airport, take a taxi from Plaza Miranda or ask for the *por puesto* that goes from the river east of the plaza. The *por puesto* stops only at the airport only for outbound passengers.

Ferries   Ferry and launch services go separately to Margarita and to Araya. For details see Margarita and Araya sections. Remember that ferry schedules are not written in stone, so be flexible. The ferry terminal is at the foot of Av. El Islote, several blocks down from the new Mercado Municipal. A *por puesto* leaves from the Plaza Miranda, between the two bridges. It is better not to walk, especially if you are alone or carrying anything. The Cumaná waterfront can be a dangerous place for the unfamiliar, the unwary and anyone with anything to lose.

Buses   The Terminal de Pasajeros is on Av. Las Palomas, another rather dangerous area. Long distance buses to Caracas and Ciudad Bolívar go west through Puerto La Cruz. There are a number of bus lines, and most departures are at night. This is the way most Venezuelans travel and the buses fill up, especially on Fridays and Sundays. Holidays such as Christmas, Easter, Carnival and all long weekends are next to impossible. Reservations are made by buying your ticket in advance. Fares in June 1993 were roughly $6 to Caracas, $5.50 to Ciudad Bolívar, $3 to Güiria (pay for Güiria and get off where you like). A bus goes twice daily, 07.30 and 12.00, to Caripe, Bs.150. All bus lines have telephones but you will waste less time and get more accurate information by going to the terminal.

Buses can be a trial for tall people and those with low noise tolerance. *Carros por puesto* leave throughout the day for Caracas and other points, at twice the bus price. You can choose one with good tyres, and a seat with leg room, or you can buy all the *puestos* and have lots of space. There are many important routes only served by *por puesto*. Cumaná Cumanacoa-Maturín is a route through the Turimiquire mountains and on to the plains of Monagas (and from there to the Delta and Gran Sabana), a route that has no bus service. This three hour trip is beautiful and highly recommended.

Where to stay

There are a number of beach hotels on Av. Universidad that runs along Playa San Luis. These are quieter than hotels in the centre, but less convenient. All have high fences with gates that are locked at dusk. Hotels Los Bordones, (093) 653783, and Cumanagoto (currently closed for renovation 1-2 years) are the best in town at about $30. Closer in is the Caribe, (093) 651777, about $15. On Av. Perimetral or Cristóbal Colón is the Hotel Savoia, (093) 314379, about $20. In the centre of town, small, friendly and inexpensive, are the Hotels Italia, Cumaná, Vesuvio, Astoria and La Gloria, about $5 single and $8 double; all are on the Calle Sucre between Plaza Bolívar and the Iglesia Santa Inés. There are other hotels, but because of their location they present problems at night and are not recommended.

Where to eat

Cumaná offers the Venezuelan standards of *parrilla, pasta, pollo* and *pescado* — grilled meat, pasta, chicken and fish. Parrillas vary in class and cost. At the top is Vitorio's on Av. Perimetral close to the Hotel Savoia where you will not pay less than Bs.500 to satisfy your appetite. I prefer a street parrilla at the south end of Calle Sucre, past Iglesia Santa Inés, in front of the Plaza Rivero. This parrilla is very popular and rightly so. You will be served, on a base of *bollitos* (maize), *yuca* or *ocumo chino*, first an excellent potato salad, then (you choose the combination) grilled steak and 2 kinds of sausage with *guasacaca* sauce. Top it off with a *parchita* juice (passionfruit), and the bill will be Bs.130. Best deal in town.

For the sweet toothed, Cumaná has a special treat, rare in this part of the world. Exquisite Italian-style **ice cream**, fruit ices and cakes are offered by Helados La Barquilla at two locations: Av. Gran Mariscal by Banco Mercantil; and Calle Blanco Fombona, around the corner from the Centro Comercial Gina on Av. Bermúdez in front of the Consejo Municipal. The fruit flavours are true to life, there are exotic icecream flavours to please any palate, and the Torta Castillo is a guaranteed diet destroyer. Personally recommended by the publisher who insisted on going twice in one day.

For *pasta* try Don Pietro's, next to the Parque Ayacucho. He serves the only homemade pasta in town and the pizza is brick-oven baked. The outdoor tables are quiet and relaxing. Hotel Savoia also has good pizza and all-around good food at moderate prices.

Pollos en brasa - chicken barbecued on a spit, and *pollo a la broaster* - deep fried in crumbly batter, are everywhere. There is one special place to get your chicken grilled over a wood fire and served with an *arepa pelada* (ground whole corn). At the edge of the Mercadito (see below) there is a woman who works afternoons and evenings preparing her speciality. A bit hard to find but worth it.

Pescado - fish, and *mariscos* - shellfish (Note: 'marisco' or 'marico' are slang for 'gay') are the basic food in this fishing town. Be sure that all seafood is well cooked, especially shellfish. Raw (as in the popular ceviche) or undercooked they can transmit unpleasant diseases, including cholera. Try the nationally famous Mercadito, a noisy collection of 20 or so seafood restaurants. Take the San Luis minibus to El Indio, a cement statue of an Indian holding a fish, said to be the only fish not consumed in Cumaná. Try the *hervido* or *sopa de pescado*, an inexpensive chunky fish soup with all the bones left in. This is a meal in itself and a mainstay of coastal diet (my wife ate it every day of her childhood). It is excellent for an uneasy stomach, and a good first food when recovering from illness. The Mercado Municipal also has a number of inexpensive restaurants offering fish and other dishes.

For an upscale (but not too expensive) treat and change from the Venezuelan style, I strongly suggest the Inkaperu behind the C.C. Gina on Callen Rondón. For vegetarian fare and variety, Ali Baba on Av. Bermúdez offers middle eastern food or 'comida arabe'. Inexpensive and excellent.

Music   Music is everywhere, from the solitary wanderer in the street singing to the accompaniment of his *cuatro* (a four-stringed guitar), to the groups of children drumming on discarded tins, to the blaring battery-powered 'minitecas' wheeled around town by sellers of bootleg cassette tapes. It is perfectly acceptable to dance whenever and wherever the mood strikes. For those who like a little more structure, Cumaná's most popular *discotecas* are La Tasca on Calle Bolívar just down from Plaza Bolívar, and the Acuario, all flash, on Av. Universidad. The recently opened 'Un Café Llamado Deseo' on Calle Sucre just past and opposite the Iglesia Santa Inés, offers a more moderate alternative. It is an outdoor bar providing live music by the excellent house band, Nacumá, and occasional special events.

What to see/do

Cumaná's historic core is conveniently compact. The centre is Plaza Bolívar and government buildings. At the NW corner of the plaza is the Bar Jardín Sport, a delightful open air bar beneath shady trees that has become somewhat of an international traveller's mecca, meeting place, and communication centre. Here you can listen to the rocola (jukebox) blare out Latin hits of the past 30 years while you beat the heat with an ice cold Polar or fruit *batido*, watch the action in the plaza, and make friends with others from near and far who have made the pilgrimage. Local hustlers abound. Be cautious, but enjoy and don't miss it.

Looking up from the plaza to the only high spot around, you see the fort, locally called *castillo*, of San Antonio de la Eminencia. Don't try to go there cross country as this area is known for its coral and rattlesnakes, as well as human dangers. Follow the signs to the Castillo/Cementerio/Carcel or take the steps up from Calle La Luneta behind Iglesia Santa Inés. Your (daylight) walk will be rewarded by a spectacular view of Cumaná's rooftops and the surrounding sea. Back at the Jardín Sport, that constantly useful thirst quenching point, you are on Calle Sucre. Turn right as you leave and head SW past the government buildings. After two blocks you will encounter the Iglesia Santa Inés, dedicated to Cumaná's *patrona* or patron saint. Alongside and up the hill are the inconspicuous ruins of the fort of Santa María de la Cabeza. At the end of the long block following, in front of the Plaza Rivero, you will see a crumbling stone wall. This is all that remains of the convent of Nuestra Señora de las Aguas Santas, built in 1641. This was a two-storey structure that served as a convent, bishop's residence, Cumaná's first university and finally a soap factory. Resist the temptation to wander up into the old section of town on the hills behind, Cumaná's colonial core built on the only high ground around. It is a tough area. The rest of Cumaná is built on filled mangrove swamp. If you visit in the wet season you will note that some parts of the city simply have no drainage.

Mercado Municipal   The new market on Avenida El Islote is a must visit in Cumaná. It is by far the best public market in all of Oriente, large, open and well organised. Wander through the airy main building where fruits, vegetables and meats are sold, and around the back to the 'playa', the part where the trucks unload and people without inside space sell directly to the public. In this section you will find the freshest produce and best prices. On the way to the two buildings that sell fish, you will have the opportunity to choose a live chicken and deliver it to be killed and plucked, get your hair cut, select some handmade cigars (a local speciality), buy shoes and clothing at the lowest prices around, eat and drink all manner of interesting things, and generally be dazzled. Off by itself alongside the main parking entrance is an *artesanía* (crafts) section that sells pots, hats, birds, herbs, handmade furniture, a good variety of hammocks and souvenirs in general. Open every day till noon, but best and busiest on weekends. During market hours almost all minibuses stop here. Look for the 'Mercado' card on the windshield. All the local colour you can handle and then some.

Beaches   Cumaná is known for its fine beaches and tranquil sea but they are unfortunately badly polluted by raw sewage and agricultural chemicals from the Manzanares River. This does not stop the Cumaneses, however, and on weekends and holidays they flock to the beach. The main beach is Playa San Luis on the Avenida Universidad reached via 'San Luis' minibuses. Dedicated beachgoers might like to walk on to the west past Hotel Los Bordones to some quieter and (hopefully) less polluted shores. Observe standard security precautions.

Hand-rolled Cumaná cigars

In a world where a real Cuban cigar can cost as much as an elegant meal, and many of the rest are made with an outer wrapper (if not part of the insides as well) of chemically treated paper, Cumaná is an oasis in a desert of mediocrity for the tobacco lover. Hand-rolled cigars, called *puros* or *tabacos*, are a traditional specialty of Cumaná, a home based industry of long standing mostly done by older women. The traditional way to smoke them (you can see it done with cigarettes as well) is with the lit end inside the mouth. Try it if you dare.

Follow your nose to the various *fábricas* along Calle Rendón on the sea side of the river, just south of Ave. Bermúdez, a main shopping street. My favourite is Tabacos Guanche, Calle Rendón 48 (heading towards the sea on Ave. Bermúdez go left one block at Bar Stalingrado), run by Canary Islander Jaime Acosta Paiz. Señor Acosta has an international as well as local following, although his production is small. He is a patient man, as fits his profession, and will sometimes treat buyers to a tour. This is for good Spanish speakers only. "The best I have smoked in 20 years," said the publisher's father when presented with a box by his loving daughter. Prices start at about $6 per box of 25 in a simple paper box. If one so desires and has time to wait, orders can be placed for big *ejecutivo* cigars with personalized rings in an elegant wooden box also handmade by Señor Acosta.

Yacht Marina   For the marine minded, Cumaná's Marina Pública Cumanagoto on Av. Perimetral, east of the Manzanares mouth, offers an opportunity to rub shoulders with the yachting set and perhaps hitch a ride or secure a crew position. The marina has a popular restaurant and a pharmacy that has a used book exchange with titles in English, Spanish, French and German. To enter the slip area you will need an invitation from someone with a boat inside as well as a pass from the office. You will need to show your passport and it is best to leave the bulk of your gear at the hotel and wear clean clothes.

Río Cancamure   When you need a break from the heat and bustle of the town, a dip in a cool river may provide the cure. Close to Cumaná is a beautiful small river, the Cancamure. Its upper reaches are quite clean, although muddy after a rain. This popular bathing area half an hour from town is served by the San Juan de Macarapana *por puesto* which leaves from Las Cuatro Esquinas, Av. Arismendi, near El Cuartel (a military enclave). Spend the day, the afternoon, watch the iguanas playing in the coconut palms. The road runs beside the river and there are picnic shelters with tables, small shops in which to buy basics and on the busier days hot *empanadas* (turnovers), *tortillas* (omelettes), chicken and pork. Weekends and holidays bring crowds. For a break, stop into the Bar Campo Lindo for a cold beer and a game of dominoes or *bolas criollas*, the Venezuelan game of bowls.

ARAYA PENINSULA

Araya is a desert peninsula whose extension from the mainland encloses the Gulf of Cariaco. Beaches on the Caribbean side are of broken shells with generally rough and murky water. For swimming and sunbathing stick to the gulf side. The gulf is very deep and the water is cooler than one would expect, but a welcome contrast to the sun's fierce heat. These depths are an important breeding ground for fish, and Araya's inhabitants are by and large fishermen.

The other industry of Araya is the salt pans. People come daily from Cumaná to join the Arayans in salt exploitation. These pans have been worked since 1499 when they were known as the world's richest. The fort of Santiago León de Araya dates from 1622 and was built to protect them. Construction of this massive fort, the partially restored ruins of which can be visited, took 47 years and was done largely at night to avoid the day's heat. You will see the fort as you approach Araya by sea. It is an easy walk from the village and has a good beach. Salt is evaporated from seawater, and the evaporation lagoon is an other-worldly pinkish mauve which must be seen to be believed. If you cross from Cumaná to the village of Araya by ferry or launch you will see a mountain of salt off to the north. Ask in the village about seeing the salt works. If you plan to visit Araya take good shoes for the rugged terrain and ubiquitous cactus. Full sun protection is called for here as there is virtually no shade. Take a hat and carry water.

Wildlife in Araya is surprisingly abundant. During the day you will see lizards and snakes, birds perched on cactus tops and feral goats everywhere. There are foxes and rabbits as well but these are more difficult to see. Chacopata Lagoon is known for its bird life, especially flamingoes. Ask Arquímedes Vargas (see below).

Getting there

Araya is accessible from Cumaná by Naviarca's open car ferry from the main dock that serves the Margarita ferry and launch. The way to the terminal on Av. El Islote, below the Mercado, is indicated by large signs in various parts of town. Sailings are variable: roughly morning, noon and afternoon on weekdays, and morning only on weekends. Remember that any 'schedule' in Venezuela is an approximation or, more accurately, a declaration of intent. Passenger fare is Bs.50. For information call Naviarca, (093) 26230.

The launches that leave from Puerto Sucre at the foot of Av. Bermúdez are faster, less expensive, more crowded and make trips throughout the day. They are known collectively as 'Tapaito' which refers to their roofs or *tapas*. Some go to the village of Araya, and you can ask to be dropped at Punta Arenas, a community with good beach and two *posadas* (see below). There is also service to Manicuare, a village further to the east known for its pottery, but it has nowhere to stay and the beach is nothing special. Be sure to ask the destination of the launch before you board.

If such services do not precisely fit your needs, you can make a deal with the owner of a *peñero*, the wooden fishing launches with outboard motor to be seen everywhere. Do not wander too far along the waterfront from Puerto Sucre. All waterfront *barrios* are tough and dangerous districts. Your negotiations will be in the strong local dialect, a challenge for anyone and prohibitive for marginal Spanish speakers. You may be asked for money 'up front' to buy gasoline for the trip. This is normal. If you are arranging for a pick-up as well as drop-off, do not pay in advance for the pick-up. In all dealings of this nature, as with taxi drivers, get an eyeball-meeting, hand-shaking agreement, or look for someone else. Avoid misunderstandings that can lead to confrontations and possible police intervention.

Araya's roads are generally rough and unmarked, and this is not a place to be lost or stranded. If you are thinking about hitching, remember that this is desert with no shade or water, dense growth of cactus and very little traffic. *Por puestos* go from Araya village to Punta Arenas, Manicuare and as far as El Guamache, but no further. There is access to Cariaco via a mostly paved road, but there is no through public transportation. Although the road is rough it has some attractive parts, especially the sea cliffs at the eastern end and lush forests on the north-south portion just before Cariaco.

Where to stay

In the village of Punta Arenas are two *posadas*, small hostels that offer beds, hammocks, meals and a very quiet, slow pace and environment, all on a beautiful beach. Rooms are small, rustic and comfortable but not private enough for honeymoon couples. Arquímedes Vargas, who speaks some English, offers bed and three meals, with refreshments, at $30 a person. He lived in the Gran Sabana for 10 years and knows Amazonas and the Orinoco Delta as well. Arquímedes offers excursions at reasonable prices to Mochima National Park, Cubagua Island (see Margarita section), and points of interest on the peninsula and Gulf of Cariaco. As there is no telephone at Villa Arenas, make arrangements through his agents in Cumaná. Call Nilo at (093) 316147, Sara Vargas at (093) 313216, or Frances Guix at (093) 652313. Frances owns an adjacent house in Punta Arenas and, following Arquímedes' example, is setting up her own *posada*.

Note: Wear beach sandals. Dogs are apparently responsible for hookworm larvae which can cause a creeping red irritation in feet. A case of such *larva migrans* has been reported from Araya. The hookworm does not develop in humans; thiabenzadole applied in a cream such as Drofen should eliminate the larvae.

EAST SUCRE STATE

The route to Paria Peninsula and Güiria

The road leaving Cumaná follows the sheltered Gulf of Cariaco. On its long tranquil shores there are three seaside places worth checking for a few days' rest. In La Chica just before Marigüitar are the small dock, beach and tennis court of the Maigualida Club (more of a hotel), (093) 91070, fax 91084. Its two new buildings have suites and rooms at about $20 single, and its open-sided restaurant makes a pleasant shady meeting spot. The Balneario Cachamaure, (093) 93045, has several inexpensive state-built *cabañas* in a large grassy park with coconut palms by a sandy cove. There are picnic and shower facilities, shelters for camping and the grounds are fenced. Hot springs, also. The Complejo Turístico Cayo Azul, (094) 314789, is a new resort with swimming pool, beach and restaurants just outside San Antonio del Golfo. The 120 air-conditioned cabins have double bed plus twin beds, renting for about $50 per cabin. The desk staff speak English.

Cariaco is an agricultural town at the end of the gulf, 13km past the fork for the Guácharo Cave. From Cariaco a paved road goes NW to Araya Peninsula, via Campoma (also turnoff for a road bordering the Gulf of Cariaco's north coast). From Campoma the scenic, often solitary road leads to **Chacopata** (about 50km), a very poor unkempt village on Araya's northern point. Nearby are lagoons where some 500 pink flamingoes come to feed. There is a passenger boat from Chacopata to Margarita which leaves early in the morning and at 14.00 (about), returning at 17.00. This Bs.250 ferry service is used mainly by residents of eastern towns who leave their cars by a Guardia Nacional post. *Peñeros* can be contracted to go to Coche Island, 40 minutes away.

Carúpano, about 55km from Cariaco, is a thriving fishery and cacao centre. It has a harbour, an attractive seaside boulevard, an airport bringing in tourists from Margarita and Caracas, some small business hotels, and a lively Carnival. Corpomedina and the Fundación Proyecto Paria have offices at No.2, Av. Juncal, (094) 312067, 315241. There are two routes from Carúpano to the Paria Peninsula (see below). Most *por puestos* to Güiria take the southern route via El Pilar, then head east, a distance of about 160km.

On the lovely Caribbean coast beyond Carúpano 10km, a headland called El Morro de Puerto Santo juts into the sea. On either side of the narrow isthmus are bays: El Morro village and a palm grove (camping not recommended) on the east; anchorage for the colourful Puerto Santo fishing fleet on the west. Swimmers here are warned of strong undertows.

Río Caribe is an attractive old fishing port, once the exporting centre for this rich cacao region. It has some fine old houses and plenty of shady avenues. The seaside Hotel Mar Caribe, (094) 61491 and 61494, has remodelled an old one-storey building which served as a maize mill, adding colonial style rooms; the kitchen has a reputation for good 'riocaribeña' cooking. Pool, 50 rooms a/c, about $25 double with breakfast.

Beyond Río Caribe a road now follows the coast; it is paved most of the way to Playa Medina. Since Medina has no phone, you could enquire here about rough parts on the coast road.

The highway for Güiria turns away from Río Caribe into lush cacao and coffee hills where Spanish moss (here called 'English beard' or *barba inglés*) festoons great trees. There is a road to Playa Medina from Quebrada Seca: turn left towards Puy Puy; at the community of Medina (6km) veer north for the coast. You will find **Playa Medina** tucked in a pretty cove between two promontories. The cape on the right was named Cabo de Mala Pascua by Columbus when a storm drove him into the bay for shelter in 1498.

Until recently the cove, fringed by a stately coconut hacienda, was reached only by sea and Playa Medina was unknown to most Venezuelans. However, developers acquired the hacienda and Club Med now has 'mega' plans. Thames Investment holds shares in the future 564-room hotel. [However, fortunately for lovers of solitude, those plans are on 'hold'.] In the meantime, there are eight charming cottages of rammed 'tapia' walls, red-tiled roofs and cane ceilings. There is a simple beachside restaurant. Reservations can be made in Carúpano (with transportation provided), (094) 315241, fax 312067. But package tours run to $200 a day (slightly less if you have transportation) including a visit to a water buffalo ranch, **Hato Río de Agua**. The Caracas offices of Corpomedina are in Edif. Galerías Bolívar, Boulevard de Sabana Grande, (02) 727234, 717328; however, they do not take reservations.

Beyond Playa Medina, the rough peninsular road from **Puy Puy** leads to an undeveloped beach. Peter Ireland described it as 'the most perfect beach I have ever seen. The trip will probably involve a mixture of hitching, *por puestos* and walking from Puy Puy, but it's worth it once you're there. Puy Puy beach is about 1km of soft golden sand bordered by palm trees. At the far end is a *caserío* with a beer shop (shuts early), a soft drink shop and a couple of general stores. You can either camp or sling hammocks between palms, though you risk a coconut landing on your head. The sea is a little rough, but the surf is great. The waves are good enough for bodysurfing; take a bit of care as there are some strange currents about.'

From here it is another two hours by jeep to **San Juan de Las**

Galdonas which has a long beach at the foot of a mountain. Still farther is the last outpost on this northern road, **Unare**. There is a 24km road linking San Juan de Las Galdonas with Bohordal on the south of the peninsula. Eastward lies Paria National Park on a mountain ridge which points to, and almost touches Trinidad.

Finca Vuelta Larga

Guaraúnos is a village between El Pilar and Tunapuy some 36km from Carúpano on the way to Güiria. This is the home (and camp) of Claus Muller who runs a large buffalo farm and nature preserve. He supports his conservation programmes by means of ecotourism. The best time to visit **Vuelta Larga**, Claus' wetlands farm, is late afternoon. If possible, stay the night on the *palafito*, an observation hut on stilts in the water. Parrots return to roost and you can see cayman, turtles, capybara and many water birds. Together with the International Council for Bird Preservation and Provita, the Vuelta Larga Foundation carries out environmental education work encouraging sustainable agriculture outside Paria park. Climate deterioration is evident in Paria, now hotter and drier with less cloud cover. Projects include a honey farm and medicinal crops. A large tract of nearby wetlands has recently been declared the Parque Nacional Turuépano.

Using a canoe with outboard motor, Claus runs camping trips (one to five days) to the delta of the San Juan River. Mangrove fringed rivers such as Caño La Brea teem with wildlife including scarlet ibis, kingfishers, cayman, giant otter, Orinoco crocodile, and, if you're very lucky, manatee. Claus provides all camping gear. He also leads hikes in Paria Park, over the ridge to the Caribbean where there is a beach shelter; walking time about 6 hours. From Santa Isabel, hikers return by sea to Carúpano. Costs run to about $65 a day.

Claus speaks German and English, as do his sons who lead excursions. His address is N°8 Calle Bolívar, Guaraúnos, Estado Sucre; telephone/fax after 6pm, (094) 69052. Telephone communication is terrible, however.

PARIA NATIONAL PARK

Paria National Park covers 375km² of the northern slope and crest forming the backbone of Paria Peninsula. Fishing hamlets dot half a dozen bays tucked at the foot of the coastal range which rises almost straight from the sea. Highest peak is Cerro Humo, 1,356m. This is an area of superb cloud forest, remarkable because it grows as low as 800m above sea level. Many palms, tree ferns, lianas, epiphytes and huge buttressed trees thrive in drenching conditions created partly by condensation recycled by the forest itself. These mountains are described as once forming part of a 'forest island' which included Trinidad and as such are the refuge of endemic species. The scissor-tailed hummingbird, Venezuelan flower-piercer, white-throated barbtail, spiny rat and black nutria live here only.

However, only half Cerro Humo is legally protected, and there are just four *guardaparques* or rangers to patrol the park. The forest is affected by farm clearing, especially in the south where villages are expanding.

The area is targeted for development. Under the name of Christopher Columbus Project, oil companies will export a daily 700 million cubic feet of liquefied natural gas. The gas, from offshore fields in the Caribbean, will be piped across the peninsula of Paria from Mejillones to a plant slated for the south coast of Paria.

Getting there

The quickest way to the Paria Peninsula: from the bus terminal in Caracas, take an *expreso* to Puerto La Cruz (5 hrs) and on to Carúpano (3½ hrs); most direct buses travel at night; about $10. A *carrito* will take you from Carúpano to Güiria. From there, all travel to Macuro and points in between (no accommodation) is by boat. CAVE flies from Margarita Island to Güiria on Mon., Wed. and Fri. (about $20). The plane should arrive in Güiria at 7.00, in time to catch the *peñeros* which leave for Macuro before 9.00.

Manacal

The following information comes from members of the Cambridge Columbus Botanical Study who spent two months near Cerro Humo (in the western section of the peninsula) in 1990: Mark Dutton, Justine Freeth, Peter Ireland and James Mead.

There is some good hiking around Cerro Humo, using Manacal as a base. The village main street is on the top of a ridge; a clearing at the end is the scene for the weekly baseball game, and the villagers

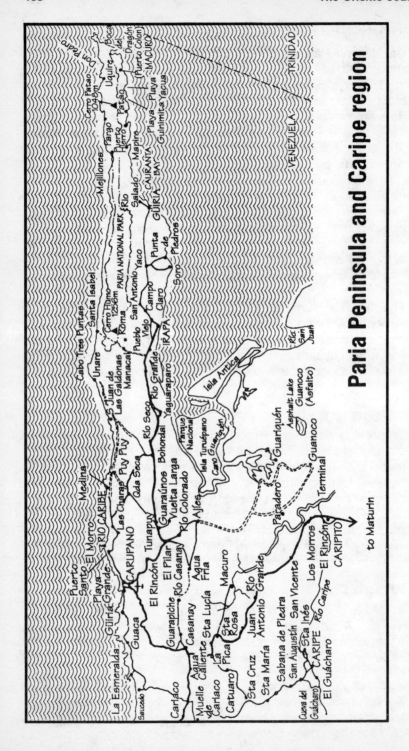

Paria Peninsula and Caripe region

will be happy for you to join in. If you want to see how hard these farmers work, ask to go with someone to their *conuco* or plot. They grow maize, roots such as ocumo (dasheen), yuca (cassava) and mapuey (cush-cush), and bananas and plantains. Just staying in Manacal is an experience in itself. Of the 30 families, 25 are evangelicals, and the others think they are mad. At night, the light outside the Evangelist church flashes in the mist instead of a bell; there is a 2-hour service every night.

Getting there

The *por puesto* to Río Grande de Irapa on the Güiria route should leave you at the entrance road (left) to Manacal; specify 'Manacal arriba de Río Grande' so as not to confuse it with another Manacal beyond Irapa. Only 4WD vehicles can make it to Manacal, otherwise it's a 3-hour hike up to 800m elevation. One or two vehicles go up each day; if you can catch a ride, it may be possible to pay the driver to go all the way (Bs.500).

In Manacal, ask for the house of the Comisario, Juan Bravo; he lives below the church on the left. Possibly you will be able to stay in a house or the school. Nights are cold, it would be best to have a sleeping bag and a hammock, too. Food in the village shop is limited to basics — sardines, spaghetti, sugar, wheat and cornflour. Or with some advance notice, ask a señora to cook up some yams or yuca; or perhaps a *dumplín* which is a great wheat arepa. The villagers are not set up for tourism in any way but are very generous. If they do not charge you, be prepared with presents: good string, lighters, cigarettes, matches, snacks, pencils, brandy or whisky (everyone has rum). [Publisher's note: if bringing presents choose them with care. Anything that increases consumer awareness for goods normally unobtainable may ultimately do more harm than good. Giving sweets to children, for instance, will create little beggars and cause tooth decay. Give to the adults to whom you owe a debt of gratitude and play with the children. This gift will last in terms of goodwill.]

Hikes to Cerro Humo, Santa Isabel

You will need a guide for hiking, not only because the way is not always clear, but because of accidents or snakes (the nearest hospital is in Carúpano). Cipriano is a good guide (about Bs.500 the day); or ask the Comisario.

The trail to Santa Isabel leads first to towards Cerro Humo and Roma, another high village on the south slope. Keep on up the ridge. After the turning for Roma, you come to a cleared area with

views north and south, as far as Irapa and the delta. You have to
step over a large stone before re-entering the cloud forest. At a high
point, 1,000m, a tree on the path is marked with an E and a K. The
K is for the path to Santa Isabel. The E stands for Entrada or
entrance to Cerro Humo. This path drops before a final ascent to the
peak (3 hrs). The actual top is a cleared plateau with a surveying
point, though trees and clouds tend to obscure the view.

From the K, the left path to Santa Isabel makes a steady descent
to the sea, crossing beautiful streams as you pass through primary
forest, then cultivations. Before you reach the village you have to
wade through the Río Santa Isabel; idyllic pools shaded by the forest
are just large enough for swimming. The whole walk is about 6
hours.

Santa Isabel, above the rivermouth, is larger than Manacal and
more used to tourists. It has a paved main street, normally covered
in fishing nets with fishermen repairing holes. The atmosphere is
different to Manacal; the people seem more industrious. The boats
come into the river to unload. The sea here is rough and there are
sea-urchins on the rocks. For swimming it's best to stick to the river.
Or continue on a path which drops into the next cove, with a long
deserted beach.

To stay in Santa Isabel, ask for Mayra's house which has a
fantastic view of the sea and a small island. Mayra provided bed or
hammock for Bs.80, and a meal of fried fish, rice and platanos for
Bs.80. To leave, you can either walk back or take the boat to Unare
(1hr 15min); the price is negotiable. You get fantastic views of forest
coming down to the beach. It is possible to arrange for a boat to
drop you off on such a beach for a day or so. Unare is at the end of
the jeep road on the north coast and there are *por puestos* to Río
Caribe.

Güiria to Macuro

Wooden lattices, fretwork and some slate-tiled roofs give Güiria a
Caribbean flavour. There are several cheap hotels. Also, economical
family style rooms (two air-conditioned, eight with fans) are rented
by Señora Leonor de Smith, La Tiendita on Calle Pagallo. Walk from
the church on Plaza Bolívar down to the beach where a kiosko
called Los Cinco Rumbos has a few tables serving fried fish, arepas,
hervido.

The Macuro boats tie up near a kiosko to the left; the trip takes 1-2
hours and a *puesto* costs about Bs.250. Larger vessels dock at the
international port on the south end of the bay. There is said to be
boat service to Trinidad run by Adrian, a Trinidadian who used to
work in London. It goes when he can get together 6-10 passengers

(the fare is $60 each way). But since immigration and customs are bureaucratic affairs, don't count on a quick departure.

Windward Island Service

Weekly maritime services to five islands has recently been started by Windward Lines Ltd. This could be the long-awaited 'bridge' between Venezuela and the Antilles. Their agents are Acosta Asociados C.A., Calle Bolívar 31, Güiria, (094) 81679, fax (094) 81112, 81682. The weekly run leaves Güiria on Wednesdays at 20.00 for Trinidad, arriving there at 07.00 Thursday. The 250passenger ship continues up the Lesser Antilles cruising at night (13.5 knots) and calling in at Grenada, St. Vincent, Barbados and St. Lucia before completing the circle back to Venezuela. Fares range from US$30 one way to Trinidad up to $90 to St. Lucia, not including restaurant or porters. Forty cabins offer twin berths at $10 a night per person. The ship is air-conditioned.

MACURO

Near the tip of the peninsula is Macuro. Columbus landed here on August 4 1498, coming from Trinidad which he named for its three peaks. He at first thought Paria was another island and called it Isla de Gracia, or island of grace because he was so impressed by its amiable natives, their farms, houses and pearl necklaces. Sailing for two days into the Gulf of Paria, Columbus finally realized that he had found a continent with a huge river mouth: the Orinoco Delta.

A bronze statue of Columbus is almost the tallest structure in Macuro. A few dilapidated wood and plaster houses remain from its heyday in the 30s. There was a governor in residence at the time and the town, then called Puerto Colón, was the head customs office (Dictator Gómez wished to sidestep a debt agreement giving the British in La Guaira rights to collect customs fees).

In an old house whose rooms are covered with amusing murals painted by an escapee from Devil's Island, a museum has been put together by Eduardo Rothe out of fossils, pre-Columbian pottery, even a hand-made aeroplane. Rothe calls Macuro 'the first and last town in Venezuela'. It has survived 500 years of solitude. Most of its 2,000 inhabitants subsist on fishing and small farm plots. There is said to be extra-legal trading with Trinidad, and the area is a natural route for cocaine traffic and parrot and macaw smuggling through the Delta.

Cristina Sganga summed up her impressions: 'Colonised centuries ago by runaway slaves, Macuro has a Caribbean feel. It consists of no more than a dozen streets with open sewers. The only stable source of employment is a nearby limestone mine owned by Vencemos. Vencemos was responsible for maintaining the power generators, but had not done so for seven months out of 12 so the residents had occupied the mine. They opposed plans to transform Macuro into a classic Spanish colonial pueblo to mark Columbus' 500th anniversary.'

In Macuro there are rooms for rent; ask Doña Angelina, or Señora Rodríguez who has four very clean rooms at Bs.200 double. She makes good food, too (chicken, fish). Or you can camp in a tent or hammock. There's plenty of firewood on the little beach and you can buy fresh fish from fishermen. Don't buy the meat or eggs of turtles which are endangered species. Other food supplies should be brought with you since they are very expensive on the peninsula. The beach is not idyllic because the water is brown from the Orinoco Delta. Macureños go up to a little rocky river for swimming.

Exploring the National Park
by Chris Sharpe

Remember you will need a permit to visit the national park. The paths in the forest above Macuro are worthwhile. See if the park guard, Chichí, will guide you, since trails constantly change course to new plots or conucos. Give him Bs.400 for a day on the trails (about 5 hours, depending on how far you want to go). Best to set off before 7am to avoid heat; water available in mountain streams. Use insect repellent.

Two trails lead from Macuro in about 6 hours to the north coast where there are crystal clear waters, rocky shores, and two villages: Uquire, and Don Pedro. Uquire is a large village with a fantastic beach, good snorkelling, and palm trees. Don Pedro is smaller, like a village 'abandoned by time'. You may have to walk to Uquire, 2 hours, if there is no boat in Don Pedro. Or return by the trail.

It's easy to spend a week travelling around the peninsula in the open fishing boats called peñeros. From Macuro you can hire a boat for about Bs.3,000 (round trip) to go through the straits called Boca de Dragón to Uquire. From here, ask Nestico, the park guard, to take you up into the forest. The lower woods have been disturbed by hunting and plantations of cacao, mango, avocado and banana, but higher up it's in pretty good shape.

SECTION FOUR

THE ORINOCO REGION

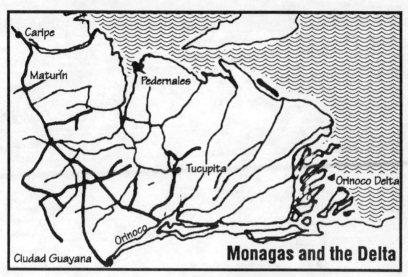

Monagas and the Delta

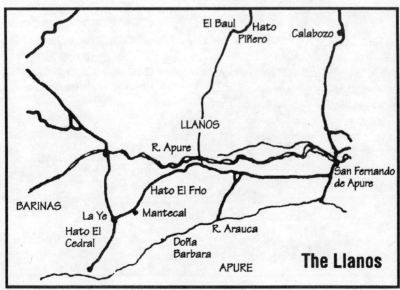

The Llanos

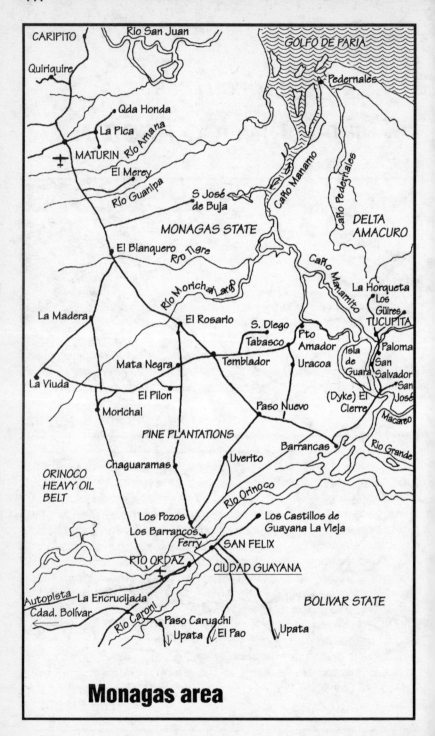

Monagas area

Chapter 12

Monagas and the Orinoco Delta

by Chris Stolley

Highlands and lowlands

Guácharo Cave, echoing with the weird clicks and flutterings of its marvellous oilbirds is located where Monagas State borders on Sucre's mountains. To the east lies a maze of rivers running into the Gulf of Paria and the Orinoco Delta, and to the south oil-rich plains drain to the Orinoco River. International travellers are slowly discovering Monagas as new hotels and river camps open up.

CARIPE

Just across from the Sucre border in Monagas State is a small mountain town, the centre of a coffee, citrus and vegetable producing area. At 900m elevation it is Oriente's mountain retreat. The pace is slow and the people are relaxed and friendly. Jeep roads penetrate the surrounding mountains to an elevation of about 1,500m, winding up through coffee plantations and cloud forest with its orchid and bromeliad festooned trees, giant tree ferns, abundant birdsong and moist coolness. Trails crisscross the area and local guides can be engaged to lead you to spectacular hidden waterfalls or to the peak of Cerro Negro, at 2,400m the highest around. Visitors find the mountain climate a welcome relief from the heat of Sucre's coast or the Llanos.

Caripe is best known for the Guácharo Cave (see page 147). The cave is located about 10km to the west of the town, above the village of Los Dos Alambres, also known as El Guácharo.

Getting there

The distance from Cumaná to Caripe is 127km (117km to Guácharo Cave) on a road turning off the Cariaco Gulf into the mountains just past Villa Frontado, also called Muelle de Cariaco. The mountain drive is very pretty. Buses to and from Cumaná take about 3hrs with a rest stop; about $3. They leave from Caripe's depot in front of the church at 6.30 and 11.30 (always reconfirm times), but can be flagged on the highway as well. There is a slightly longer route from Cumaná via Cumanacoa, so you can make a circle. There is a *por puesto* service to Maturín from the centre of town. Look for the congregation of cars.

Where to stay/eat

There are two hotels that I recommend in Caripe. Hotel Samán, (093) 51183, is in the centre of town and has the best restaurant. Some of the rooms are of the traditional cave-like type, very small with no exterior windows and wall-to-wall beds. There are newer, more comfortable rooms as well, with more space and exterior windows. Be sure to specify when making reservations. The Samán also has a new solar heated swimming pool with poolside bar. A short walk to the west of town is El Guácharo Hotel, (092) 51218, older and slightly more rustic but off by itself in a very peaceful setting. There is an unheated swimming pool with bar. I do not recommend the restaurant. My preference is to stay at El Guácharo but eat at the Samán. Both hotels are in the $20 per night range. There are several less expensive hotels of the cave-like bed-filled type. The best of these with adequate restaurant is the Hotel Caripe on the main street.

As Caripe is a popular family vacation spot there are many *cabañas* available with cooking facilities and space for six or more people. To stay in these you really need a car. Most have no prepared food. Cabañas Bellerman, (092) 51326, high on the hill overlooking Caripe at 1,200m, are very comfortable and well-run bungalows. Located east of Caripe in **Teresén**, Hacienda Campo Claro, (092) 551013 (and in Caracas (02) 9876081), is a working coffee, citrus and dairy farm. They have horses to ride, cabañas with kitchen, smaller rooms just for sleeping, and there is a new restaurant. It is a delight to be served a relaxed breakfast of coffee, orange juice, homemade bread and jam, butter, cheese, milk and eggs, all from the farm.

When planning your trip, remember that Caripe facilities will be booked solid at Christmas, Easter and Carnival, as well as school holidays, roughly July-Sept.

A highpoint of Caripe is the natural wine made from *mora* (blackberry) and *fresa* (strawberry). These wines are sold exclusively by their maker, an elderly German, at his highway stand between Caripe and Hotel El Guácharo. I recommend them highly. I have passed many an evening with a friend and a bottle of *mora*, without suffering a *ratón* (hangover).

The Cave of the Guácharos
by Chris Stolley

The Cueva del Guácharo is named for, and is home to, approximately 18,000 guácharos or oilbirds (*Steatornis caripensis*). The Spanish name refers to one who sobs or laments, as they do. The English name refers to the fact that the young birds were once hunted and rendered for their tremendous fat content. The adult bird weighs about one third that of the young, the difference being solid fat. The young fatten on oilrich nuts of *seje* palm, and at adulthood purge the oil by eating the fruit of the *cobalonga* tree.

This unique bird has several features found in no other bird. It is the only bird known to fly in complete darkness finding its way like a bat by the echo of sounds made by clacking its beak. You will hear this sound in the cave. It is the only nocturnal bird that is not carnivorous and it eats only on the fly, grabbing food in its beak. There has been much speculation, often conflicting, about the habits of the guácharo. The birds were once thought to fly as far as Brazil in their nightly search for the 32 kinds of fruit that make up their diet. It is now thought that they fly no more than 50km. Guácharos live in a number of other caves, 30 to 87 by various counts. Guácharos share their home with other cave-adapted creatures. There are fearless smooth-furred brown rats. Bats, unable to manage a peaceful coexistence, live in their own part of the cave. This is the Hall of Silence, so named for the abrupt absence of bird sounds. The entrance is a bottleneck through which the birds cannot pass. You may also see unpigmented crickets with very long antennae, spiders, millipedes, centipedes, mice, crabs and fish.

The cave has been known to Europeans since 1660. In 1799 Alexander von Humboldt, the famous German explorer, visiting the cave, described and named the oilbirds. His Indian guides would only permit him to go as far as the entrance to the Hall of Silence, to them the entrance to the world of the dead. In 1953 electric lights were installed. The birds abandoned the cave in great numbers, but returned when the lights were turned off. Calcium carbonate encrusted light bulbs can still be seen.

Parque Nacional el Guácharo

The highway crosses the national park and dips down from the mountain crest, passing in front of the park office. Directly opposite is the mouth of Guácharo Cave which faces west. The cave was named Venezuela's first natural monument in 1949 and in 1975 627km² were declared national park.

The cave is open to the public daily, and there is a museum and restaurant. One can enter the cave only with a guided group. The cave guides are very poorly paid, so if you get a good one, please tip him. A good guide is Carlos Luna, son of a 30-year veteran guide. He speaks adequate English and is a fountain of information. Flashlights and flash cameras are prohibited in the cave. A dawn or dusk visit will be rewarded by a view of the clamourous exit or entry of the guácharos. Take a jacket as it can be chilly.

The cave has 9½km of galleries and visitors are allowed to penetrate a distance of a little over 1km. The entrance cavern, named after Humboldt, is a vast chamber where the guácharo birds roost on high dim ledges. There are stalactites and stalagmites in the immense tunnel that leads 759m into the mountain and there are no birds in the Hall of Silence beyond. Cavers wishing to explore further should contact the speleological groups and secure written permission from the National Parks division of Inparques. (See *National Parks*.) Include details of passports and allow 60 days.

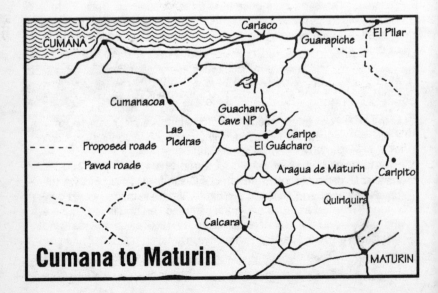

MATURÍN

Maturín, the state capital, has little to offer tourists, but is the access town for excellent river trips. The Hotel Mallorca, (091) 413287,26620, in the centre of town offers all the basics at less than $10 per night. Maturín is an oil boomtown and accommodation can be hard to come by. It is worse during the week than on weekends. As there is little of interest in this businesslike city, holidays present no problems. Maturín is served by six daily flights from Margarita and Ciudad Bolívar. There is a good bus service from Caracas, also.

Río Morichal Largo

The management of Hotel El Guácharo runs day tours and operates a camp on the Morichal Largo River, a 45 minute drive to the south of Maturín, state capital. This river, although heavily used by the tourist traffic in season, has an abundance of wildlife including the troops of howler and capuchin monkeys, and the remarkable hoatzin. This bird, called *chenchena* or *guácharaca de aqua*, is distinguished by its raucous call and disagreeable strong musty odour. They are clumsy flyers and are easily heard as they flounder about in the trees. Several features single them out among birds: their diet (leaves) and digestive process (two stomachs, like a cow) and the presence of a hook at the 'elbow' of wings of fledglings, which allow them to escape predators by dropping into the water then climbing back to their nests, using these hooks and their strong feet. You may see cayman or *babas*, the infamous anaconda and piranhas or *caribes rojos* as they are locally called.

On its way to join the Mánamo in the Orinoco Delta the river runs through forest and *morichales*, the stands of mauritia palms. This palm is a principal source of food and fibre for rope, baskets and hammocks for the Warao Indians who live there. You will see them in their stilt houses (known as *palafitos*) along the bank, and in their canoes. For those who do not have the time, endurance or money to go on a full-fledged river expedition, this is a good chance to see this type of country. Prices run from $25 per person for the lowest priced day tour, to $75 for an overnight at the riverside camp. All food and drink is included, and you can arrange for transport from Caripe or Maturín. Ask at the Hotel El Guácharo, (092) 51218, or call (091) 41097 in Maturín. Guide Jefferson Valero speaks good English.

Route to the Delta

From Maturín a highway runs 90km to a fork at El Rosario. The southern route heads for the Orinoco River (82km) and a ferry linking

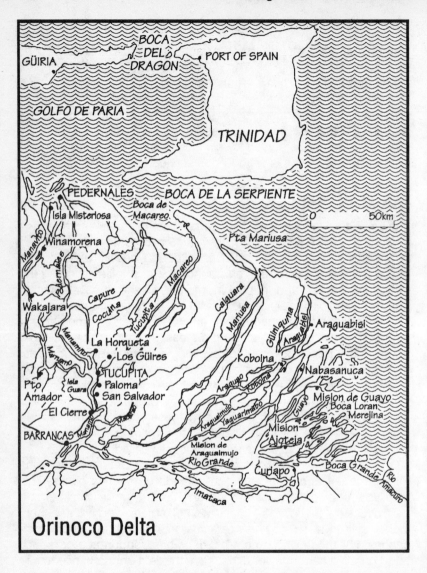

Orinoco Delta

Los Barrancos (not to be confused with Barrancas) and Ciudad
Guayana. On the way you cross vast state plantations of Honduras
pines around Chaguaramas. Intended for a pulp and paper plant,
the pine trees cover 400km² and have converted arid sandy plains
into a greener, cooler ecosystem now supporting a variety of birds
as well as animals such as deer.

Off the SE route to Tucupita (122km) there is a new bungalow
complex called Balneario Cabañas Rio Selva just before San Antonio
de Tabasca. You follow a road from Temblador about 25km east. In
the middle of 'nowhere', the 'jungle' resort has a large pool (you pay

by the day), bar and lunch spot. The developers offer day trips on tributaries flowing into the Delta: the Tabasca River down to Caño Mánamo and Tucupita; the Uracoa and Caño Mánamo to Warao communities such as El Pajal and Santo Domingo. (Sadly, Rio Selva was last reported to be temporarily closed.)

A paved road now continues from San Antonio de Tabasca to the nearby village of Uracoa, with its old palm-thatched houses and *gallera* or cock pit. From here to Tucupita is about 95km.

THE ORINOCO DELTA

The Orinoco Delta seldom appears on travel agendas. Inhabitants are few and services are primitive in the vast estuary. The maze of changing rivers and islands is mainly a target for wilderness travellers who can get around with the locals, stop where they stop and sling a hammock at night. I advise asking the "*comisario*" or "*prefecto*" in each village for local orientation.

The local people are the Warao or Guaraúnos in Spanish. Excellent fishermen, the Warao long kept intact their way of life as the 'canoe people' (*wa arao*), safe in the outer delta marshes. 3,300km² of this area have recently been declared the Parque Nacional Mariusa. Using trunks of mauritia palm, the Warao still build riverside houses on piles, linking dwellings into villages. These *moriche* palms also give them food, wine and fibre for ropes, dugout sails and the baskets and hammocks which have made Warao crafts sought after in Europe and North America. Numbering about 19,000, the Warao are Venezuela's largest native group after the Wayú (Guajiros). Neither Carib nor Arawak, the origin of their ancient language is still debated. Today under pressure from farmers moving in, many Warao families are moving out to Monagas and Bolívar States in search of a livelihood.

Thirty-six major outlets fan over the Delta's 40,200km². Now Venezuela's 21st state, it is called the Delta Amacuro after a river flowing from the border near Guyana. At the fan's apex by Barrancas the Orinoco spreads 22km wide. The main channel flows to the Atlantic through the Río Grande. In Warao language the name of this outlet is *wiri noko*, 'to row, place', perhaps the origin of 'Orinoco'. Less than 15km from the delta lies Trinidad which Columbus named on the first landfall of his third voyage. The year was 1498 and the day August 4, height of annual floods, when his ships passed through the Serpent's Mouth. Columbus was amazed by the Orinoco's fresh-water 'mountain range of waves'. This outpouring has been calculated at 1.1 billion cubic metres yearly, depositing tons of silt and creating new land.

Temperatures average 26°C, cooling a little at night. Rains are often irregular — starting in April, pausing in July, then trailing into October and sometimes December. This is malaria country; take anti-malaria pills *before* arriving in the Delta.

Tucupita

With its shady Plaza Bolívar, band concerts and esplanade called the Paseo Mánamo where people watch the river go by, Tucupita has some small town pleasures. It is the trading, supply and banking centre for more than half of the Delta's 92,000 inhabitants. The capital lies opposite Monagas State in the angle where Caño Mánamo is joined by Caño Tucupita, some 110km from the sea. The road to Tucupita crosses the Caño Mánamo over a dyke that closes off this large river, separating the central delta from the northern delta. (Unfortunately, the 1969 scheme to reclaim land for ranching and farming was dampened by salt water backing up from the sea). This point on the dyke is called the *cierre*; there is a guard post or *alcabala*. Except for a few kilometres from Tucupita to La Horqueta and Los Güires, there are no other roads in the delta. In the sporadic communities outside Tucupita, expect to find only rudimentary shelter and the barest of supplies.

Getting there

Scheduled airlines were not flying to Tucupita at press time (June 1993), Avensa having suspended service. The fare was about $40. The airfield is 3km from town and taxis are reliable. Buses drive overnight from Caracas to Tucupita, covering the 730km in 11½ hours; fare about $10. Expresos Camargüi, (02) 4438623, and Rápidos Guayana. The buses return to Caracas leaving Tucupita at 19.00. *Por puesto* cars from Puerto Ordaz charge about $5 a seat.

Where to stay

Among hotels, the Pequeña Venecia near the waterfront, (087) 21558, has low-priced lodging, small restaurant. Julian Singleton stayed in the centre at the Pequeño Hotel on Calle La Paz, recommending it as 'friendly, clean, safe. $6 for a single with fan'. The Gran Hotel Amacuro near Plaza Bolívar, (087) 21057, 25 rooms a/c and restaurant, appeared to be 'good, more expensive' ($10 single). The Hotel Delta, Calle Pativilca, (087) 21219, has 16 rooms, a/c. At the entrance to Tucupita is the 2-storey Hotel Warauno, Av. Cocalito, (087) 22600, 40 a/c rooms, lacklustre restaurant. In San Salvador, about 12km south of Tucupita, there is a newly built hotel, the Parque Venezia.

Julian reports that 'Tucupita is a pleasant town. It's quite lively at night, there's usually music and dancing going on somewhere, often near the waterfront. There are numerous bars. I recommend the Posada Delta bar, it has good music and a friendly atmosphere.' El Alcaníz and Restaurant-Cervecería Tucupita are the busiest restaurants.

Luis Armas has other suggestions: 'It may also be useful to visit Radio Tucupita, a station used much like a telephone for relaying messages in the delta so that everyone knows what's going on. The radio station is 200m from Plaza Bolívar. Crafts are best bought from the Indians themselves rather than Tucupita middlemen. Take a *por puesto* from the bus stop on Plaza Bolívar to **Paloma** out of town where there is an Indian centre or Casa Indígena called Ikariyene. Good hammocks and baskets of *moriche* palm, carved animals.'

Missions

Tucupita's one-storey profile is broken by the looming new Cathedral, La Divina Pastora, and the older Mission Church of San José de Tucupita. Missionary work among the Warao began in earnest when the Araguaimujo Mission and boarding school were founded in 1925. This was followed by the missions of Amacuro, Tucupita, Guayo, Nabasanuka and Ajotejana. The Capuchin fathers in Tucupita may be asked for permission to visit the missions (go to the Casa Parroquial). Travellers are given shelter but are reminded that donations are welcome and food is scarce, also clothing, medicines. Journeys to most missions start in Barrancas.

River travel

Travel in the delta is by open boats — fishing craft or *peñeros*, motorised launches, large dugout bongos. For travel to the northern delta, principally on the Mánamo, Pedernales, Tucupita or Macareo rivers, ask at the *bomba* or service station on Calle Tucupita where boatmen buy gasoline. *Por puestos* go from the marketplace to the *muelle*, a small port called El Volcán towards the *cierre*. A public launch goes twice weekly to Curiapo and Pedernales; this *transporte fluvial* costs Bs.200 per person.

In the central delta, ocean-going vessels navigating the Orinoco use the Rio Grande. The channel is regularly dredged to allow passage of ore carriers from Ciudad Guayana. River boats to communities such as Araguaimujo Mission, Sacupana, Curiapo and Guayo Mission leave from Barrancas. Travel time varies according to the engine used: with a 40hp, the run from Barrancas to Guayo takes 8 or 9 hours; with a 75hp, time is 3 to 4 hours. It also varies seasonally. During the rains the river is full and calm, making travel easier; during low water, the current, waves and eastern trade winds are all stronger. Barrancas is rated as 'horrible'; travellers go to this pueblo only to arrange a *curiara* but return to Tucupita for the night.

Tours

Three-day trips to San Francisco de Guayo and Curiapo are offered by Mánamo Tours, Calle Dalla Costa No.22, Plaza Bolívar, Tucupita, (087) 21156. All river transportation, food and camping gear are included in the package at around $150 a person, based on a group of 4. Mary Lou Goodwin advises contacting Abelardo Lara or Jairo Córdoba at Delta Tours, Calle Pativilca No.75, (087) 22986, 21095. A new service is offered from Tucupita to San Francisco de Guayo, 4 days/3 nights, organized with German efficiency by Tom Tours, (02) 334177, 2621210, fax 2621905; $300. Lobster's Tours goes from Ciudad Guyana to the Delta. Their Caracas address is Oficina 8-B, Edif. La Roca, Calle Villaflor, Sabana Grande, (02) 7613440, fax 7625636.

The French connection

'Definitely recommended,' said Cal O'Neill of a 10-day tour which took him from Monagas State to the Delta and Paria Peninsula for about $500. The tour is organised by Natura Raid, a company run by two Frenchman, Dominique Jacquin and Gilles Cros. They have offices in Porlamar, Margarita, (095) 611626, fax 614419. Gilles Cros has a Caracas telephone, (02) 349200. 'The guides and boys on the boat were all very eager and helpful,' Cal noted. 'Our fishing boat carried bottled water, food, and we cooked on board. We ate hot "dumplings" — sort of pan-baked dough — and fresh fried carite (kingfish), shrimp, palm heart salad.

'Indian paddlers took us in dugouts through caños a few yards wide where we saw monkeys and macaws. We spent four nights in native stilt houses sleeping in hamocks with mosquito netting — the Indians just moved out when our party showed up. In these *palafitos* built over the water there are no walls or bathrooms. Except for a lack of amenities, the camps were very good.'

The travellers' *peñero*, a 12-metre fishing craft, was equipped with four 65HP motors. Navigating through the delta by way of the Mánamo and Pedernales Rivers, they crossed the Gulf of Paria (3 hours) back to terra firma near Güiria. Here the group stayed at the new Posada Turística Playa Dorada, (094) 81665, fax 81112, in Punta de Piedras. The 4-room beachside inn is run by Asdrubal Marin; about $50 single with all meals, hammocks (no individual bathrooms).

The *peñero* continued around the Paria Peninsula to the north coast, stopping at San Juan de Las Galdonas where Cal reported that there are now two small hotels. He recommends the French-run Posada de Las Galdonas as good quality.

American enterprise

A young American, Anthony Tahbou, has opened the first real tourist camp in the Delta. His base is near Guamal on a branch of the Mánamo, two hours by launch from Tucupita. Tahbou relied on native labour and materials to build the riverside structures raised on stilts; boardwalks link the dock to a dining room, sleeping area and bathroom. Across the narrow caño there is a small settlement of Warao Indians. Some work with Tahbou, speaking Spanish as well as Warao. Other guides are English-speaking, helping on trips to a second, remoter camp near Guaranoco. During the 2-hour boat ride Indians spot toucans and parrots, monkeys and cayman, or catch large fish such as *sábalo* and *morocoto* with a hand line trailing behind the boat.

Cost is $80-110 per day depending on group size, all inclusive from Tucupita. Ring Tucupita Expeditions, (087) 22496, fax (087) 21547. In Caracas, call Linda Sonderman, Alpitour, (02) 2836677, 2855116.

Delta tour

Julian Singleton, writing about his Delta travels, said that 'guides in Tucupita hang around the Plaza Bolívar; they'll find you. For a regular Delta tour, Rafael is said to be good. (I didn't go on one of these, but other travellers recommended him.) For 3 days, the price was $50 a person (I think there's an extra charge towards food). The trip by motorboat stops first at a small homestead on the Mánamo River; there you go horse riding. Next, on to Morichal Largo (hammock and mosquito net essential); then to Isla Misteriosa to visit an Indian village before heading back via the Pedernales River. The boat frequently goes down narrow rivers so it's possible to see wildlife.'

For the more adventurous, Julian shares his own experience of five days in a dugout which he rates as 'one of the highlights of my trip'.

Five days in a dugout canoe
by Julian Singleton

For someone who enjoys sleeping among the trees in a hammock, hunting and fishing and cooking food by the campfire, I'd strongly recommend this trip. It's sensible to be fairly fit. We paddled for about four hours non-stop each day till I thought my arm would drop off. I got fairly filthy and was drenched by the occasional rain shower.

To make the trip, locate Rafael. He's a tour guide but knows people who live in the delta. Rafael told me I could arrange to make a canoe trip with his friend Jóvito (or El Diablo as he's otherwise known). Jóvito owns a farm growing coconuts, cocoa, etc. in Morichal Largo in the Pedernales region. Negotiate with Rafael for passage to Morichal Largo. I paid about $30 to Rafael for passage there and back. It may be possible to pay only one way with Rafael as many boats pass by Jóvito's heading for Tucupita ($5 to $8). Rafael is a good friend of Jóvito's and wrote a note introducing me. Without his help I couldn't have made the trip. Bargaining is essential with Rafael, though. I should say here that it's important to know some Spanish, the more the better.

The journey to Jóvito's takes 4-5 hours. Once there negotiate with Jóvito to hire one of his workers. It's an idea to bring along a bottle (rum) for this. I hired an Indian called Erme, a very competent guide. He knows how to survive in the delta off the land, fishing, hunting and preparing camp. Jóvito has a shop of sorts where I bought flour, salt, sugar and rice. You can hunt and fish the rest. Erme supplied everything needed for cooking.

During the mornings we paddled. Later we fished from the boat or went down a narrow *caño* to hunt with the gun. We cooked our day's catch on the campfire. You can learn so much more on a trip like this. I saw a fair amount of wildlife, mainly birds, toucans, macaws and others I couldn't name. I saw turtles basking on rocks and on one occasion I saw what looked like an otter (*perro de agua*) poking his head out of the water. We met some Indians along the way. They still live pretty much as they have since the first ships arrived from Spain. At night we strung our hammocks under shelters made from palm fronds, used by passing Indians or fishermen. Mosquitoes are rife at this time (November) so a hammock (which you can buy in Tucupita) with mosquito net (probably better to buy at home) is essential.

Here's a list of other equipment I think is necessary: poncho or waterproof, plastic sheet to cover pack in boat (buy at a *ferretería*), mosquito repellent, long shirt and trousers, hat, sunscreen. A machete is a good idea for clearing camp. Take some coffee.

Besides the $30 I paid to the guide, I gave Jóvito some money for food and board. I stayed a couple of days on the farm after my trip — Erme was needed back at work. On the farm Jóvito's family and the workers were very friendly and made me feel at home.

Humboldt, man of science

Alexander von Humboldt was not yet 30 in 1799 when he reached Venezuela, almost by accident. His long-planned scientific journey to the Nile had been cancelled by Napoleon, as was an invitation to circumnavigate the world. But the baron from Berlin was unstoppable. With a young French botanist, Aime Bonpland, he hoped to catch a boat to Smyrna, and they set out for Spain on foot. Handsome and single, Humboldt charmed his way to King Carlos IV. More than his talents in Spanish, biology, astronomy and meteorology, it was Humboldt's knowledge of geology and mining that won passports from the Spanish king — with permission to use instruments for geodetic, astronomical and physical observations. Humboldt was ecstatic. Until then, Spanish America had been off-bounds to foreigners, a scientific *tierra incognita*.

When typhoid fever struck their ship, the captain changed course from Cuba to Venezuela. 'Had not the fever broken out on board the *Pizarro*, we should never have reached the Orinoco, the Cassiquiare,' he wrote. Humboldt and Bonpland went on to ascend Colombia's Magdalena River and Ecuador's volcanoes, then descend the deserts of Peru before heading to Mexico and the United States. When he returned to Europe in 1804 he had such a cargo of measurements, notes, dried plants, insects and minerals, that it took him decades and most of his family inheritance to classify 6,000 new species and write the 3-volume *Travels to Equinoctial Regions of America*, and *Cosmos*, his 2,000 page masterpiece examining the physical world.

The German king made a medal in commemoration of *Cosmos*, showing Humboldt, a Sphynx and an electric eel.

The latter was a constant source of curiousity to Humboldt. The electric eel, *Electrophorus electricus* is not, in fact, an eel but is related to carp. In his travels through Venezuela, Humboldt arrived at Calabozo in 1800 determined to measure the electric eel's discharge. Thirty horses and mules were driven into a pool; as they were 'electrocuted' in the ensuing frenzy some drowned. But when the fish exhausted their discharges, most animals recovered and Humboldt got his wish to make the first scientific examination.

'I do not remember ever having received from the discharge of a large Leyden jar a more dreadful shock than the one I experienced when I very stupidly placed both my feet on an electric eel that had just been taken out of the water. I was affected for the rest of the day with a violent pain in the knees and almost every joint.'

However, the electricity remained a mystery: it didn't register on Humboldt's electrometer, it gave off no spark of light at night, nor was there a magnetic effect. And despite dissections, Humboldt could not answer the question: why don't electric fishes electrocute themselves?

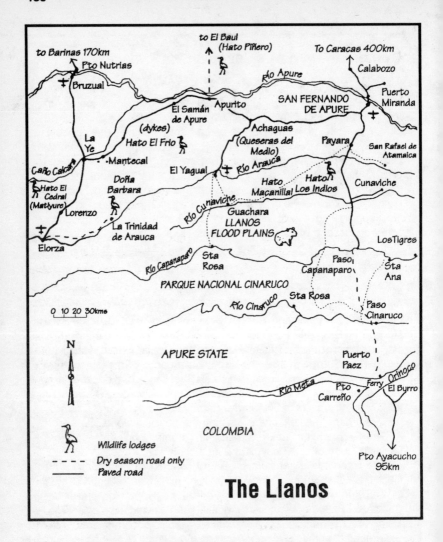

The Llanos

Map labels:

to Barinas 170km · Pto Nutrias · Bruzual · La Ye · Caño Calco · Hato El Codral (Matiyure) · Lorenzo · Elorza · Mantecal · Doña Barbara · La Trinidad de Arauca · Hato El Frio · El Samán de Apure · (dykes) · El Yagual · to El Baul (Hato Piñero) · Apurito · Achaguas (Queseras del Medio) · Río Apure · SAN FERNANDO DE APURE · Río Arauca · Payara · San Rafael de Atamaica · To Caracas 400km · Calabozo · Puerto Miranda · Río Cunaviche · Hato Macanilla · Hato Los Indios · Cunaviche · Guachara · LLANOS FLOOD PLAINS · LosTigres · Río Capanaparo · Sta Rosa · PARQUE NACIONAL CINARUCO · Paso Capanaparo · Sta Ana · Río Cinaruco · Sta Rosa · Paso Cinaruco · APURE STATE · Puerto Paez · Río Meta · Pto Carreño · Ferry · Orinoco · El Burro · COLOMBIA · Pto Ayacucho 95km

0 10 20 30kms

N

Wildlife lodges
- - - - Dry season road only
———— Paved road

Chapter 13

The Llanos

Vast grasslands border the lower Orinoco, from the Andes to the delta, forming one of the great natural features of the continent. These flat *Llanos* stretch over 660,000km² in Venezuela, and another 220,000km² in Colombia. More cattle than people live on the plains. Traditionally, life has been hard for both the *llaneros* and their cattle. Cattle ranches are called *hatos* (the 'h' is silent, as in *hacienda*).

Today, instead of leaving herds to range semi-wild over unfenced tracts, many ranches are modernising. Despite technology, the image lingers of tough *llaneros* on horseback battling sun or floods, jaguars or piranhas. And dearest to Venezuelans is the music of the Llanos, particularly the fast *joropo*. The *Alma Llanera* is a national favourite...*Yo nací en una ribera del Arauca vibrador/ Soy hermano de la espuma, de las garzas, de las rosas/ Y del sol...*

A few ranches have turned to ecotourism and photo safaris to support conservation (and bring in hard currency). Although mostly flat, the plains harbour a variety of ecosystems in gallery forests, mauritia palm swamps, dunes and marshes known as *esteros*, and outcrops called '*galeras*'. Private wildlife sanctuaries list over 270 bird species, 50 mammals and 40 reptiles and amphibians, not to mention fish. The owners of Hato El Frío and El Cedral have helped the government to set up the Guaritico Wildlife Refuge along a river between their lands.

It is a harsh environment of sun and drought alternating with rain and floods. 'Summer' on the Llanos is the dry season, from December to April. This is called *verano*, the time when most visitors come. It's dusty, but easy to move around by jeep, and mosquitoes are few. Grass withers and cattle must be brought in to waterholes. The ground cracks in dry stream beds and the last remaining ponds seethe and groan with too many fish and too little oxygen. Fishermen take advantage of thousands of large striped catfish and peacock bass trapped in such pools. Thousands of wading birds do the same. A friend who spends New Year's fishing on the Capanaparo is usually gone no more than three days and returns with his cooler stuffed with bass.

Spring comes in May with the first rains. Frogs, turtles, and even fish emerge from the softened mud after months buried in a dormant state called aestivation. New grass sprouts for the cattle to eat. Creeks turn into rivers. Fish spread out through the Llanos to spawn. By July, the Orinoco is in flood and rivers become lakes. On the lower floodplains of Apure, *llaneros* give up horses and jeeps in favour of boats and aircraft. Cattle which have not been rounded up to higher ground may drown. This season is called the *invierno* or winter.

Fauna

Many animals and birds on the Llanos are adapted to water. The first reptile seen is usually the spectacled cayman or *baba*, 2-3m in length. The biggest reptile, the Orinoco crocodile, which once grew to 8m, has been hunted almost to extinction and is now being reintroduced in one or two areas. You won't see a crocodile in the wild, and the chances of seeing an anaconda are slim. Not so with piranhas, here called *caribes* (which means flesh-eater and is the root of our word Caribbean, and cannibal). *Caribes* live in most of the plains rivers and are the easiest fish to catch.

You should also see family groups of what look like rotund, giant guinea pigs. They are capybaras, the world's biggest rodents, which munch plants at the water's edge, their slightly comic snouts lifted to sniff danger. They swim and dive like beavers. These *chigüires* weigh up to 60kg and are hunted for food. On ranches where hunting has been banned, you may see families of giant otters (or hear their snorts). A mature male may measure 2m head to tail. River dolphins can be spotted in the turbid Orinoco tributaries when they surface to "blow". Shyer, solitary and rarer are the tapir, giant anteater, tamandua, armadillo, fox, tayra and spotted cats, big and small. But peccaries run in bands, as do coatis. The opossum is so ordinary as to be despised, while the tree-porcupine with prehensile tail is charming; both are nocturnal.

Birds

Water and wading birds gather by the thousands for a feast at shrinking ponds. Herons, egrets, scarlet ibis, glossy ibis, roseate spoonbills, wood storks, jabirus, boat-billed herons, anhingas, cormorants, jacanas, gallinules, Orinoco geese, whistling tree-ducks, as well as many birds of prey, may be seen on a single ranch. The hoatzin is a bird often seen in riverside bushes. Its young swim and have hooks on their wings making it easy for them to scramble up the water's edge. Hoatzins digest toxic tree leaves by means of foregut fermentation rather like a cow.

San Fernando de Apure

San Fernando de Apure, the gateway to the Llanos, lies in the south of Guarico State on the Apure river. It is a hot, cheerful place, well supplied with budget hotels and restaurants. For *hatos* (wildlife lodges) near San Fernando see page 165.

Where to stay

There are many business hotels around Plaza Bolívar. Hotel Gran Plaza, (047) 21255, is the best kept-up. La Torraca, Paseo Libertador, (047) 25003; $8 double, shower, TV, restaurant. La Fuente, Av. Miranda, Plaza Negro Primero, (047) 23233.

Getting there

By plane   From Caracas, San Fernando is 45min by jet (about $35). Avensa flies in the morning and Aeropostal in the afternoon; both flights continue to Puerto Ayacucho (about $45). Las Flecheras airport is at the east end of town.

By road   The road distance from Caracas is 400k, the last two hours very hot and straight over the plains. Expresos Los Llanos takes 8 hours; about $9. The bus station in San Fernando is a 10min walk from the town centre.

Other routes   A straight road runs south from San Fernando to Puerto Páez (210km) on the Orinoco. However, it is paved only as far as the Capanaparo (120km) and is being improved after there. The road goes on top of an embankment or *terraplén* which ends at the Cinaruco. The Capanaparo and Cinaruco rivers are crossed on *chalanas*. These flatbed barges, pushed by surprisingly small craft, operate from sunrise to sundown, Bs.100. But during the rainy season the Cinaruco ferry suspends work for 4-5 months and so all traffic halts south of the Capanaparo.

In the dry season drivers go south of the Apure River (*llano adentro*) in 4WD vehicles, taking spare gasoline and food (also rope, hammocks and mosquito netting as some cattle areas have vampire bat problems). It is possible to go across country to remote ranches, steering by compass.

A bus runs between San Fernando and Puerto Ayacucho (Amazonas), taking about 8 hrs and costing $12. After Puerto Páez the road is good.

Cinaruco-Capanapara Park

This is the only park to include part of the Orinoco, as well as several of its islands. The eastern boundary of this Llanos tract of 5,840km² is formed by the Orinoco, the northern by the Capanaparo, and the southern by the Cinaruco. Officially it is called the Santos Luzardo National Park. Other nearby islands in the Orinoco have been declared a wildlife refuge because in the dry season the arrau turtles go there to lay eggs. In practice, the Orinoco is out of reach and there are no facilities of any sort, but the highway itself is an open invitation.

At the Capanaparo River, just beyond the old ferry crossing, a park visitors' centre is planned. Visitors will be requested to get a parks permit here, for a small sum. Enquire about fishing season and limits at Inparques, Calle Palo Fuerte, San Fernando, (047) 25530. According to the Bioma management plan camping facilities will be provided with guard service. Bioma is encouraging neighbouring ranchers to offer lodgings.

Adjacent to the park, the islands of Pararuma, Ramonera, Loros and Isla del Medio and half a dozen islands more in the Orinoco, have been declared a wildlife refuge. It is hoped that here the endangered Orinoco turtle, the *tortuga arrau* (*Podocnemis expansa*), and the very rare Orinoco crocodile (*Crocodylus intermedius*) will be protected.

This part of Apure, which is largely under water during the floods from June to August, has many habitats other than the open Llanos or prairies. For a start, there are extensive sand dunes that are generally covered by shrubs and grasses. Gallery forests thrive along the creeks and rivers — which all flow into the Orinoco. Among the *morichales*, dense clumps of Mauritia minor palms, which favour marshy hollows, live associated plants typical of Amazonian and Guayana flora, which here grow north of the Orinoco.

The 'Galeras del Cinaruco', a Precambrian geological formation like a small steppe (recalling a raised galley) support different flora again. In the eastern part of the park are two lagoons, Las Mercedes and Araguaquén, marked only by a ring of treetops when the Orinoco is in flood. Nearly 300 species of plants have been identified in the area between the Capanaparo and the Meta.

Wildlife and conservation Fauna listed by a Bioma census include 333 bird species (5% of the world total), more than 50 mammals, 345 kinds of fish, 67 species of reptiles, and 26 amphibians. Among severely endangered species of large mammals are: the giant otter (*Pteroneura brasiliensis*), the manatee (*Trichechus manatus*), a 500kg relative of the sea-cow (*Sirenia*), the once plentiful jaguar (*Panthera onca*), and the giant anteater (*Myrmecophaga tridactyla*). Even the nearly extinct giant armadillo or 'cuspón' (*Priodontes giganteus*) is listed.

None of these animals has suffered such loss as the arrau turtles, whose main breeding grounds were islands in the Orinoco, including Pararuma, now part of the wildlife refuge. Stopping here in 1800, Alexander Humboldt estimated that 33 million eggs were laid every dry season.

In the days when José Gumilla, a Jesuit priest, wrote his *Orinoco Illustrated* back in 1745, he believed that the great number of such turtles (which can grow to 1m in length) would make the Orinoco unnavigable if the eggs were not taken. 'It would be as difficult to count the grains of sand on the shores of the Orinoco, as to count the immense number of tortoises which inhabit its margins and waters.' Then, several hundred Indians of different tribes would assemble in late March for the egg harvest. Some tribes even came from the upper Orinoco. Turtle-egg oil was sold for lamps in Ciudad Bolívar.

Today, during low water, some turtles still come to nest on the same sandy islands. The most southerly of the big nest sites is Pararuma, now part of the refuge. Only a fraction of the 33 million eggs which Alexander Humboldt estimated in 1800 are laid now. The half-dozen park rangers will try to prevent the nests from being robbed in the future, but the distances are great and the laying season covers three months.

Visiting the park   Local fishermen and birders like to make their own way. Mary Lou Goodwin shares a tip for birdwatchers (with jeep): 'One of my favourite camping spots is known as Laguna Brava. After you leave the Capanaparo ferry, drive for about 50 yards and turn right towards the road going south. Counting the *Welcome* sign at the junction as kilometre one, you will reach a sandy road going west at 4.6km. Turn right on this road and continue for 6.8km when you veer towards the left. At 8.3km turn left. The Lagoon is 9.6km from the Capanaparo. Here I have seen not only almost all the savanna and water birds listed for the park but also the scarlet macaw, red-bellied macaw, blue-crowned parakeet and festive parrot.'

Wildlife lodges

An inquisitive traveller's guide to the Llanos
by Edward Paine

I worked in Venezuela for four years, most of them spent between the Apure and Arauca rivers, in the heart of the Llanos, and my addiction for the area developed slowly as I worked first as a cowboy, progressing to manager of a 100,000 acre ranch. As with all the remote parts of the world, you have to work hard to get beyond initial impressions and begin to understand the local culture and traditions.

Firstly, as a transient visitor there is the problem of access: only one paved road loops its way through these immense plains and you won't see much from a vehicle. However, here are some of the ingredients that make up the Llanos.

The cattle: the large white ones with humps are probably Brahman — descended from the Zebu cattle of India they have revolutionised the local cattle-breeding industry with their resistance to ticks and the heat, and are replacing or being crossed with the original *criollo* animals brought over from Europe by the early colonists.

The cowboys: still fiercely independent, the *llaneros* share with their Argentine cousin the *gaucho* a reluctance to go anywhere on foot when a horse or mule is available. Their main diet is, of course, meat, although as killing day is normally weekly the menu progresses through thinner and thinner *sopas* until there are a few bare bones and some spaghetti swimming around in hot water. As in all people who live by the hours of the sun and do not depend on watches, they are early risers. While you may find everyone asleep by 8pm, there will be activity in the bunkhouse several hours before dawn, soon after the cock crows. I soon learnt not to place too much trust in this natural alarm clock: one morning, after a night at one of the outlying corrals, we rose when the cock crowed, caught the horses, saddled up and set out on the eight-hour ride back to the farm centre, only to find that after five hours riding the sun still had not risen!

The wildlife: by a happy chance the ranch economy has not conflicted with their habitat, so take a good guide and wonder at the bright colours and sheer numbers of birds as they fly from one lagoon to another.

The music: so often a short-cut to a good understanding of other cultures, you should plan to stop at any of the scruffy towns on the Llanos during the Patron Saints' *fiestas*, and listen to the same cowboy who that morning was up at dawn training his favourite fighting cock as he sings his heart out to his companions — companions whose agility on a horse has been converted to agile fingers moving over the strings of a harp, accompanied by the four-stringed *cuatro* and maracas.

Most lodges accommodate about 20 people in comfort, providing full board, excursions; children up to 12 pay half. Costs are estimated for foreigners but Venezuelan residents often benefit from special prices. Swimming in rivers is discouraged and pools are the exception. These private ranches all have their own radio transmitters and landing strips. Of the well-known *Hatos* listed below, the first is in Cojedes State. All others are in Apure, and guests are ferried by car or plane from San Fernando or Barinas.

Hato Piñero is remarkable for its 45-year hunting ban. As a result its fauna is quite trusting. Owls, macaws and iguanas spy from great trees above the lodge. On a river outing, the boat may be surrounded by hoatzins, ignored by a passing capuchin troop, peered at by agoutis and curassows, and certainly preceded by herons and anhingas. Foxes, ocelots, giant anteater, fishing bats are spotlighted at night from an open-topped safari truck. Piñero is located in the *llano alto* or upper plains of Cojedes State and on its 800km² are many habitats from cattle pastures and wetlands to hills, rivers and forests. Such variety combined with wildlife management has given Piñero international prestige. 5% of net profits go to conservation, education and a biological research station. Piñero is a 5-6hr drive from Caracas, via Valencia and Tinaco; 60km before El Baúl, a sign (by Escuela Barbasco) points east. However, you must still cover 22km and pass four gates. The lodge has 10 rooms with fans, shower. A stay of 3 days/2 nights costs over $300 a person during the two high seasons (Jan.-Apr., July-Aug.), and less the rest of the year; closed Dec.16-31. Try for a weekend as the excursions are tops). For transfers, not included, and reservations, enquire (in English) at Bio Tours GBS (Caracas), (02) 916965, or fax 916776.

Hato El Frío was the first of several cattle ranches to protect its wildlife for biological research. Scientists from the Coto Doñana in Spain interrupt their work to act as nature guides, ecotourism bringing in funds for research. For this reason El Frío is still the best introduction to the lower Llanos ecosystems. Covering over 1000km², the ranch harbours thousands of capybara, deer, spectacled cayman. Crocodiles are being reintroduced in the tributaries or *caños* such as the Guaritico which has been declared a Wildlife Refuge. Best months to see birds nesting in the *garceros* is the mating season, May-June, or December when waters recede. In July-August the station is sometimes flooded. Although the biological station now has 20 rooms with fan and shower, guests are limited to 15. A fee of $60 a day covers three meals and two excursions by jeep, but guests must find their own way to the ranch. El Frío is located some 180km along the San Fernando-Mantecal road; taxis charge about $75 from San Fernando. Reservations through Fundación La Salle, Av. Boyacá, Maripérez, Caracas, (02) 7828711 ext. 228, fax 7615732. The Mantecal bus will drop you at the entrance.

El Cedral has long been a wildlife refuge where you can see a horizonful of birds. Formerly the King Ranch, it was owned by the Rockefellers in the 1950s. They invested in levees which provide water in the dry season and high ground during the rains, making the ranch an excellent choice year-round. Nesting time (May-Oct.) is impressive as herons, egrets, spoonbills and ibises literally clothe trees and bushes in the *garceros* or rookeries. Conservation has been kept up and an incredible diversity of fauna breeds on its 530km² (One section along the Matiyure River is advertised as a sanctuary but is really the same as El Cedral.) El Cedral's facilities are almost luxurious — seven air-conditioned cabins, bar and swimming pool. The ranch is located west of the main road from Mantecal to Elorza, 2hr from San Fernando by car, 3hr by bus. Reservations are taken in Caracas by Turven, (02) 9511833, fax 9511176. Prices are lower in the rainy season, April-October, about $70 a night; high season $90.

Los Indios Adventure Camp is part of Hato Macanillal's 320km², located deeper south near the Cunaviche River. The camp is modern and complete with pool. Tour prices are about $100 daily. The lodge is 2hrs by a Llanos track from the main road. Ring Flavio Freites in San Fernando, (047) 26946, for information about transfer by vehicle or aircraft; in Caracas (02) 7816945, fax 7817421. — Charter services from Caracas, such as Amazonair, are a good idea if your party is large; (02) 2836960, fax 2832627.

Hato Doña Bárbara is part of a 360km² working ranch, La Trinidad de Arauca. The fourth and fifth generations of the Estrada family here have built 21 rooms double-roofed for coolness, with fan, shower. The Estradas have much to tell (they speak English) about the character of legend and literature called Doña Bárbara, who lived here and is part of Llanos lore. Access is by light planes from San Fernando, dry-season jeep track from Elorza, or launch down the Arauca River. Cost of about $100 a day includes excursions by jeep, river, horseback, accident policy and transfer from San Fernando. Their agency in San Fernando is in the Hotel Torraca, Mezz, Paseo Libertador, (047) 25003, fax 27902. Compared with other ranches wildlife such as capybara is scarce, but the friendliness of the family makes up for it and there are plenty of birds.

'I loved seeing the huge numbers of scarlet, green and buffneck ibis and egrets round the water holes. I feel that by the time all the Estrada's many plans have been realized and there will be much more wildlife to be seen. The whole Estrada family were so kind and welcoming, and we had endless long and fascinating conversations about everything that happened on Doña Bárbara and life in the Llanos generally.' (Robin Wise.)

Fishing Probably the most comfortable fishing lodge in Venezuela is the new Cinaruco Bass Lodge on the edge of the savanna just south of Apure's Santos Luzardo park. Fishermen fly from the USA prepared to pay $2,000 to catch fat peacock bass. Four cabins, each with two doubles, hot water, three course meals. Fax Alpi Tour in Caracas, (02) 2856067.

The birds of the Llanos. A 19th Century engraving by Kinnersley Johnson.

SECTION FIVE

THE GUAYANA REGION (THE SOUTH)

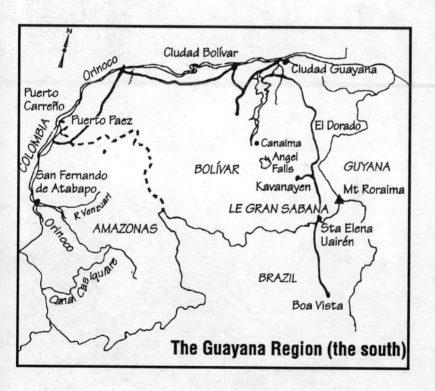

The Guayana Region (the south)

Ciudad Bolívar, at the Orinoco Narrows, when it was called Angostura.

Roraima, with Kukenán (2,600m) on its left.

Chapter 14

Bolívar State

GRAN SABANA, 'TEPUIS', ANGEL FALLS

A glance at a map will show a huge area of uplands, bordered by the Río Orinoco to the north and west and Brazil to the south. This is Bolívar State, by far the country's largest. The mountains that make up the Guyana Highlands are shared by Venezuela, Guyana and Brazil and are one of Venezuela's most interesting areas. The new road that leads eventually to Manaus makes this an increasingly popular overland route.

The chief attractions of the region are La Gran Sabana, a huge rolling savanna with unique topography of tablelands or *'tepuis'*, and Angel Falls, the world's highest — both within Canaima National Park. The giant mesas conjure images of Arthur Conan Doyle's *The Lost World*. Conan Doyle was fascinated by reports of the walled mountains which defied ascent by 19th Century naturalists. When Roraima was at last climbed in 1884, members of the Royal Geographical Society packed the meeting to hear the explorers' account. Today the tepuis are equally fascinating, and a lot easier to get to.

ACCESS TOWNS
Ciudad Bolívar

Historically important as the Orinoco's major port and capital of Bolívar State, Ciudad Bolívar retains much charm. Jostle with shoppers along the Paseo Orinoco's arcade, or have a drink at a metal table overlooking the deep and yellow river. The river rises as much as 18m (from a low of 3m) during high waters in mid-August. Then the city feasts on zapoara fish, caught in circular nets called *atarrayas*. And on the Paseo, a week-long *Feria del Orinoco* celebrates with local food, arts and crafts, cultural and sports events.

Upstream you can see the Angostura suspension bridge, somewhat taller than Ciudad Bolívar itself. The city was built in 1764 on a rocky rise (54m alt.), taking advantage of the narrows or *angostura* after which it was first named (like the bitters invented here). The Orinoco is less than a kilometre wide at Ciudad Bolívar, 450km from the Atlantic. Although its importance as a river port has declined dramatically since the days of rubber, hides, chicle and tonka beans, Ciudad Bolívar is now the air supply centre for missionaries and miners. Many gold and diamond buyers have offices in the old centre. The airport, located conveniently right in town, is also a hub for travellers to Canaima and the Gran Sabana.

Old Ciudad Bolívar was one of five cities in the hemisphere selected as historic patrimony of the world in conjunction with the 500th anniversary of the Discovery of America (others were Quito, Ponce, Tlalcotalpan and Joao Pessoa). This meant renovation of buildings around Plaza Bolívar, where five statues personify the countries Bolívar liberated. The city of Angostura was renamed in Bolívar's honour in 1846. On the upper side of Plaza Bolívar is a balconied house which was the colonial Governor's residence; on the east is the Cathedral of Our Lady of the Snows (the city's *Fiestas Patronales* on August 8 celebrate the *Día de Nuestra Señora de las Nieves*). On the west is the seat of the 1819 Angostura Congress and the Government Palace of Bolívar State; on the north, the Casa de la Cultura, Escuela Heres, and old Maradey House.

On the Paseo Orinoco are two handsome old buildings, now museums: the Correo del Orinoco where in 1818-21 Andrew Roderick printed the republic's first newspaper, *The Orinoco Mail*, in Spanish and English; and the Carcel Vieja or gaol where the Archivo Histórico de Guayana is housed at the corner of Calle Igualdad. Of interest here is the **Museo Etnográfico** which displays photographs and crafts from major Indian tribes of the Guayana region: the Yekuana (Makiritare), Pemón, Kariña and Warao. The State government was the first (1990) to appoint an Indian to head its Indian affairs bureau known as DAI, the Departamento de Asuntos Indígenas. Ciudad Bolívar is the seat of several newly organised Indian movements which publish a monthly paper, *Orinoco Indígena*, at Edificio Mancini, Calle Bolívar No.40.

Little **Zamuro Fort**, still in the old centre, gives a great view over river and city. To its east is spacious Quinta San Isidro, a former coffee hacienda where Bolívar stayed. With its tall ceilings, simple elegance and ample gardens it is a most attractive museum (like all museums here, closed Mondays and midday). The entrance is on Avenida Táchira at 5 de Julio. For the Jesús Soto Museum of Modern Art, continue south on Av. Táchira towards the airport and go east 2 blocks on Calle Briceño Iragory. Soto, Venezuela's leading kinetic artist, was born in Ciudad Bolívar in 1923.

Ipostel, the post office, is on Av. Táchira. The CANTV telephone centre is not far away; you turn east on Av. 5 de Julio.

What to do

'A road skirts the Laguna del Medio and another runs east along the Orinoco riverbank from the new tile-roofed Mercado La Carioca near the Club Nautico. It's nice to sit and watch the riverboats cross to Soledad, have a drink at the club. Beer is cheap and there's a disco. At the corner of the airport there's a park full of mango trees (season March-August) and cashews. (People cook the red fleshy cashew fruit, *merey*, but the nut at the end has a caustic shell containing cardol; do not bite it.) Nearby on Av. Upata are three large informal *campestre* restaurants where the grilled beef and chicken is tasty and economical: Said Morales, Los Caobos and Marahuanta. You can sit to eat or buy steak/checken by the kilo (about $7) to take out, also fabulous fresh cheese called *queso de mano*. They are near the Canaima Hotel.' (Richard Sydney Coles)

Airport

Jimmy Angel's restored plane is now parked outside Ciudad Bolívar's airport. The terminal's location must be one of the handiest of any airport, at the end of a city street, on Avenida Táchira, 3km from the Paseo Orinoco. The airfare from Caracas was Bs.3,500 in 1992; Aereotuy's Gran Sabana flight cost Bs.4,500 to Santa Elena. This service flight (no food) in high-wing Twin Otters crosses fantastic tablelands, jungle and rivers; for a view of Angel Falls, sit on the right. On Thursdays the flight takes five hours, stopping at missions and mining settlements in Kamarata, Uriman, Wonken, Icabarú and El Paují. On Mon., Wed. and Sat. it goes direct to Santa Elena in two hours and returns in two to four hours. Be at the airport before 7am and, better, buy a ticket in Caracas because these turbo-prop planes take only 20 passengers and are usually full up. Aereotuy is firm about a 10k baggage limit. It is possible to negotiate flights in single-engine planes from Ciudad Bolívar to Angel Falls (an hour) or to remote gold mines with air taxi services such as Aerobol, (085) 26279, and Transmandu, (085) 21462.

Bus terminal

Located on Avenida República, the Terminal de Pasajeros is about 2.5km south of the Paseo Orinoco and 2.5km west of the airport.

'Excellent terminal with a seat area and all-night cafe. It is safe to sit here with all other travellers waiting for night connections.' (J.M. & M.D.) The bus from Caracas costs one fifth of the airfare. Expresos La Responsable, Guayana and Oriente cover the route in anywhere from 8 to 11 hours, often driving at night. Rápidos Guayana is the first to leave at 6.00. If you buy a ticket you can probably deposit your luggage at the line's office. Ask for buses to Caicara, Puerto Ayacucho, Maturín, El Dorado, Santa Elena and Boa Vista, Brazil.

Hotels

Budget travellers can try the small Hotel Panamerican or even smaller Caracas and Italia hotels (all about $6 double) at the Paseo Orinoco's east end. The splendidly old-fashioned Gran Hotel Bolívar, (085) 20100/02, is right in the middle of the Paseo ($20 double). Paul Weatherstone writes: 'We stayed at the Gran Hotel Bolívar (£7 each per night — hot showers, air conditioning) which was spartan but clean. I would recommend a room at the front of the hotel overlooking the river.' A respectable hotel near the airport is the Valentina on Av. Maracay, (085) 22145, at about $18. Economy hotels (about $8 single) include the Florida, (okay Italian food) and the Táchira, both on Avenida Táchira. The Emperador and Canaima, Av. Upata (double $12, poor restaurant), are near east end of airport. 'The Canaima staff were very friendly and were able to provide us with scales to pack our rucksacks in accordance with the Aereotuy 10k limit. They provide early morning calls, which we arranged for 5.00.' (J.M. & M.D.)

Banks

Some useful advice comes from Peter Weinberger. 'If you rely, as we did, on cash advances with your credit card, you can easily find yourself without one bolívar. As far as I know, there's not one bank in Ciudad Bolívar accepting international credit cards (eg. Visa, Mastercard). The best deal is changing US$ traveller cheques. It often happens that the banks don't have the current exchange rate, but at least the Banco de Comercio changed our cheques after 16.00, which seems to be some banks' deadline for exchange transactions.'

Roraima excursion

Harald Baedeke recommends that you do *not* arrange a trip to Roraima in Cuidad Bolívar. Sta. Elena is a better centre for this.

Ciudad Guayana

This is really two towns at the confluence of the Caroní River with the Orinoco. On the Caroní's left bank is **Puerto Ordaz**, an iron ore port founded in 1952. On the right bank is old **San Félix**, a worker's town which dates to 1576. The airport is in Puerto Ordaz, the bus terminal in San Félix. They were joined in 1961 into Ciudad Guayana, the planned centre of burgeoning heavy industry powered by cheap hydroelectricity. The state body which plans regional development is the Corporación Venezolana de Guayana (CVG) with interests in everything from hydroelectricity and gold to pine trees and parks. In fact, Ciudad Guayana is a company town. For information about any aspect including tourism (maybe a city map or *plano*) ask at CVG headquarters in Alta Vista district: Edificio CVG, Calle Cuchivero, near the Plaza del Hierro, Puerto Ordaz, about 3km east of the airport. Public tours are organised at Sidor, the steel mill, and at most of the aluminium smelters.

'Puerto Ordaz has one of the highest cost-of-living indexes in the country,' reports Debbie Quintana. 'A large mall in the centre has boutiques, electronic and sporting goods shops and restaurants that reflect the tastes of a largely middle class population of white-collar workers. But the planned city lacks what gives most cities a heart and soul.

'The other face of Ciudad Guayana, across the Caroní bridge, has more of a traditional flavour with its Plaza Bolívar (remodelled as Plaza Bicentenaria), cathedral, nearby city offices and CANTV telephone centre. The market bustles in the early hours.' The bus terminal is on Avenida Gumilla, about 1.5km south of the quite small *centro* and 6km east of the Caroní bridge. Urban problems besiege San Félix: lack of security, health, housing, education. Many of Ciudad Guayana's half-million people are new arrivals in this fastest-growing city in Venezuela.

Christopher Leggett writes: 'I prefer the part of town on the other side (east) of the river, San Félix. The bus station is there; quieter, and cheaper hotels (around $6 single). I stayed at the Hotel Guayana, which was OK, but there are many similar ones (that no taxi driver in the airport of the posher Puerto Ordaz side would know about).' In the old centro are Hotel Excelsior and Hotel Joli.

In Puerto Ordaz, hotels start with the Intercontinental Guayana; next the Rasil (pool) and new Embajador. A good moderate choice is Hotel Tepuy, Carrera Upata, (086) 220102, $15 single; near pizza and parrilla restaurants. Downscale are the St. George and the *antiguo* Embajador.

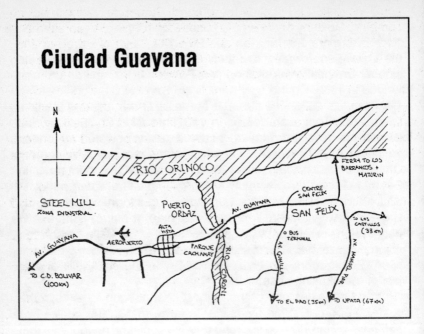

Ciudad Guayana

Ferry to Los Barrancos

The large Orinoco ferry carries vehicles and people from San Félix over to Monagas State. It takes about ½hr, but you may have to queue for an hour. The terminal is at the north end of Av. Manuel Piar, east of the old town centre. From the village of Los Barrancos the highway goes 120km to Maturín, crossing a vast forest of Honduras pines planted for pulp.

What to see

Cachamay Park This fringes the Caroní's banks by the road leading to the bridge and the Guayana Inter-Continental. Here, the dark river, 6km wide, breaks up into cataracts embracing half a dozen islands. The adjacent **Parque Loeffling** has a small zoo of native fauna including anteaters, tapirs and armadillos.

Saltos La Llovizna To reach these splendid falls on the east side of the Caroní, you must start from San Félix: head south on Avenida Gumilla (towards El Pao); some 7km from the bus terminal, turn right at the CVG-Edelca sign for Macagua Dam. It is 2.5km from here to the guardhouse where public buses run (free) to the beautifully kept La Llovizna Park. The Caroní thundering down the gorge throws up spray, *llovizna*, and shakes the ground. Superb for picnics, but no camping. Go early because the buses stop running in mid-afternoon and visitors are shepherded out. Below La Llovizna's drop of 20m, the Caroní soon meets the slow Orinoco, its dark current flowing side by side with the yellow waters.

Castillos de Guayana   A pair of old forts are located down the Orinoco, an hour or so by launch, or 38km east of San Félix by road. Built in the 17th and 18th Centuries, the forts guarded against the successors of Sir Walter Raleigh who in 1595 made a foray up the Orinoco which led him to write *The Discoverie of the Large and Bewtiful Empire of Guiana*. In 1618 Raleigh's men returned to raid Santo Tomás, killing the Spanish governor but losing many men and Raleigh's own son. Raleigh, who had been too ill to fight, lost his head to the wrath of King James. Santo Tomás was eventually moved well upriver, refounded as Ciudad Bolívar. You may be able to hitch to the forts which are individually known as San Francisco and San Diego de Alcalá (the higher).

Further afield

Guri Dam   Waters from Roraima and Angel Falls mingle in the Caroní which drains most of the Guayana highlands. At the Necuima Canyon on the Caroní, 90km up from the Orinoco, is the giant dam officially called the Central Hidroeléctrica Raúl Leoni. Completed in 1986, its potential of 10 million kilowatts made Guri the world's largest (now second to Itaipu in Brazil-Paraguay). At the foot of the dam face (162m high) are the turbine houses, reached by plazas where art strives to compete. One plaza has a huge stainless steel 'Solar Tower' by Alejandro Otero; the other, called the Plaza del Sol y la Luna, has a great sundial by Esther Fontana and Lisette Delgado.

The Guri compound is 20km from the main highway and another 75km from Puerto Ordaz. Visitors to the *represa* should not miss the bus tour (9.00, 10.30, 14.15 and 15.45) from the gatehouse to the dam. The compound has an airfield, hospital and golf course. You may request permission to cross Guri to the Upata road. There is a Club Náutico, La Churuata guesthouse (private) with a restaurant (not private), Club Guri (coffee shop, tennis courts). In a shopping centre with supermarket, there is a 62-room Hotel Guri, (086) 229411, about $30 a double, with restaurant and pool open to non-guests. It is the base for Guri Lodge fishermen (some come from the USA, paying $300 a day).

Guri Bass Camp is run by Orinoco Trips, (086) 606254/6. They arrange fishing boats for $100 a day. Fully equipped cabins are let for about $70 daily: three rooms (six people), refrigerator, washing machine. Guri Lake, which flooded an area of forest and savanna nearly the size of Trinidad, has become a fishing resort internationally famous for plump, plentiful peacock bass. This is the same *pavón* that inhabits rivers of the Llanos.

Cerro Bolívar   The iron mountain whose discovery in 1947 set off the area's development lies 54km south of the Guri turn-off. The road (to La Paragua) rolls through plains studded with *moriche* palms. On the horizon rises a mammoth pyramid, tiered by 40 years of mining. Cerro Bolívar's high grade ore is loaded onto railcars and hauled in long trains to Puerto Ordaz. Some ore is shipped down the Orinoco for export; much goes to the national steel mill. Iron was nationalised in 1975, a year before oil. Permission to visit the Ferrominera Orinoco installations may be requested in Ciudad Piar.

THE ROAD TO BRAZIL

Beautifully graded and entirely paved, the Gran Sabana highway is now the finest in the country. There are fairly regular buses and *por puestos* from Ciudad Bolívar to Santa Elena de Uairén and, over the border, to Boa Vista in Brazil. The road covers 345km from the El Dorado fork to Santa Elena. For most of the way it goes through the Imataca forest reserve and the Canaima National Park, noted for such fauna as the giant anteater, bellbird and orange cock of the rock. Do not expect to find banks or posh hotels here, so change travellers cheques before leaving Puerto Ordaz (ask for small notes).

The Gran Sabana is a grassy plateau of some 900-1,200m elevation above which loom *tepuis* or table mountains. The base of these giant mesas is the Guayana Shield, an igneous and metamorphic formation, 2,000-3,000 million years old. The tepuis themselves are said to be 1,700 million years old, and the sandstone they are made of qualifies as among the world's oldest rock. These sediments are thought to be made of sand washed from the grand-daddy of all continents, Gondwana (Pangaea). In places the layers of Precambrian sediments in the Gran Sabana are 2,000m thick. Over the aeons, most of this sandstone was eroded away by ancient deltas and lagoons. Left standing today are isolated tepuis — remnants known as the Roraima Formation. Diamonds may be one of Venezuela's links with the time when South America and Africa were part of the same super-continent. It is believed that Gondwana was the source of the diamonds now washed down rivers such as the Caroní.

The route to the Brazilian border takes you from Ciudad Bolívar or

Ciudad Guayana (San Félix) in 4-5 hours to **El Dorado**, a gold miners' village although not much glitters there. Expresos de Oriente buses cover the 1,000km from Caracas in 18 hours; cost about $10. The bus leaves Caracas at 18.00, stops in Ciudad Bolívar, arriving at noon the following day in El Dorado. Basic lodging includes Campamento Turístico on the banks of the Cuyuní. Miners pay high prices, so ask before taking a room at a dingy hotel. (However, since the highway south bypasses El Dorado, travellers not in a rush may find it more convenient to make a break earlier in Tumeremo or El Callao, a pleasant pueblo famous for its calypso-style Carnival. The gold rush of 1860-80 centred on El Callao. Today the British company Monarch has 49% of a high-tech plant to reprocess tailings of once fabulous mines.)

The recent big strike has mushroomed near **Las Claritas**, 83km SE of El Dorado. Just before the market clutter of Las Claritas, a road on the right leads to the mines. Of all ages and nationalities, miners live in rows and rows of tin-roofed huts. Beyond, prospectors sluice clay banks with high-powered hoses and dig open gold mines along forest creeks. Like *bachacos* or leaf-cutter ants, they strip the earth of everything green. Anaconda Tours have a classy set-up in Las Claritas with eight handsome bungalows in a walled garden, a polished bar, kitchen with chef. We also saw Anaconda's tents near the Aponguao Falls. For prices of 3-5 day tours, ring their office in Centro Comercial ANTO, Puerto Ordaz, (086) 223130, fax 225672; in Caracas, Pool de Aventuras, (02) 2619918, fax 2613521.

Warning   Working in deplorable conditions, many miners suffer from malaria, spreading the disease from Brazil to the Orinoco. Even if you are taking anti-malaria tablets, wear long trousers and long sleeves, use repellents, and burn spirals at night. This applies to Santa Elena also.

In **San Isidro** or **Kilómetro 88**, miners tank up on *aguardiente* and beer. In turn, buses and *por puestos* stop to fill up with petrol before the ascent. This begins at a giant rock called the Piedra de La Virgen (410m), the road climbing *La Escalera* or 'stairway' to the Gran Sabana proper (1,430m). The climate changes sharply. Campers should have rain gear and warm sweaters here.

After passing the military checkpoint known as **La Ciudadela** in some kilometres, you see the Ilú-Tramen tepuis outlined in the east; beyond them is Guyana. On the right, 17km beyond the Luepa turn-off, is **San Rafael de Kamoirán**, an Indian town. A separate entrance leads to a stern-looking house with a large petrol tank in front (often as not empty). The inn and good-looking restaurant built of stone currently offer travellers the only formal accommodations until Santa

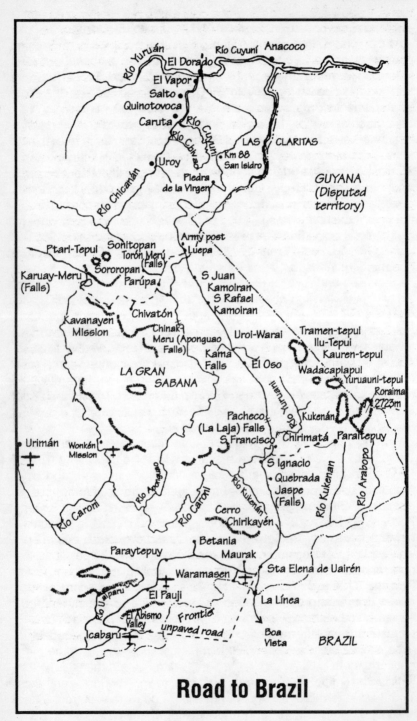

Road to Brazil

Elena. If you want to get out of the cold, there are rooms at Bs.800, single, double or triple. The Kamoirán River runs behind the inn.

As the road runs over the plateau, it dips to the warmer, *moriche* palm-studded savannas of Santa Elena de Uairén (800m). Look for splendid waterfalls on the way. Watch for the Kamá bridge at Km 198; on the river to your right are a few Indian huts. Here, **Salto Kama** slips over the savanna's edge in a lovely 50m curtain. At **La Laja**, also known as Quebrada de Pacheco, there are very pretty falls called Arapán Merú to the left of the road, and some metres off to the right at the lower end are almost unvisited falls, unseen from the road (Km264). This is a popular camping area. The **Yuruaní** bridge is a short distance below a wide stretch of falls. Swimming is good in the dry season, but gnats and other *plaga* are pestiferous the year round. Most astonishing of all in its vibrant red and yellow bed of solid jasper is **Quebrada Jaspe**, a wooded stream which is a short way to the left at Km262. The falls are small, intimate, lovely. There is *plaga*.

Santa Elena de Uairén

Soldiers and gold-seekers of several nationalities pass through this frontier town, 15km from Brazil. Missionaries and Indians live to one side. It was first settled in 1922 by a prospector, Lucas Fernández Peña, who named the place after his daughter — he had some 27 children. In 1931 the Franciscans arrived and their big stone mission is an impressive sight, west of town. More impressive to modern travellers is a hospital, and radio-telephone service.

Lodging

Among hotels, Las Fronteras is moderate and has a popular patio restaurant. Other lodgings such as the Macking are primitive. Señor Polley's Hospedaje Uairén has been mentioned. Among pleasant newer accommodations are the Friedenau's clean cabins equipped with stove and refrigerator, in the Cielo Azul district. 'Hotel Nona is right around the corner from the very small international bus terminal. Triple room with private bath $12; very clean. The proprietor is very helpful and changed a small amount of US cash at a rather fair rate, considering we arrived at 20.00. We found a small restaurant on the same street. There you also can change money, even until 22.00.' Peter Weinberger.

Transport

Aereotuy   From Santa Elena, Aereotuy's high-wing Twin Otters fly five days a week to Ciudad Bolívar. Monday's flight stops at Icabarú, Wonken, Urimán and Kamarata. It is worth taking this slow run almost brushing the tepuis. 'The plane departs from a small airstrip some kilometres south of Santa Elena, reached by taxi (no public transportation). Try to be there before 11.00 otherwise your seat reservation may be cancelled even if you bought your ticket just one hour before. Before proceeding to the "departure hall", a thatched roof without seats, register at the nearby military post. The plane will arrive somewhere between 12.00 and 14.00 depending on weather conditions,' says Peter Weinberger. He spent some time hunting up the Aereotuy representative in Santa Elena to buy a ticket, locating the office in an unmarked garage at the south end of downtown. 'Follow the main street until you reach the hospital, 15min., and a group of one-storey white houses. The last one says Residencias El Gato; the office is in the garage to the right. To find the manager, the best time is between 9.00 and 10.30. US cash will be accepted, but don't expect him to have change.'

Bus   There is daily service to Ciudad Bolívar by Línea Orinoco; about $8. The bus leaves at 5.00 from the little international terminal in the centre. *Por puestos*, also.

To/from Brazil   The Boa Vista buses leave daily at 8.00 and 13.00, arriving at Boa Vista, 220km, in 5hr. Cost, about $13. A visa is essential from the consulate in Santa Elena; this requires 24 hours during the working week. However, no papers other than passport or *cédula* are needed to visit the border settlement called Pacaraima (Estado do Roraima). There's a statue to Emperor Dom Pedro on the border. Pacaraima, dusty and bare, depends on Santa Elena for petrol and many necessities, while Venezuelans go there to buy medicines at the pharmacy and eat at the restaurants. Hotel Palace Pacaraima quoted 10,000 cruzeiros (Bs.500) for a double.

  Peter Weinberger entered Venezuela from Brazil: 'The bus drove across the border, waiting for the exit and entry formalities of Brazil and Venezuela, and went to the international bus terminal in Santa Elena.' He adds a **warning**: 'Because I didn't have a visa yet, I went to the Venezuelan consulate in Boa Vista, Av. Benjamín Constant 525E; Mon.-Fri. 812. One passport photo and $10 in US cash (no cruzeiros accepted). But this consulate is issuing only 72-hour transit visas (even if you prove financial solidity and can show an airline ticket to Europe).'

Excursions

Apart from Roraima, there are some interesting places to visit. Kavanayen, described by C. Leggett, enjoys an exceptionally beautiful setting ringed by tablelands. There are almost no facilities along this 60km side road, except for Chivatón, a simple 12-room lodge (no restaurant, no phone), with a stream-fed pool; 45 km from the highway.

Camping is superb by brooks and waterfalls. The rough track (17km) to tall Torón Falls leads right at a fork before Parupa; at the first ford look for campsites and explore the rocky creek downstream.

Aponguao Falls

Half way down the Kavanayen road, a rough track turns off SE towards a beautiful waterfall (pictured on the front of this book). If you have a camera, be sure to go early when the sun is on the falls: they are over 100m high and almost as wide. To reach the falls, called Chinak Merú in Pemón, go 5km beyond the CVG agricultural station at Parupa; look for jeep tracks on the left over the savanna. They bring you to Iboropó, a Pemón community at the Aponguao, about 3km from the falls. If you wish to walk, cross the Aponguao, paying the Pemón to ferry you over, and pick up the trail. An Indian dugout with motor is usually moored at the river, waiting to take visitors to the head of the falls. The price depends on the *motorista* and the number of people (6 to 12). Plenty of open camping at Iboropó, but midges, too.

Kavanayen

'A very pleasant place, with a good side trip to Karuay waterfall, and the chance to stay in a mission (you pay a little). Take a bus south from Km 88 to the Ciudadela or army checkpoint and stay on the bus until the Luepa side road, the only turning, sign-posted 'Kavanayen 70km'. From here you can start walking, or wait for a ride. There is very little traffic, so be prepared for a night out. It is high, so cold at night. There is one hotel along the sandy road (Chivatón, not checked out).

'The mission does not provide food, but there are two local shops, one of which will prepare food for visitors for Bs.65. The Karuay waterfall is about 18km away (5 hours walk) along a very rough road with beautiful views. It is safe to swim in the large natural pool below it.

'Ask around for rides back to the road. The bus back to Ciudad

Guayana passes the checkpoint at about 10am, and south to Santa Elena at about 3pm.'

Gran Sabana by vehicle

A package tour can give a valid sampling of the Gran Sabana. I saw four marvellous places new to me, despite many camping holidays with my family. And you don't have to cook. The operators of Keyla Tours have a base camp complete with tents, folding cots, sleeping bags, kitchen, showers, loos. We took the early jet (50min) from Caracas to Puerto Ordaz. There the driver waited with a 10-seater van and we began the first day's 400km drive, mostly through hot lowlands. We by-passed El Callao and El Dorado, old and new gold towns, but paused at **Las Claritas** boomtown (and other places to drink a *refresco*, try *cachapas con queso* -maize pancakes with fresh cheese, and lunch on steak). Finally, the van eased up the curves of La Escalera onto the Gran Sabana, stopping soon at a base camp by a cool river.

On the second day we piled into a big dugout to see **Aponguao Falls** (Chinak Merú) where for the first time I hiked to the falls' foot (nice swim), and we picnicked at other falls. On the third day we stopped by more waterfalls including red **Jasper Creek**, my favourite. From the frontier post of La Línea we crossed into Brazil (another first). Returning in the hot afternoon I made two excellent discoveries. First, hidden 1km west of the highway (opposite Roraima), was a perfect camping spot — **Río Soruape**, a broad rippling stream with smooth rocks, swimming ponds, mauritia palms and no *plaga* (biting insects). Second, 1-2km north of La Laja, we turned east onto a track to a lone hill which gave us a superb spectacle as the tepuis of Ilú, Yuruán, Cuquenán and Roraima emerged from clouds under a full moon. After this, everything else was anti-climax. But the last day held another first for me: a detour in Las Claritas to see vast pits scoured out of the rainforest for grains of gold.

You will find a spare pair of track shoes useful, and a sweater and waterproof. Similar tours can be arranged in Ciudad Guayana with Keyla Tours, tel/fax (086) 291021; or in Caracas with Turismo Colorama, Centro Comercial Bello Campo, 2 blocks SE of Altamira metro station; (02) 2617732, fax 2621828. Four days cost about $350 including airfare to Ciudad Guayana.

RORAIMA

'This is a brilliant walk; I've done various hikes in South America including the Inca Trail and the Torres del Paine National Park and although it's obviously impossible to make comparisons, I think that overall Roraima tops the lot.' (Huw Clough)

For several reasons, Roraima is the most important of all the tepuis. On its top is the three-way boundary marker: Venezuela on the west, Guayana on the east, and Brazil on the south. The mountain called by Indians 'Mother of All Waters' drains into three watersheds: the Orinoco, the Essequibo, and the Amazon. With an altitude of 2,810m, Roraima is the tallest massif (although you start climbing from the savanna at about 1,100m).

In 1912 geologist Leonard Dalton used Roraima's name to typify the tableland formation. It was also the year that Arthur Conan Doyle, inspired by Roraima, published his adventure classic about dinosaurs. However, the tepui tops are unable to support any animal larger than an opossum, the environment being extremely harsh. Not surprising since they have been exposed to the sun, wind and rain for over 500 million years. Clinging in crevices are mosses, lichens, tough-leaved shrubs and twisted trees. Some orchids grow on baking rocks. Of the plants, many species live only on the tepui tops, as do some birds and rodents. The small endemic black frog (*Oreophrynella quelchii*) which crawls clumsily and sinks in water appears to have adapted to the tepui conditions by pretending to be a stone.

Roraima drew a series of explorers and naturalists in the 19th Century after it was reported by Robert Schomburgk on a Royal Geographical Society expedition. All parties approached from British Guiana and all failed to scale the 600m cliffs and were driven back by storms, cold, fog and lack of food. Excitement ran high in Darwin's England, and the Spectator challenged in 1874, "Will no one explore Roraima and bring us back the tidings which it has waited these thousands of years to give us?" In 1884, Everard Im Thurn and Harry Perkins finally made the ascent after a two-month expedition. It was December 18, and very wet.

Journey to the Lost World

by Bill Quantrill with additional information by Justine Freeth

Getting there

The first thing to be decided when planning the Roraima hike is how to get to the point from which you start walking. The best thing undoubtedly is to have a four-wheel drive vehicle, or hire one (National Car, when available) in Ciudad Guayana. However, the driver must pay some $90 a day and be over 25. It is about 300km from Ciudad Guayana to El Dorado (in fact a pretty scruffy town), and another 280km to the Pemón Indian settlement of San Francisco just after the Yuruaní bridge. The road leading in to Roraima is a jeep track which leaves the highway on the left about a kilometre beyond San Francisco, coming back at a sharp angle and leading round the face of a range of low hills just to the south of San Francisco. It is not sign-posted but it is not difficult to find.

Justine Freeth flew by Aereotuy from Ciudad Bolívar to Santa Elena. She writes: 'From Santa Elena it is possible to take a jeep to Paraitepuy, but it is expensive, about $100. There are buses to San Francisco, just over 1 hour; the afternoon service to Ciudad Bolívar leaves at 3, 6, and 9pm. There is a National Guard post at San Ignacio and my driver instructed me not to mention Paraitepuy, but to say I was going to San Francisco.'

This is the standard advice for independent climbers. Although Roraima lies just outside Canaima National Park it is an environmentally sensitive area and the authorities are not keen on allowing too many people to climb it. Rightly so.

And Mark Dutton adds: 'The trail to Paraitepuy was very hot; there was no water for several hours. Walking fast, it took 6 hours 15 minutes. Perfectly possible to camp, but nasty biting gnats and lots of ants.'

If you do not have your own four-wheel drive vehicle, San Francisco is as far as you will be able to get by public transport. From here it is about 25km (7 hours on foot — lovely scenery — or you may be lucky enough to hitch a ride) to the hill-top village of Paraitepuy, which is where we parked our jeep and started walking. Whether on foot or in a jeep, the track is not difficult to follow — it has been heavily eroded in places and you may have to go back on your tracks from time to time if you choose the wrong way round a particular hillock or dip, but all the tracks lead to the same place in the end. At one point you are faced with the choice of going straight ahead over a fairly substantial hill or going off round to the left around the hill. Both routes lead to Paraitepuy, but the one to the left avoids a particularly tricky ford through one of the many streams which have to be crossed. Otherwise the only thing to look out for is the point at which the road to Paraitepuy branches off at a right angle to the right — if you miss this turning, as many people do, you will find yourself in the village of Chirimatá, where you can ask somebody to put you on the right road for Paraitepuy.

Guides

It is not required that you hire a guide, but you are urged to do so for a variety of reasons: by taking a local guide you are doing something for the village; it is the people from this village who keep the track open and waymarked; it is easy to get lost when hiking on the top, and your guide will know the very few camping places. Make sure you bring enough food for your guide as well as a blanket. The best known guides are the Ayuso brothers. Guides charge Bs.1000 a day (1991) but they help to carry some equipment.

The Trail

Paraitepuy is regarded as the normal starting point for the Roraima hike. You will almost certainly be greeted on arrival by the village headman, who can provide a guide for you.

'Anything you do not require for the hike you can leave in a locked hut in the village for Bs.50. The village is a typical Indian settlement with thatched huts but it is increasingly geared towards the many tourists going to Roraima. There are shelters specifically for hikers; there is plenty of tent space and it is even possible to hire tents in the village for Bs.400 a day, but these are not of good quality.' (J.F.)

The first night in Paraitepuy can be spent camping by a little river. From the village you set off along a former jeep track down into the next valley. At the bottom of the valley you cross a stream then go through a gate. The jeep track then winds away to the right to get to the top of the ridge in front of you. The footpath cuts diagonally up across the face of the hill to the left, rejoining the jeep track at the top. You then have a lovely steady walk along the ridge, with the two tepuis of Kukenan on the left and Roraima on the right getting steadily closer as you advance. Mostly the footpath follows an old jeep trail, with occasional short-cuts on the steep up and downhill bits. After about three hours of steady walking, you come down into a valley with a slightly bigger stream than any you have come to so far, with beautiful deep, blue swimming holes. You can cross this stream dry-shod, unlike the next one, about 15 minutes further on which has to be waded at the point where the jeep track fords it. Half an hour beyond this is the biggest river of all — the Kukenan

River. If it has been raining within the last 24 hours this can be quite a difficult crossing, especially with a full pack on your back: thigh-deep rushing water and an uneven, slippery bottom.

If, like us, you set out from Paraitepuy at around mid-day, you are likely to arrive at the Kukenan River in good time to set up your camp, have a swim (but the sand flies can be very bad here) and prepare your evening meal as the sun goes down. If, however, you started in the morning, you will reach the river at about lunch time, and can then continue for another three hours or so in the afternoon to one of the most exquisite campsites I have ever seen. Known as the *campamento abajo*, this is a flat meadow right under the shadow of the sheer cliffs of the Roraima massif. Two clear streams run through the meadow, which is alive with birds and, at night, fireflies. The view back over the route you have come is superb. The track from the Kukenan River to the Campamento Abajo is not difficult to follow. It goes along the left hand bank of the river to begin with, then rejoins the jeep trail and follows that until it peters out where the Roraima foothills begin. You then have a fairly stiff climb up through the foothills until you reach the meadow.

From the Campamento Abajo to the top of Roraima is about four hours hard climb. You can see the trail winding upwards through the trees from the eastern end of the meadow — the opposite end from the one in which you arrived. For the first two hours or so you are scrambling through the trees, over rocks, even, at one point, along the bed of a stream — all the time going relentlessly upwards. Eventually you come to the face of the cliff itself, at a point where an icy-cold stream shoots out of the cliff-face. The path changes and for the next couple of hours you work your way up a diagonal ledge up the cliff face. It is quite a broad ledge, well covered in vegetation. Most of the time you are hardly conscious of the fact that there is an increasingly high sheer cliff a few metres away to your left, though occasionally you come out of the undergrowth and can get an idea of your progress. At one time you have to drop down 50m or so to get round a rock buttress. Finally you come to a point where you have to pass under a cascading waterfall — (a nasty cold shower, but there is no avoiding it) then scramble up a rocky gully that eventually brings you out on to the summit.

It is not easy to move around on the summit. The surface consists mostly of huge rock formations surrounded by bog. Camping is not easy. There is one area, known as *El Hotel*, which is an extent of dry sand under a rock overhang sheltered from the prevailing wind and which provides space enough for two or three small tents at most. Other areas which look flat enough to camp on usually turn out to be waterlogged: if not already so when you find them they quickly become so once the inevitable evening downpour starts. The route to El Hotel is marked with red painted arrows, going off to the right almost immediately after you first arrive at the summit. If this space is already occupied, the best choice is probably to find a flat rock to pitch your tent on, attaching the guys to rocks. We tried camping on what looked like a relatively dry patch of sand, but were inundated by rain running off the surrounding rocks during the night.

'Our guide knew sheltered camping spots before the top of the trail. Once on top, the walk to the triple boundary marker is not too tough, about eight hours there and back. But it is complicated and should not be attempted without a guide. Just before the marker, you walk some distance beside a huge mysterious lake, and from there you pass through the Valley of Crystals. This is a spectacular canyon paved with white and pink quartz crystals. (Please do not pick the crystals.) Twenty minutes beyond the marker is the most beautiful waterfall I've ever seen. Water trickles over the surface of the tepui to cascade into a pool about 10m below. The sun makes amazing rainbows in the waterfall. Just above the amber pool, pillars of rock like stalactites project into the water; between these, luxuriant plants give the impression of hanging baskets. A little further on is what is called "the great labyrinth of the north", but we didn't have time to go there.' (J.F.)

Warnings

Many people will be only too familiar with the pestilential little biting gnats known as *jejenes* or simply as *la plaga*. They infest the Gran Sabana and can make life miserable to anyone who is susceptible to their itching bites. Covering up well and using an effective insect repellent help to alleviate the problem but don't solve it altogether. The only place free of the little beasts is the top of Roraima where I suspect the altitude is too much for them. The other pests are the human litterbugs who have moved in since the paved road up to the Gran Sabana was opened. I am told that after Easter Week the National Guard collected over a thousand beer and soft drink cans from the road going into Roraima, and the rubbish along the main highway was indescribable. The National Guard, who are responsible for controlling the area, realise that something will have to be done and may place tighter controls on access to the region.

Huw Clough, who took a group up Roraima without guides, would not recommend others doing the same. By using a guide you are helping the local economy and perhaps preventing abuse of the area by trekkers. Huw concludes, 'I would also appeal to campers' "green" conscience, respecting the unique ecosystem up there by keeping to the camp sites. Since I first went to Roraima three years ago, there are already disturbing signs of pollution (open-toilet remains by the camp sites) and litter scattered all over the place.

'Roraima does seem to be getting to be one of the most popular hikes in Venezuela. It's just outside the Canaima National Park so not protected by the same laws. But I hope that the authorities will either incorporate it into the park, or impose some controls and regulations on visitors going there, before it's too late.'

Campers, remember to bring a shovel.

A message left by Jimmie Angel

When pilot Jimmie Angel landed on top of Auyantepui, he made a mistake. Not only was there no gold, but the surface was so boggy that the plane remained stuck. Goldless (and largely foodless), Angel, his wife Marie, Gustavo Heny and his gardener Miguel, survived only because the route down had been scouted for them in advance. But before they started walking, Angel left a paper in the cockpit with a scrawled message. Their way had been previously established by Félix Cardona and Gustavo Heny. Is the fact that the escape route already existed evidence of thoroughness, or perhaps of Angel's intention to leave the plane? Perhaps Angel was as much a publicity hound as fortune seeker. Who was the message for? An air rescue team? Years later it was found and kept by Alejandro Laime and is reproduced here.

By Jimmie Angel
This Flamingo Airplane was landed here Saturday Oct 9, 1937 at 11 45 AM the landing was intentional, switch was cut also gas. We were on the ground 750 feet before we hit soft spot Plane nosed up. And tore entering edge on left wing tip. And pulled one hose connection loose on oil radiator, No more visable damage done passengers my Angel Gustavo Heny Miguel Delgado today is the eleventh of October we are walking out in good Health

ANGEL FALLS

If one place alone draws travellers to Venezuela, it is Angel Falls, highest in the world with 979m free fall. The falls can vary daily with the rain; in the dry season the water turns to mist by the time it reaches the ground. Consequently June to December may be the best months for a visit although, of course, there will be a lot of clouds. After heavy rains, literally hundreds of waterfalls pour off the cliffs of the giant mesa called Auyantepui.

The romantic name comes not from heaven but American bush pilot Jimmie Angel. For many years Angel's abandoned plane glinted in a bog atop the mesa where he landed in 1937 looking for gold. All the stuff of legends. But Angel eclipsed the falls' early discoverer, a prospector and rubber hunter named Ernesto Sánchez La Cruz who in 1910 reported the cascade as Churún Merú. This is its name in the language (merú = falls) of the Pemón Indians who of course knew all the time it was there. Four years after Angel died (1956), his son returned to Venezuela to scatter his ashes over the falls. Jimmie's plane (it was borrowed) was later removed by the Air Force. Restored, it is now displayed at the Ciudad Bolívar airport.

Angel Falls still draws adventurers who scale the canyon's face, walk tightropes, drop in parachutes... But, aside from a barricade of permits, the hazards are terrible. In 1990 French climber Jean Marc Boivin lost his life tragically in a paraglide jump over the falls.

Small planes and helicopters offer breathtaking tours of the falls from Canaima's airstrip, penetrating 'Devil's Canyon' deep into Auyantepui. A seat in a Cessna costs about $60. Apparently the Avensa jets no longer swing over the falls. The Aereotuy excursion to Kavac, $165 from Ciudad Bolívar, flies over Angel Falls, weather permitting.

Canaima

About 40km north of Angel Falls, at a bend where the Carrao River spills over seven lovely waterfalls into a lagoon, is Canaima. Canaima's camp of 90 cabins, restaurant and souvenir shops is more than a bit touristy.

'Monopolistic,' says Peter Ireland who was camping. 'In the store, prices are about double; in the hotel, dinner is $9-10. But it's a truly idyllic setting. I just stared at the tepuis over the falls in amazement. I camped beyond the Guardaparque's hut where I checked in, on the beach with ultrafine white and pink sand. You could sling a hammock (even rent one from locals at Bs.250). Mozzy net recommended, but not an absolute necessity. I left my pack at the Guardia's while I went to explore. There is an Indian settlement with

The Angel Falls area

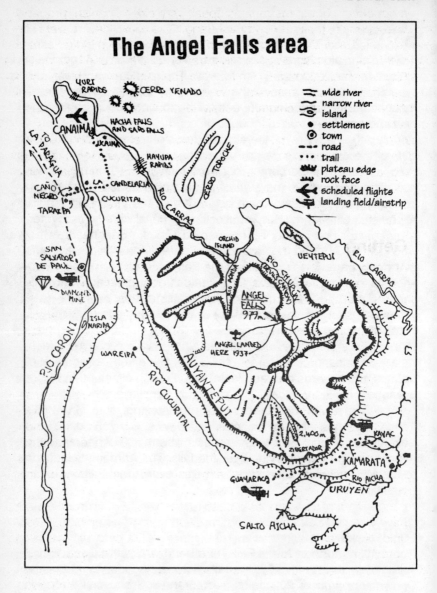

Legend:
- ⎯ wide river
- ⌇ narrow river
- island
- • settlement
- ⓞ town
- - - - road
- ··· trail
- plateau edge
- rock face
- scheduled flights
- landing field/airstrip

YURI RAPIDS
CERRO VENADO
HACHA FALLS AND SAPO FALLS
CANAIMA
UKAIMA
TO PARAGUA
MAYUPA RAPIDS
CAÑO NEGRO
LA CANDELARIA
CUCURITAL
RÍO CARRAO
CERRO TOPOCHE
TARAIPA
SAN SALVADOR DE PAUL
DIAMOND MINE
ORCHID ISLAND
UEYTEPUI
RÍO CARRAO
RÍO CHURUN (DEVIL'S CANYON)
RÍO AONDA
ANGEL FALLS 979 m.
ANGEL LANDED HERE 1937
ISLA MARIPA
RÍO CARONÍ
WAREIPA
AUYANTEPUI
RÍO CUCURITAL
2,400 m
LIBERTADOR
KAVAC
KAMARATA
GUAYARACA
RÍO ACHA
URUYEN
SALTO ACHA.

a couple of shops; the Indians speak very clear Spanish, probably because it's their second language. The next day, I went on excursion (not that well organised) to Wareipa: 45 minutes across the savanna in a trailer pulled by a tractor, and then one hour up the Río Cucurital by dugout to Wareipa rapids. Took a shower in a waterfall; it's still a novelty swimming in tea. Excellent views of Auyantepui's 1000 columns, totally fascinating in the setting sun's red light.'

Note   Canaima beach has stray dogs and as a result jiggers or *niguas*, nasty sand fleas that burrow into your feet; you dig them out with a needle. The sand used to be pure, as well as the clear, brandy dark water. This can no longer be guaranteed.

Getting there

At noon every day, Avensa's jet lands at the Canaima airfield. The Canaima flight was listed (1993) at Bs.10,000 from Maiquetía with a stop in Ciudad Bolívar (or Bs.6,264 from CB). But Avensa charged visitors staying at the Canaima camp only Bs.6,500 from Caracas. CAVE also flies propeller planes from Barcelona, Porlamar, Puerto Ordaz and Valencia; if anything these flights are more expensive.

Most tourists buy Avensa's package which covers 1 or 2 nights in Canaima; Avensa may deny there are seats available if you do not buy the package. Despite its high cost (about $200 from Caracas, 2 days/1 night; no single-occupancy cabins), the package is popular, so bookings during Venezuela's high season (school holidays) should be made well in advance. Address: Avensa, Esquina El Chorro, Av. Universidad, Caracas, (02) 5640098, fax 5623196. Avensa does not take bookings for expeditions or river trips.

Independent travellers wanting to buy only the air fare from Avensa have been made to wait for confirmation until 48 hours before flight time. However, hikers can stand on their rights by having a parks permit. This is an Inparques *Permiso de Excursionismo*, a form issued by the Director of Parques Nacionales that states passport number and parks to be visited. (See Chapter 3 — *National Parks*.)

A Cuidad Bolívar airline, Rutaca, flies charters to Canaima at about $125 per person. Enquire at their office in the hangars, Av. Jesús Soto, (085) 24010; open 6-11, 3-5; from Caracas, charter lines such as CAVE and Aeroejecutivos offer day tours to Canaima with a flight over Angel Falls, weather permitting. Aereotuy leaves from Porlamar ($240) and Ciudad Bolívar ($165), daily except Monday. All provide picnic lunch and a spin on the river. Check with any travel agent.

Paul and Tracey Weatherstone were wary of getting involved with an organised tour but, having been told by obstructive airport staff that all Avensa flights were full, they booked a tour with Turi Express for $250 for a three day excursion. Paul writes: 'I have to admit to being pleasantly surprised by the distinct lack of organisation. The trip was one of the highlights of the holiday. The price at first might seem prohibitive but ... to put together our own "package" would have been more expensive than the option we chose.'

Upriver to Angel Falls

Once you are on the river, you are on the edge of Eden. However, in the dry season (December to April) it is not possible to find organised river trips to the base of Angel Falls. Because shallow rapids mean troublesome portages, operators only offer river trips in the rainy season, which is when the rivers (and falls) are guaranteed to be full.

Like other operators, the Jiménez Brothers of Excursiones Canaima run 4-day trips May through mid-October. Their motorised dugouts take off the same afternoon you land by Avensa: three days travel upstream, and one to return. They provide all food; trekkers sleep in hammocks. The cost is about $250 a person in groups of six minimum. They use native Spanish-speaking guides (who have been known to turn back in mid-stream for private reasons). Reservations should be made 60 days in advance. Excursiones Canaima have a desk in the national terminal in Maiquetía, (031) 44793, and an office in Hotel Macuto, Urb. Alamo, La Guaira, (031) 552462, fax 519549. 'They were a great contact and helped us to get there in the cheapest way.' (C.Nacher) Ask them to book your Canaima flight. Another company doing Angel Falls trips (three days for about $200) is Canaima Tours, telefax (02) 413696; ask for Sandra Benellan. Kamarakoto Tours, an Indian group, is represented in Caracas by Organización Epsilon, Centro Empresarial Don Bosco, Of.23, Av. Miranda, (02) 348544, fax (02) 346714.

Ucaima Camp

This is located above Canaima's Falls, reached by a ½hr hike. It is a family affair, small and exclusive, about $150 a day without airfare. Ucaima was built by Rudy Truffino, the Dutchman who first led expeditions to Angel Falls and Auyantepui. He schedules 4-day river trips by powered craft to the base of Angel Falls from July to November only. Rudy has built two cabins upriver where trekkers sleep in camp beds. The cost is about $500 a person (minimum 5). You arrive on Sunday's Aereotuy flight, and return to Caracas on Friday. Write: Apartado 61879, Caracas 1060A; tel (02) 6619153, fax 6611980.

Kamarata to Angel Falls

One way to avoid Canaima where the tourist trade detracts from the wilderness is to approach Angel Falls from Kamarata, by going down the Akanán and Carrao rivers on the east side of Auyantepui, then up the Churún. The first night's camp is usually at Iguana rapids or Iwanamerú, a spot with lovely walks and beaches in the drier months, and a view of the Aparamán range. The Akanán feeds into the Carrao River; here campers hang their hammocks at Arenal, an old miners' camp near the mouth of the Churún River. The stony Churún sparkles like brandy when the water is shallow. Base camp is often made on Isla Ratoncito, farthest point reached by motor craft. From there, 1½ hours through tall forest bring walkers to an outcrop in front of Angel Falls.

Guillermo Cuellar reports that in Kamarata there is a very efficient group of Pemón guides headed by Tito Abati. Abati provides curiaras, outboard motors, hammocks and men to run the dugouts and make camp; you provide food. The 5-day trip to the falls and then down to Canaima costs about $200 a person, in groups of six to 10. Tito makes this river run from May to December. His outfit, called Macunaima Tours, also arranges food and lodging in Kamarata (with beds, bath). Messages may be sent via Aereotuy to Kamarata. Or contact G.Cuellar, (014) 272119, fax (02) 773610. — He arranges charters to Uruyen which, like Kavac, is close to falls that spill from Auyantepui's flanks into a deep hidden bowl. This is far from crowds, far from anyone at all.

Note: Photographers should be aware that the falls face east and receive sun only in the morning.

As on any river travel, a hat is a must. Since it will probably rain, expect to get chilled as well as burned. Old canvas shoes are a good idea for beaches because of *niguas* or jiggers. Mosquitoes may bite at night and malaria has been recorded in the area. Malaria can only spread where there are people who already have the disease, so it is unlikely to be a threat up remote rivers or on tepuis.

Overland to Canaima

by Paul Rouche

During dry weather jeeps and pick-up trucks use a miner's road of about 120km from La Paragua to San Salvador de Paúl, an old diamond camp. Before reaching Paúl, a track forks to the Caroní River where *curiaras* (dugouts) can be hired to take passengers across to Puerto Cucurital. There remains a hike of about 2½ hours to reach Canaima camp.

Kavac Canyon

Aereotuy's turbo-props fly daily excursions (except Monday) to Kavac from Ciudad Bolívar ($165) and Porlamar ($240). It's a wonderful flight over Angel Falls and Auyantepui, landing on a savanna strip SE of the massif. A dozen attractively thatched Indian houses provide shelter here, half for tourists during the day, more for guests overnight. Aereotuy asks $100 a night with food. The place was built with local materials by the people of Kamarata, a village two hours walk away.

Peter Ireland reports: 'It's a lovely place to stay, with Auyantepui in the background. You can pay for a hammock or a bed, or you can sleep on the floor for free. There's a shower which has warm water. At a small shop you can get a few basics, and cold beer for Bs.60. After all the tourists have left, Kavac becomes a very picturesque pueblito; the locals, except for about 15 people, leave too for their homes in Kamarata. There is a *carro* which takes people to Kamarata, though it costs Bs.300 because petrol is so expensive.'

To reach Kavac Canyon and its waterfall, you walk towards Auyantepui; after ½ hour, there's a natural jacuzzi-type pool. Further up the Kavac River, you swim into a canyon so narrow you touch both walls, into a dark pool where a waterfall plunges from a hole overhead. (Kamarata's drinking water is piped from Kavac Falls.) If you are not on a day trip, you must pay Bs.500 to join the group.

AUYANTEPUI

Doing it independently

by Peter Ireland

Auyantepui is huge. Its 600km² top is as big as the island of St. Lucia. In shape it resembles a heart, about 40-50km long, with a deep gorge in the middle; this is where Angel Falls plunges over a cliff. Rock climbers such as David Nott have scaled the face near Angel Falls. However, the only trail up Auyantepui is the southern route which was opened by Félix Cardona/Gustavo Heny 55 years ago to rescue Jimmie Angel. It rises from 1,000m at Guayaraca savanna to 2,400m on top.

An expedition up Auyantepui depends on hiring Indian guides in Kamarata, starting point of the trail. Aereotuy's Gran Sabana flight goes from Ciudad Bolívar to Kamarata on Thursdays, and from Santa Elena to Kamarata on Mondays. Few people hike to Auyantepui because it is remote.

Kamarata is a large Indian settlement where people are still genuinely very friendly. A helpful man for advice about guides is Lino who teaches at the school and speaks good English. There is a well-stocked shop, a place to eat, even a 'hotel'. We camped by the volleyball court in front of the big Catholic mission. There are several taps with drinking water, and you can swim or bathe in the river.

We agreed with our guide Justiniano to meet in Kavac in the morning. The hike was said to be 10 days and we agreed with Justiniano on Bs.7,000, although we planned to cover it in 9 days. The hike is hard so we stocked up on plenty of food for Justiniano, too. It's a 2 hour walk to Kavac, easy but hot, and there's a river half way.

The first day's hike is across savanna to begin with. It was the dry season, very hot, and the path was hard. About 4 hours from Kavac we bathed in the last river before the trail starts to climb; hard work in the sun. In about 2-3 hours from the river we were on top of the first level and in another hour we reached a river and campsite called Guayaraca. The river is beautifully refreshing (fine for drinking, as is all the water on the tepui). Some wooden frames have been constructed where you could use plastic sheeting for a roof, convenient because all other sites up the mountain were under huge rocks and so no other protection from the weather is needed. We were in the forest and saw several huge purple orchids and timid hummingbirds.

The next day's hike climbed from forest to a kind of dense tepui vegetation on a shoulder called Danto, then up more steeply to El Peñón (1,700m). This is a huge rock with 10 beds cut in the sand underneath. A perfect shelter but chilly because wind funnels through it. There's a stream 5 minutes away. You can see, below, the plateau and the savanna path; Kamarata and Kavac are already out of sight to the east; to the south are other tepuis.

We left behind our tent and some food, out of reach of rodents, for the return. The path goes up steeply, then over a tangle of wet tree roots, emerging at the base of a huge vertical wall. We couldn't see the top as it was cloudy. We skirted the wall, climbing steeply, using ropes (already in place) a couple of times. Scaling the final rocks to the tepui's top is great. The huge columns of rock are incredibly shaped and pitted, mysterious in the clouds. On the rock to the right as you come up is a bronze bust of Bolívar, brought up by the Universidad Central de Venezuela in 1956; hence this point (about 2,400m) is known as Libertador. Breathtaking views, both into and out of the tepui. There is a rock here that you can camp under, but we continued on to another rock known as El Oso (the bear). We walked over black rock dimpled with pools of water. Each pool is full of mosses or plants. We climbed carefully across a near-vertical slope, jumped other crevasses many metres deep.

The water on top of the tepui is red like tea and tastes pretty good (the colouring comes from tannin, especially from the Bonnetia trees). The trail goes through some Bonnetia forest to El Oso camp. The next day we hiked 4 hours to Borrachito (meaning 'little drunkard', perhaps for the weird rock shapes?). There is a fair amount of small forest, orchids, birds. Hummingbirds darted to within a foot of my head. Borrachito is on the banks of a lovely, deep red river, the Churún, which eventually passes over Angel Falls. There is a dark cave where we slept. The next day was spent scrambling through forests, around crevasses, to Boca de Dragón where the river disappears under rocks for a space. The rock bed is 30m wide but the river covered little of it then (watch out if it should rain, however!). About an hour's walk downstream we discovered a lovely waterfall, about 30m high which Justiniano hadn't seen before.

Return — Day 6. To have enough time to get to El Peñón, you need to be at El Oso by noon, Libertador by 3pm. Day 7. We got back to Guayaraca by noon. Here I set off on my own for Kavac to try to arrive in time for a flight. Although I was there at 4 pm, the last flight to pick up people for Canaima at 14.30 was full. A warm shower and some beers cheered me up. The others arrived at 16.30, having come via Uruyén, a village close to the path from Guayaraca. Day 8. It seemed likely there would be planes to Porlamar, Ciudad Bolívar and Canaima. However, we took a plane to La Paragua which had just brought some cargo to Kavac — a fantastic flight below cloud level. In La Paragua everyone snarls at you. It's a gold and diamond town and we were fairly thoroughly searched at the National Guard post as we left by *por puesto*.

Note about flights   At any airfield around the tepuis you could ask a pilot if he had places. You can hitch lifts on the daytripper planes that are not full, or on a returning cargo plane. Even if you are likely to pay a fair amount, the flight is worth it, especially in the little single engine Cessnas which the pilots drive like cars. They fly so low the views are always spectacular. Aereotuy: there are representatives in each town on the Gran Sabana route. They are very helpful. In Kamarata, if you want to make a reservation, you talk to Dionysius.

Organised treks

A way to save time and preparations is to join a guided trek for a small group to Auyantepui. Edith Rogge's Alechiven trek appears to be the best, if not the only one. The cost now runs over $1000 for 10 days, but it is all inclusive from the time you land in Venezuela (bring your sleeping bag), and Alechiven takes care of permits. Hikers walk from the savanna at Kamarata westward to Kavac camp in 3-4 hours;

then in 6 hours from Kavac around to Auyantepui's south end, crossing many streams which flow from the massif. The ascent itself is made in two days from Guayaraca. 'As we approach the wall, the last stage of the climb,' says Edith, 'it seems impossible that special skills are not required. But the Indians lead the way through a sort of huge stone doorframe and up a stairway of jumbled rocks.' They spend one night on top of the mesa where rockscapes evoke the moon, and the panorama of distant savanna and tablelands is unforgettable.

Alechiven, (041) 211828, fax 217018, is a hard-working company which maintains a base and radio in Kamarata. From April to December, they do river trips to Angel Falls, arranging all transportation from Maiquetía.

La Paragua to Caño Negro

Not on most maps, this dodgy road starts opposite the old river port of La Paragua, last point for taking on petrol and supplies. I went with my wife in 1987 in a Toyota 4WD packed with food, fuel and spares. A car ferry or *chalana* over the wide Paragua River operates until 6pm and there is a small charge for cars. We found excellent campsites by savanna creeks and in the forest (two nights along the road, then three nights in Canaima). Although it was April and the track itself was mostly dry, countless potholes, ruts and gullies kept our average speed down to 30kph.

21km beyond the Paragua is the Río Chiguao ferry (a bridge was under construction). Some distance beyond, the road deteriorated into a deeply rutted track. The mud started. And about once every kilometre the road crossed a stream or ravine, at times on a bridge of girders or felled logs. We saw few people along the track beyond half a dozen vehicles. 72km from the Paragua River is the entrance to Las Bonitas, an Indian village (1km to the left). At 96km from the Paragua we spotted obscure tyre tracks veering left to the Caño Negro: this is the best place to cross the Caroní for Canaima, via Puerto Cucurital. Because the tracks swerve through the savanna without any sign — the river is nowhere in sight — drivers should pay close attention to the kilometre reading. Jeeps can drive 6km towards the river and park by a hut at the Caño Negro. With the help of the family living there, we paddled across the Caroní River by dugout. Wide, deep and fast, the Caroní is superb, dark as steeped tea.

We tied up at a little landing on the east bank not far from the Cucurital tributary. Sightseeing tours from Canaima occasionally visit Puerto Cucurital by jeep. The Canaima trail began 100m to the right of a hut. Leading through forest and crossing many creeks, it emerged onto open savanna with Auyantepui's massif straight ahead. At the end of an hour's march from Cucurital — the last stretch over clear but swampy ground — we arrived at a log bridge. From here, the sandy jeep road to Canaima camp led across a very hot savanna with little shade.

Half an hour brought us to a fork where we took the left hand; at the next crossing we went right, and at the third, left. The jeep road brought us to Canaima airfield. My non-stop walking time from the log bridge was 74 minutes; double this if you are tired.

Crossing via Taraipa

It's possible that when you arrive in Caño Negro the *curiara* owner is not at home. In that case, alternative arrangements can be made at Taraipa, a Kamaracoto village 14km farther south on the main jeep road to Paúl. Taraipa is a 20min walk from the river. Etiquette may require a consultation with the *capitán* or village head about parking your vehicle and crossing the Caroní. If the bargaining (Bs.500?) for the *viaje* includes your return crossing, insist on a *fixed hour and day* (I know friends who were stranded anyway). Once across the Caroní, you pick up the path northwards, skirting the river, to Puerto Cucurital. I'm told this stretch takes 1½ hours.

San Salvador de Paúl is 8km south of Taraipa. Its tin-roofed houses sprawl along the Caroní. There is a Guardia Nacional post with radio links to Canaima and La Paragua. Some *abastos* sell overpriced plastic canteens, hammock ropes, tinned sardines... and beer! Some miners still sieve the river gravel for diamonds. The camp is named after a prospector called Paul whose good luck started a rush in the 1960s. Beside the airstrip is the miners' cemetery, a sad affair with pieces of tin for grave markers.

Remember   Miners' tracks such as the one to Paúl are not engineered and during the rains they may become impassable. Best time would be year-end to Easter. In any event, drivers should invest in a heavy tow rope and a spade.

THE CAURA RIVER AND PARÁ FALLS

The Caura is a southern tributary of the Orinoco, in western Bolívar, and a great river in its own right, tumbling darkly over boulders and rapids. It gathers into spectacular falls, the Saltos Pará, seldom visited because they are 200km upriver. The Caura basin has some of the heaviest rain in the country, nearly 3m a year. Its average water flow (2,700m³ per *second*) is exceeded only by the Caroní and the Orinoco.

The best time to travel is the dry season, December to April, when rock formations, emerging beaches and absence of mosquitoes make camping superb. The people who live up the Caura are mostly members of the Yekuana tribe, formerly known as Makiritares. Some speak Spanish as well as Yekuana, a Carib language. 'Yekuana' means 'men of the river' and these Indians are indeed master makers and handlers of dugouts — slim, elegant (and tippy) craft hollowed from single trunks. Such *curiaras* measure 6m to 16m and longer. Because of the Caura's many intricate rapids, the Yekuana are the only real navigators of its changing currents. Few outside travellers penetrate above Pará Falls.

Maripa

On the Caura's banks by the new kilometre-long bridge, Maripa makes a good river base. The pueblo is famous for making and selling *curiaras*. A dozen dugouts are usually moored below the bridge and men can often be seen hollowing out camphorwood and sassafras trunks with axes and fire. For a riverman the big investment is not his curiara but an outboard motor.

Although the present Maripa was built by the government on a grid plan, the village of some 3,000 inhabitants dates back to 1773 when Franciscans founded the settlement as San Pedro de Alcántara. It was once an export centre for tonka beans used to make perfume and cigarettes (Lucky Strike) and today the *sarrapia* nuts are still gathered and dried. Largely a Yekuana village, Maripa means 'bat' in Carib. The village has no pharmacies or doctors; a nurse attends a small dispensary. Because malaria is a problem, visitors should bring preventive medicine. There are no telephones but the Yekuanas have radio contact with Ciudad Bolívar and Caura settlements.

Caicara-Ciudad Bolívar buses stop at the Estación de Servicio Maripa on the eastern outskirts.

Getting there

By bus   As the road south of the Orinoco now has excellent bridges, getting to Maripa is relatively easy from Ciudad Bolívar, 220km, or Caracas, about 630km. From the Caracas terminal, Colectivos Caicabo, (02) 5413029, go to Caicara for about $10; you will have to change buses in Caicara for Maripa (136km). There is another line starting from Valencia which runs a through service to Ciudad Bolívar, passing Maripa.

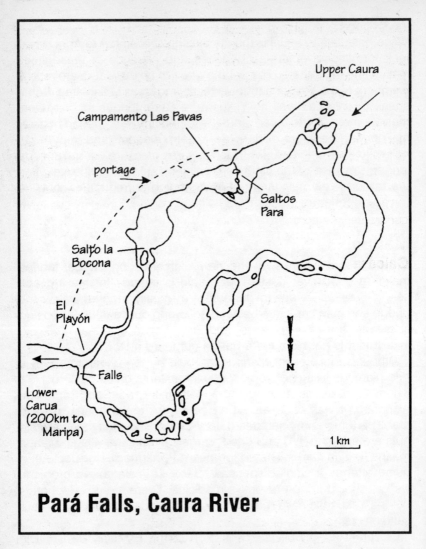

Pará Falls, Caura River

By car   The drive from Caracas can be made in one day only with a very early start to catch the Orinoco ferry before sunset. The first mountainous stretch to Chaguaramas on the plains, a distance of 300km or so, takes nearly 5 hours (with lunch). Most people use the Charallave-Cua route. Chaguaramas has a petrol station with scruffy snack bar. Although paved and straight, the Llanos road south from here is tricky because of pot-holes. If you are hungry you might stop like the *llaneros* do at the *cachapera* on the left before Las Mercedes; their maize pancakes (*cachapas*) are very good with fresh cheese. 55km beyond Las Mercedes a sign points west for Aguaro-

Guariquito National Park (possible campsite?). Aside from cows and twisted chaparro trees, there is little else until Santa Rita, 60km before the Orinoco. It has two service stations and two restaurants, the Manapire at the Corpoven station and the better choice, Mañiño's, where good, economical fried chicken is served.

Ferry   The Orinoco ferry or *chalana* is an open barge which runs hourly from 6 am to dusk between Cabruta and Caicara. In periods of low water the crossing downstream takes ¾hr; when the Orinoco is full the return may take an hour or longer. Expect to find a long queue of lorries, cars and buses waiting to board. Passengers do not pay to cross; cars pay Bs.200. If you have no car, try the faster curiara service across the Orinoco.

Caicara

This small town is growing with new avenues, districts, depots, restaurants. Hotels with simple accommodation include the Miami on Antigua Calle Carabobo, the Venezuela on Av. Bulevard, and the Bella Guayana on Calle Merecey; don't be surprised if the air-conditioning doesn't work or there is no water. A good pension is Residencias Dina on Calle 23 de Enero. The newer Hotel Redoma is by the airport traffic circle on the road out of town.

Ten kilometres beyond, the road divides right for Puerto Ayacucho and left for Maripa. The lovely highway crosses palm-studded savannas interrupted by rivers and huge black boulders. Although there are new fences and more Zebu cattle, settlers are still scarce. *Bodegas* selling bottled drinks or anything at all are few.

Where to stay/eat

In Maripa a shopowner, Caramelo, has converted an old house on the Calle Principal into an attractive hostel, the Villa Maripa, with garage space. The four large rooms with fans and shower are low-priced. A small restaurant in town, La Entrada, serves economical hot meals. Some shops sell basics such as *arepa* flour, oil, tinned tuna, soft drinks, beer, batteries, hats, rope.

Campamento Caurama is a guest lodge on a ranch north of Maripa called Hato El Retiro. Cattle and water buffalo range over its 150km² bordering the Caura, and owner Ilio Ulive uses his ultra-light plane to reach annually flooded pastures, dropping fodder and salt. Ulive, a film maker, has used Caurama's forests and rivers as settings. There are 14 double rooms with ceiling fan, bathroom, thatched diningroom, bar, swimming tank. Packages include full board, use of horses, canoes, fishing gear, excursions to gold camps. Costs run over $110 a day without land/air transportation. For information ring Ilio Ulive, (02) 7817511; or Amazonair which flies light aircraft from Caracas, (02) 2836960, fax 2832627.

Tours to Salto Pará

There is a road which forks 22km east of Maripa and goes south to the tiny Caura 'port' of Trincheras (53km, last part unpaved). No buses, but transportation can be arranged in Maripa at a stiff price. Camps in Trincheras such as the one operated by Tom Tours run trips to Salto Pará. A 5-day excursion costs $350 from Ciudad Bolívar. Tom Tours' Caracas address, opposite the Torre Británica, is: Of.708, Edif. Terepaima, Av. Roche, Altamira Sur; fax 2631812.

Campamento Wasaiña organises 6-day trips to the falls and 12 days to the upper Caura ($770), picking up passengers in Ciudad Bolívar. Contact Woken Tours in Caracas, (02) 2640365, fax 2613533. Including flight from Caracas, Preference Tours offers 7 days boating and hiking led by multilingual guides, $636; (02) 7932148, fax 7932229; ask for Raso.

An alternative excursion by *curiara* is described below.

In Maripa we went straight to see Germán Rodríguez, a Yekuana Indian, on Calle Ruiz Pineda where he has built a thatched roundhouse. Germán was at home and agreed to leave next day for the Saltos. The rental of a curiara or dugout with a good outboard motor and the services of pilot and helper or *marinero* for five days runs to about $300 and so is only economical for a group of six people. As we offered to buy and help load two drums of petrol plus 18 litres of 2-stroke oil, and as Germán needed no helper, costs were lowered and we struck a bargain for four people. We took up Germán's offer of hammock space (also garden shower stall) for the night.

In the early morning we pushed off upriver in Germán's 10m *curiara*. On board were hammocks, tarpaulin, lamp, machete, food for ourselves and Germán. The crocodile-coloured Caura slid past our prow for 3 hours to Trincheras, a *criollo* pueblo on the east bank. Jabillal, the adjacent village, is also said to have curiaras and launches (*rápidas*) for hire. The second stage to the falls (like the third) takes another 3 hours, up to the mouth of the Nichare. The river, now swifter and clearer, was broken by jagged rocks. Germán scanned boulders and rapids. For our picnic and swim he chose a *laja* or flat boulder by Raudal Cinco Mil, rapids where a man's *curiara* once sank along with his fortune. It was a good site shaded by a huge copaiba, jacarandas and kapok or silk cotton (*ceiba*) trees.

The sun dropped early behind the forest wall; the river darkened and the breeze chilled. Many parrots nested in old trees; scarlet macaws flew over in pairs, squawking. Near the Nichare's mouth a red clay bank rose steeply to Germán's own settlement. A path led through banana plants to a clear brook polka-dotted with small tadpoles. Beyond was Germán's plantation of pineapple, sugarcane, yuca and cacao. Germán has built his family about five *churuatas* by the river. A little roundhouse serves as medical dispensary where his daughter is the nurse in charge. Everyone except the very young and old had gone down to Maripa for Christmas. A Sanemá family from Brazil camped under a shelter. Germán, a Yekuana, hired these Sanemá as labourers. A *grulla* or trumpeter bird patrolled the grounds, chirping sweetly. By making a booming noise, trumpeters announce intruders; they are useful for eating snakes, too.

We slung our hammocks under a tin roof beside the radio generator. Germán can speak to Santa María del Erebato, Campamento Las Pavas, Maripa, Ciudad Bolívar and the Nichare biological station. This small research station two hours up the Nichare is sponsored by the Amigos del Nichare, Econatura and the New York Zoological Society, among others studying the area's rich fauna. The Nichare is important, in Germán's view, as a fish reserve. When the Caura rises in May the fish go down to the Orinoco to spawn in shallow lagoons; in October they return upriver. But there are no regulated fishing seasons on the Caura and commercial fishermen use *trenes* which are 100m-long nets to trap half a ton of fish nightly—morocoto, cachama, pavón (*peacock bass*), boquiní. Four-legged fauna appear to be depleted, too. We heard howler monkeys only once, saw few turtles and a single cayman; crocodiles have all been killed. Birds: fishing eagle, white egrets, black hawks, grey skimmers dipping to black waters, snakebirds all aligned on a sunny boulder, toucans flapping hard. There are stingrays, Germán said, and the way to avoid them is to shuffle your feet through sand or mud rather than step gingerly on the bottom.

The second day Germán piloted us through a maze of islands. Stopping at a dwelling called Soapire, we met a Yekuana family. They were roasting a whole tapir for the year end fiestas. A great deal of yuca had been harvested and flat *casabe* cakes dried. More islands, fast water, the Caura narrowed and at last we pulled up at **El Playón**, a fabulous expanse of beach facing three cataracts. This was the end of the Lower Caura and the beginning of Saltos Pará, an 8km series of falls. From here the Yekuana carry petrol and gear up to a landing on the Upper Caura where they keep other curiaras. I watched as a Sanemá family and eight dogs came down the portage and piled into a curiara. One dog had painfully swollen paws. Six days later I remembered this dog when my inflamed feet showed embedded sand fleas or jiggers (chigoes). Extracting the *nigua* egg sacs was both horrible and fascinating but without side effects.

Exploring hot rocks by foaming water, stripping for a wash, stringing our hammocks in a great fallen tree: El Playón was idyllic. Not one fly or mosquito. Two Indians strolled to the cascades with fishing line and worms. When they returned carrying a pair of 10-pound morocotas, Germán said *'hasta mañana'* hastily and went to share their supper.

In the morning we walked up to the main falls. The well beaten trail, a 7km trek through forest, starts at shelters by El Playon's landing. Half-way, there's a sign for 'Campamento Las Pavas — 3km'; go straight (a boat portage bisects the trail). We were not alone: many Yekuanas were heading to fiestas up at Entre Ríos and Santa María del Erebato (2-3 days by dugout, another drum of petrol).

Pará is a crescent of half a dozen dazzling falls spanning the east arm of the Caura. The waters first plunge about 50m (Niagara's drop is 52m), and dive later over smaller cataracts known as La Bocona halfway to El Playón. A west arm leaves the main flow some 2km above Pará; the two arms join again at El Playón.

Added to the falls was a surprise: **Campamento Las Pavas**, a neat set of cabins in a park-like clearing. Engineers built six houses in about 1975; when they completed feasibility studies for a dam they left the camp in the Yekuanas' charge. A nephew of Germán's showed us around the dispensary and study hall. A visitors' house has spartan bunks at Bs.400 a night. The Yekuanas will help to portage visitors' gear up to the camp. Ask for the name of the camp *encargado* and settle all prices (in Spanish) with him. The Yekuana ask high prices for their basketware and are hard bargainers.

When we got back to El Playón some German tourists were setting up tents. They had left Jabillal that morning. In fact, our return to Maripa the next day was fast, just 8 hours nonstop downstream. After a group photo in Maripa, we swapped our plastic crates for Germán's baskets and turned our backs on the Caura. Making camp by the road, we felt the 'mozzies' home in as the breeze and a yellow/purple sunset died away. Clouds hid the stars and satellites.

"Man and his productions almost disappear amidst the stupendous display of wild and gigantic nature". Alexander von Humboldt.

A traveller's life on the river has not changed much in a hundred years, apart from the important addition of outboard motors.

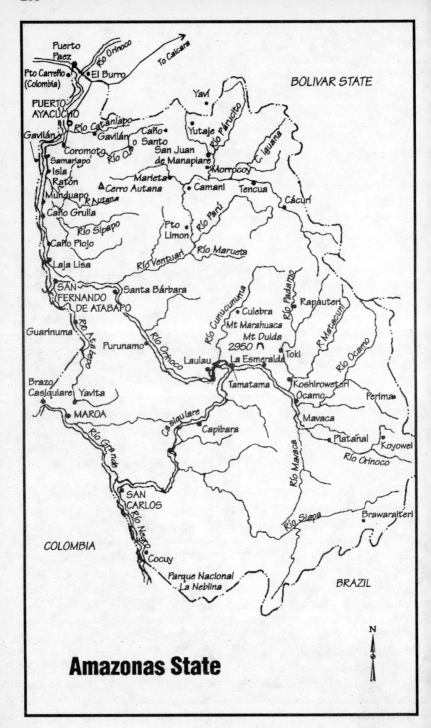

Amazonas State

Chapter 15

Amazonas

With information by Florence Smith, Sandrine Tiller, Marco Crolla

Amazonas was recently declared Venezuela's 22nd state. This territory of 175,750km² extends to 1° from the equator and includes the Orinoco River headwaters. Southern Amazonas was largely undisturbed by white men until gold-seeking *garimpeiros* invaded from Brazil in the 1980s. Despite this, population is still sparse. The principal ethnic groups in Amazonas are the Guahibo, Piaroa, Yekuana (Makiritare), Baniva, Yanomami (Waika) and Sanemá. The Yekuana are noted for their long dugout canoes called *curiaras* or *bongos* and their beautifully designed communal houses (see Chapter 14). These huge conical structures accommodate several families. The Piaroa make baskets, stools, carved animals and now mobiles of birds and butterflies. Their traditional roundhouse or *churuata* is also spectacular: it is like a 100-person seamless hat, 12m tall and thatched from ground to tip.

Venezuelan law requires special permits to visit Indian territory. The creation of an 83,000km² biosphere reserve in 1991 was intended further to restrict travel. However, Catholic missions were established centuries ago. La Esmeralda has a long history of Franciscans who ran a mission in the 18th Century and Salesians who have run a large school and mission since the 1940s. The Salesians also have missions in Colonia Coromoto, Isla Ratón, San Fernando de Atabapo, San Juan de Manapiare and Ocamo. New Tribes missionaries have operated for nearly 50 years from remote airstrips. The evangelist missions of Tama Tama, Padamo and Mavaca are reached by river.

La Esmeralda now has an environmental research station, the Centro Amazónico Alejandro de Humboldt. This is built on the savanna (partly funded by the German government) and is run by SADA, an autonomous service for the Environmental Development of Amazonas. Four national parks in Amazonas cover a total of 53,000km² (mostly on paper): Duida-Marahuaca, Neblina, Yapacana and Parima-Tapirapeco. However, a large section of these parks falls within the new biosphere zone.

PUERTO AYACUCHO

Capital of Amazonas State, Puerto Ayacucho was founded in 1924 where the great Atures and Maipures rapids divide the Orinoco. The lower Orinoco is navigable for 900km to the Atlantic, and the upper Orinoco goes south and east for another 1,160km. The town was built on a conventional plan — the church, mission school, town council and government offices surround Plaza Bolívar. Across the river (here at its deepest, 50m) is Colombia.

All cargo to the upper Orinoco must be trucked 85km around the rapids. Controlling river and air traffic, Puerto Ayacucho is the regional administrative centre. Orinoco barges once brought all the town's fuel, vehicles, beer and cement, while planes supplied perishables. But with the opening of the new road to Caicara, times are changing fast. Today, large numbers of campesinos and Indians, some from Colombia, have moved in from remote areas. About half of Amazonas' 80,000 inhabitants live in Puerto Ayacucho and the city is as full of vendors (and thieves) as a Turkish bazaar.

Puerto Ayacucho (alt. 110 m) receives some of the heaviest rains in the country, almost 2m a year falling mostly between June and October. Depending on when you go, then, the weather will be hot and wet (30°C) or hot and dry (26.5°C).

Before you go

Remember this is a malaria region. Bring insect repellent, mosquito net, spirals. Electricity is variable so always have a flashlight.

Getting there

By plane Aeropostal flies every afternoon, and Avensa every morning and afternoon; both stop at San Fernando de Apure. The airfare is about $45. Taxis from the air terminal, 7km south of town, cost about Bs.150.

Air taxis Air taxi lines such as Wayumi, (048) 21635, calculate flying time at about $175 an hour for a 5-passenger craft, $300 for seven passengers (1993). When estimating costs for flights to jungle camps, add the pilot's return time to Puerto Ayacucho.

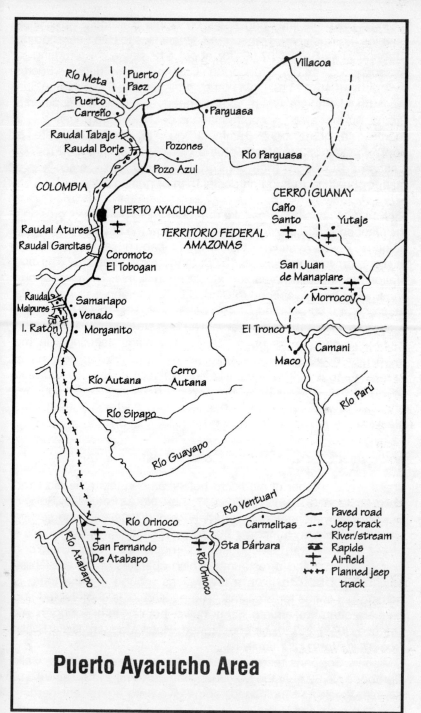

Puerto Ayacucho Area

Single travellers may find seats on flights to remote Amazonas pueblos. For instance, Transporte Camani flies to San Fernando de Atabapo Mon.-Sat. at 07.00, for about $12 single, — returning to Ayacucho at 14.00. Transporte Camani, Av. Orinoco, Puerto Ayacucho, (048) 22418. Light planes charge some $14 a seat to San Juan de Manapiare where Axel Kennedy runs the Campamento Piraña. Further away, accommodations become more primitive — a room in a home or a hammock on the porch. The fare is approximately $32 to Maroa on the Guainía River, and $40 to San Carlos de Rio Negro (one pension with board). It becomes less a matter of getting to such outposts, than of getting *back*.

By bus   Caracas coaches take the route via El Sombrero, crossing the Orinoco at Caicara; from there they follow the beautiful motorway 364km to Puerto Ayacucho. Colectivos Caicabo buses leave Caracas at night, arriving next day at 13.00; the fare is about $15. 'The bus station has a seating area and a cafe open till late. There are 2 bus lines going from Ayacucho to Ciudad Bolívar in about 11 hours. We took one at 8.00 but others leave before and after this. The journey was certainly our most enjoyable. The bus stops at major towns en route and often picks up or drops off Indians seemingly in the middle of nowhere. The scenery is fantastic: vast plains, rocky formations that jut from the plain, like mini tepuis, often surrounded by small areas of picturesque forest. An hour after Caicara we changed buses and could no longer see anything through the blackened windows of the new bus.' (J.M. & M.D.)

Where to stay

There are a number of mediocre hotels, among them the old Gran Hotel Amazonas, (048) 21962/22237, three blocks from Plaza Bolívar. Despite renovations, the government-owned hotel varies in service and food. It has a Humphrey Bogart movie ambience, but there's a newer section with air-conditioned rooms and bar. There's a swimming pool and a restaurant which operates on an availability basis so it's best to have a few rations around in case there is nothing but coffee for breakfast. The parking lot is unprotected and cars are often broken into. Other newer hotels: Hotel Tobogán, Av. Orinoco, (048) 21320, air-conditioned; Hotel Maguari, Calle Evelio Roa 37, (048) 21120, family-run.

Michele Coppens recommends the Residencias Rio Siapa, Calle Carabobo No.39 near the Don Juan cinema, (048) 21138; about $10 double. Small air-conditioned rooms give onto a pleasant garden. She also mentions Residencias Aragüita on a side street opposite, recently enlarged with air-conditioned rooms, simple and reasonable, about $12 double. Both have fenced parking areas. Marco Crolla stayed at the Residencias Internacional, Av. Aguerrevere, (048) 21242; 'comfortable rooms with fan, Bs.500, or less without bathroom; very friendly people'.

Set in large grounds outside Ayacucho, **Calypso Camp** has 60 beds in thatched cottages with room dividers; good mattresses, fan. Bathrooms are in a separate building. The camp is on the road to Samariapo, a 15 minute walk from the airport to the north, 15km from Puerto Ayacucho. Prices cover full board. They have radio but no phone. In Caracas, ring Calypso Tours at (02) 5450024, fax (02) 5413036.

Camturama is a pricey *selva* resort at Garcitas Rapids on the Orinoco, 15km south of Ayacucho. Sixty doubles in air-conditioned thatched bungalows, restaurant, disco, pool. Caracas reservations through ABC Tours, (02) 7828413, fax 7930890; 3 days/2 nights with flight from Caracas and all meals for $240. Hotel Carcitas, a modest jungle resort also on the Orinoco, is opening just next to Camturama.

Permits

A new government body is coordinating activities in Amazonas including tourism. No travel (or mining) is permitted in the Orinoco headwaters region or Alto Orinoco Biosphere Reserve. The Servicio Autónomo para el Desarrollo Ambiental del Amazonas (SADA) has an office in Puerto Ayacucho: MARNR, Av. Los Lirios, via Aeropuerto, (048) 21059. In Caracas SADA occupies the same temporary building as Parques Nacionales on Av. Rómulo Gallegos near Estación de Metro Parque del Este, (02) 4081822, 4081026.

What to see/do

'The artisans' **Mercado** is fantastic. Best time to go for the best selection is 6am on a Friday. You can buy hammocks of any kind and mosquito nets. Delicious fried fish can be had in houses in the town. The señora puts a huge pot of oil to boil in front of her house and you sit outside as her kids bring out the table, fork and beer. Just ask "Dónde venden pescado frito?" The **Museo Etnológico del Amazonas** is very cool, very intelligent and has a good library'. (S.T.)

A good souvenir shop is run by Vicente Barletta: Típico El Cacique, Urb. Andrés Eloy Blanco, (048) 22519. 'Sr. Vicente has been in the tourist business for over 30 years and will bend over backwards to help.' (M.C.)

Excursions

Nearby is the village of Pintado and the immense boulder called **Cerro Pintado** where, like Humboldt, one may view pre-Columbian petroglyphs carved at a seemingly inaccessible height; one is a 150ft serpent. These are difficult to see and a guide is useful. Another attraction in this area is **Parque Tobogán de la Selva** on a side road 35km south. The 'toboggan' is a smooth, steeply inclined rock over which water runs — quite exciting in the rainy season. Picnic tables, shelters; refreshments on weekends. The park gets crowded on holidays (it is possible to camp during the week). Near Tobogán you may visit the Coromoto community of Guahibo Indians.

Tobogán Tours have a lot of experience in day trips by jeep and dugout to nearby petroglyphs, rivers and nature spots, plus longer trips on the Orinoco, sleeping in hammocks. Ask Pepe Jaimes for an English-speaking guide. Address: Av. Río Negro No.14, Puerto Ayacucho, (048) 22138/21700, fax 21600.

The latest in Amazonas adventure is white-water rafting down the **Atures Rapids**, a novel and hair-raising way to court the angels. The expert, Jorge Buzzo, shepherds you through mammoth waves in 15ft rubber rafts of his own design. Luke Tegner and Katharine Lewis recommend Expediciones Aguas Bravas: 'Jorge Buzzo and his wife Claudia own Expediciones Aguas Bravas. For US$30 Jorge takes roller-coaster fans white-water rafting down the rapids of the Orinoco, just south of Puerto Ayacucho. Their rubber raft has been especially built for these waters and is powered by outboard motor. For expert rafters the levels are 3 and 4. It's a good thrill and the advantage of the outboard is that Jorge can return and run any rapid as often as his crew want. The office is on the main avenue towards the airport. You can call them on (048) 21541. Reservations preferred but not obligatory.'

Adventure tours and camps

Marco Crolla reports that 'between holidays, it is very difficult to get a tour (and expensive) unless you have a group of four. You can waste a lot of time and energy looking for responsible outfits. From Puerto Ayacucho a 2 day/1 night trip costs roughly $130, everything provided; 4 days/3 nights, $200 (much more worthwhile). This does not include flight from Caracas. I recommend the Autana Adventures people, (048) 21962, 22237, as very professional. They do trips up the Rio Parguaza to visit Piaroa communities. We camped and slept in hammocks.' Luke Tegner and Katharine Lewis also liked this company: 'It is managed by Henry Mora and Cesar Jaramillo who are both extremely professional and knowledgeable of local lore.

They will arrange trips to suit your agenda.

C. Nacher recommends a trip organised by Javier Cubillos of Internacional Tour, Av. Aguerrevere No.18, Puerto Ayacucho, (048) 21242. 'They offered a very exclusive and spectacular tour through the Orinoco into the Río Tomo in Colombia, and Tupamaro Park, trekking on the savanna to the beautiful tepuis.' The address is the same as the Residencia Internacional.

Tucan in Ayacucho has served as reliable base for many Amazonas expeditions. Bilingual guides lead treks of 2 to 10 days exploring various ecosystems from rivers, rainforests and rock formations to savannas with mauritia palm swamps. Costs, all inclusive from Puerto Ayacucho, run about $65 a day. The lodge has 10 double rooms with bath, near Ayacucho airport. In Caracas, ring Alpi Tour for information on excursions to their Parquaza River camp and lodging at Tucan's hotel not far from the airport (also known as the Genesis), (02) 2831433, fax 2856067. In the fishing season from October to mid-May, 10-day expeditions head for the lower Casiquiare where a converted Brazilian riverboat, the *Voyager III*, is docked. Serious fishermen come for 'the big ones', 5kg peacock bass. Capacity is 8-10 people who pay about $150 daily. From June to September the riverboat may run tourism excursions.

Many distant camps, all reached by light plane, give a real chance to see jungle, rivers, and sometimes Indian cultures in a short time. The fees of such camps cover all activities and food, but not always the flight. **Yutaje** camp, half a dozen cabins on the headwaters of the Manapiare River, has lovely falls, birds, good fishing, fresh water dolphins. Information in Caracas: Amazonair, (02) 2836960, fax 2832627.

The operators of jungle camps such as Camani and Junglaven have formed an association in Puerto Ayacucho called Asoturama, (048) 22122; president Hugo Borrel. **Junglaven/Camani** are located on the Upper Ventuari, 45min by light plane, or 2 days upriver. Excursions are made to Tencua Falls and San Juan de Manapiare. For information on bird watching (268 species) or sport fishing, ring (02) 919587, 915083.

Alechiven, a tourism firm of professionals, keeps a *bongo* (dug-out canoe) stationed on the **Casiquiare Canal**. This may be the far-out traveller's most efficient way of seeing some of **'Humboldt's Route'**, with English-speaking guide. Alechiven maintains shortwave contact with their base in San Carlos de Rio Negro. For fixed departure dates and prices, contact Edith Rogge, Alechiven, Local A-18, Centro Comercial Siglo XXI, La Viña, Valencia; (041) 211828, 212660; fax 217081. Alechiven also has an office in Puerto Ayacucho: Urbanización Monseñor Segundo García, no 2458, opposite Fundacion del Niño.

Brazo Casiquiare flows to the Amazon

The name of Amazonas State is rooted not only in flora and fauna similar to Brazil's. A unique river, the Casiquiare Canal in fact joins the Orinoco and Amazon basins. In Spanish it is called *brazo* or 'arm'. The Brazo Casiquiare leaves the Upper Orinoco and, depending on the season, carries off roughly one fifth of the Orinoco's waters to the Río Negro, an Amazon tributary. The Casiquiare empties near San Carlos de Río Negro (a pueblo with an airstrip and little else). A day's journey farther is the frontier post of San Simón de Cocuy.

In 1800 Alexander von Humboldt and Aime Bonpland started their great inland adventure. With their carriers toting trunks of instruments and boxes for plant and animal collections, they went by mule over the Llanos, by boat to the Orinoco where their dugout was hauled through the Atures and Maipures Rapids. Then with Indians again paddling, they went up the Atabapo to its headwaters. 23 Indians from the mission of Yavita dragged the bongo 11km over to the Guainía's headwaters. Continuing what is today still called 'Humboldt's route', they went down to the Río Negro. Humboldt was at last in a position to prove the existence of the Casiquiare Canal as a link between the Amazon and Orinoco basins. His party paddled from the Río Negro up the waterway linking the two huge river systems which brought them to the Orinoco below La Esmeralda.

The Casiquiare, 320 km long and about as wide as the Rhine, has an evil reputation for year-round clouds of biting midges and mosquitoes. Humboldt and his party were distracted from insect torture only by their floating animal collection: a mischievous toucan, hyacinth macaw, parrots and several other birds, and eight monkeys. Today, travellers using outboard motors can luckily go faster than the insects.

UP THE ORINOCO

South to Samariapo is no problem — there are buses — but to go further you must get a seat on a bongo, and there is no organised service. A river trip is always fascinating; take along food, waterproof, hammock. According to SADA in Caracas, no permits are needed to go up the Orinoco as far as La Esmeralda (beyond this point travel is prohibited). At the *puerto* show your identification to the Guardia Nacional and state that you are an *excursionista* and wish to go only to the next pueblo. **Samariapo** is the embarkation port during high waters and Venado, about 9km beyond, during low water. The road ends at Morganito.

The Cuao and Sipapo tributaries are 1½ hours up the Orinoco. The rivers flow from a dramatic mountain, **Cerro Autana**, rising like a mythical tree trunk to a height of 1,200m. This *tepui*, sacred to the Piaroa Indians, has a cave traversing it near the top. Julian Jaramillo, Av. Amazonas 91, (048) 21369, has led groups up the Sipapo, camping and sleeping in hammocks. His charges are about $50 daily per person. The Piaroas currently discourage tourism on the Sipapo River but this may change.

San Fernando de Atabapo is the next important pueblo up the Orinoco, a day's travel from Samariapo. Here the black waters of the Atabapo River meet the brown Guaviare and lighter Orinoco. San Fernando, founded in 1765 by Capuchin missionaries, was a *balatá* centre in the early 1900s. It will again see rubber exports if and when the CVG plantations mature. Among new facilities today are air service by Transporte Camani and a tourist camp called Campamento Piraña.

Coming from/going to Colombia

From Puerto Ayacucho, bongos and launches take day shoppers across the Orinoco for about $1 to Casuarito on the Colombian side where jewellery and leather goods are well made. The pueblo of Casuarito appears to be built on a single vast rock or *laja*. Formalities are limited to showing your passport.

Drivers can head north of Puerto Ayacucho to El Burro and cross the Orinoco on a ferry-barge to **Puerto Páez**. This small Venezuelan port lies at the junction of the Orinoco with the Meta. It has an army post. On the Colombian side of the Meta is **Puerto Carreño**, a little town with the necessary DAS office to stamp you into the country; it also has a Venezuelan Consulate (you should get stamped out of Venezuela before leaving Puerto Páez). Puerto Carreño is connected to Bogotá by a reasonably good road. There is a twice-weekly air service (Satena). The only hotel is the Samanare, with a genial owner, Jairo Zorro. Restaurant and disco.

Venezuelan drivers go from Puerto Páez to San Fernando de Apure, crossing the Llanos on an unfinished road. This route is not practicable in the rainy season.

The Lancers of the Llanos, who fought the with the Patriots 1811-23. See Box on page 224.

SECTION SIX

THE WEST

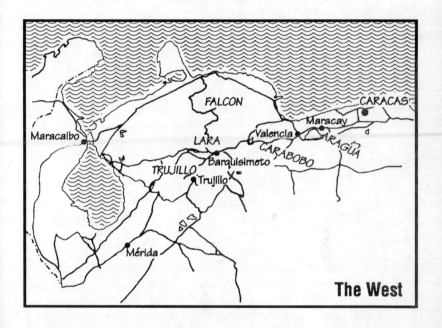

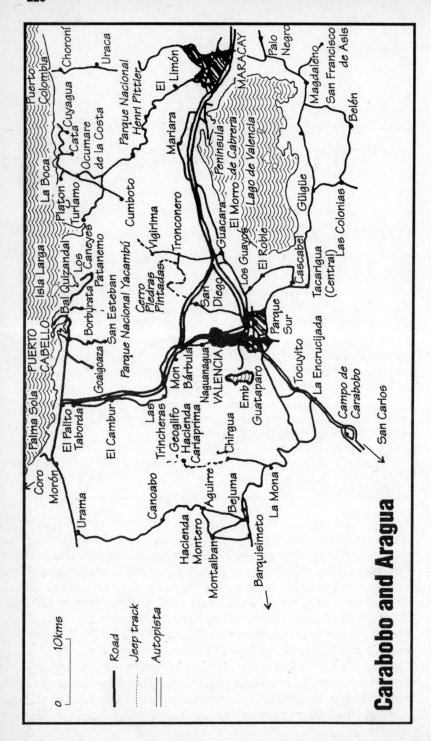

220

Carabobo and Aragua

0   10kms

Road
Jeep track
Autopista

Chapter 16

Aragua and Carabobo

TWO MID-WEST STATES

Traffic courses through the Aragua Valley to Maracay (110km from Caracas) and Valencia (159km), capitals of Aragua and Carabobo States. Between Maracay and the sea, a large tract of mountain wilderness was declared Rancho Grande National Park in 1937 and later renamed Henri Pittier after the naturalist who worked to preserve it from axes and fire. Still threatened by flames every dry season, Venezuela's first national park is an irreplaceable refuge for the animals and birds, trees, ferns and orchids of the Cordillera de la Costa cloud forest. There is less development on the Caribbean side where the crescent bays of Cata, Cuyagua and Choroní have beautiful beaches. Other bays such as Chuao and Cepe have no road and are reached by few outsiders.

ARAGUA STATE
Maracay

Green plantations of sugar cane border the *autopista* to Maracay which is a pleasant city once you get through rings of factories. This is the take-off point for Choroní (NE) and Rancho Grande-Cata (NW). It bears the stamp of dictator Juan Vicente Gómez who turned Maracay into his private 'capital' from 1910 until he died in 1935. Eldest of 13 children of an Andean farmer, Gómez had a Bolívar fixation. He was born on Bolívar's birthday and died on the day of Bolívar's death, having already prepared his family mausoleum in Maracay. He built many government buildings, barracks, bull ring, aviation school (now an aeronautical museum), and the former Hotel Jardín. Gómez, an illiterate, was so tyrannical that his motto of '*Paz y Trabajo*' was taken by many to be 'Peace in the Cemetery and

Work on the Roads'.

A small zoo (closed Mon.) functions in an old Gómez estate in Las Delicias. Its animals, although mostly caged, include a wide variety of Venezuelan species such as capuchin monkeys and capybaras, plus a hippo, elephants, tigers, llamas. A large central lagoon has an island of nesting herons and egrets, and many iguanas, turtles, ducks, pelicans.

Where to stay

Bigger hotels such as the Maracay, (043) 416311, Byblos, (043) 415344, and Pipo Internacional, (043) 412022, have ample facilities including pool. More economic central hotels are the Wladimir, 27 Av. Bolívar Este, (043) 332444, with a good Italian restaurant; the Bermúdez with a busy restaurant opposite Cuartel Páez, (043) 23291; the Micotti, south of Plaza Bolívar, (043) 349087; and the Traini, Calle Prez Almarza Norte at 19 de Abril, (043) 25597.

Buses

The bus terminal is on Av. Constitución at Av. Fuerzas Aéreas, an easy walk from Plaza Bolívar. Buses leave for Ocumare-Cata and Choroní-Puerto Colombia hourly until about 16.00. Some three blocks north of Plaza Bolívar, Las Delicias Avenue veers NE to the cordillera and Choron, passing the Jardín Zoológico, Hotel Maracay entrance, Hotel Pipo's tower and lastly the community of El Castaño.

Choroní

From the guardpost at Parque Nacional Pittier a mountain road spirals up to cool heights then drops to the Caribbean, some 56km in all. Buses take nearly two hours over this hairpin road. It was built by convicts in Gómez' era as an escape to the sea. Today it is an escape from urban chaos into enchanting forests where mists top the ridge and crystal streams splash over fords down the Caribbean slopes. At the bottom in the hot Choroní Valley you can spot red-fruiting cacao under great plantation trees.

Choroní conserves its delightful atmosphere of a colonial village isolated beyond the mountains. Beautifully painted cottages line a long street paralleling the rushing river. There are a couple of abastos selling supplies. The 300-year-old church of Santa Clara on Plaza Bolívar has a mural of saints.

Puerto Colombia faces a pebbly bay, about 2km farther. It is still a small village, although quite active since adopted by a young European crowd. Travellers are now greeted by pensions, restaurants, telephones and even a gasoline station. At night the *malecón* or seafront walk vibrates to song (and a certain amount of drink). In the morning some fishermen haul in nets while others take visitors to solitary beaches such as Cepe or Bahia Bajo Seco for about $20 per boat, round trip. Choroni's fine beach, Playa Grande, is on a lovely crescent bay 5min walk around the rough headland. There are snack bars and a changing room open Fri. to Sun. Hammocks swing from coconut palms. But unsightly rubbish attracts vultures, and the turquoise sea hides a dangerous undertow or *resalue* at the far end. Bathers use the west end.

Lodging

About 5km before reaching Choroní, there is a new hotel, La Gran Posada. Look for the sign to La Planta de Electricidad. It is small, comfortable, in a lovely lush mountain setting. In Caracas, ring (02) 9633985; room fee is about $40. At the entrance to Puerto Colombia is the village's oldest hotel, the Alemania, (043) 911036; 10 rooms with fan, well-run restaurant where dinner costs around $8. A single with breakfast is about $15. The former German owners run the plain, clean Posada Alfonso opposite; $16 double. On the same street, right before the police checkpoint or *alcabala*, is the signless Posada Humboldt, (043) 911050. Owned by a German-American couple, the Humboldt is a quiet, flower-filled enclave in the colonial style; purposely not air-conditioned. Price, about $60 a day, includes all (excellent) meals, juice, beer; must reserve in Caracas, telefax (02) 2847247.

The Club Cotoperix on Av. Morillo is the hotel that launched Choroni's fame with its remodelled colonial houses and all-inclusive package, about $70. You must reserve. In Caracas: Edificio Unión, next to Cine Broadway, Boulevard Sabana Grande, Chacaito, (02) 9528617, fax 9517741. The Cotoperix occupies two charmingly remodelled village houses brimming with plants and hammocks and a third modern house by the waterfront. Some of the 38 double rooms have four-poster beds, some shared bathroom; no TV or air conditioning by policy. The package includes all meals (with local fish, fruits, vegetables, coffee, chocolate), picnics, launch to solitary beaches, excursion in the national park, and often local music at night. Round trip from Caracas by car can be arranged for about $40. Cotoperix is good value and very attractive, although the service is poor.

Hotel La Montañita, Calle Morillo No.6, (043) 911132, is two doors from the sea. Its dozen rooms, run by the friendly Rodriguez family, are pleasant, about $16 double with fan. Breakfast and supper to order. Reservations in Maracay, (043) 832560.

The Hotel Playa Grande's 2nd floor rooms are over the crowded Tasca Bahia, Av. Los Cocos, at the river crossing to Playa Grande, (043) 915410; small, plain, about $10 double with fan and $16 with air-conditioning. On a side street nearby is Hotel Maitin, basic rooms around a dark roofed patio; same rates.

Chuao

Chuao chocolate was long equated in Europe with the world's finest. Today some cacao plantations are being renewed (with Japanese investment). There is a trail from Choroní over the range to the east and down to the old plantation village and bay of Chuao. This is an easy hike in view of the possibility of returning via fishing boat to Puerto Colombia. In colonial times a muleteer's road linked Chuao with Turmero in the Aragua valley and it is still possible to follow this.

Carabobo Battle broke royal power

After a decade of wars for Independence, the battle which put Venezuela's reins firmly in patriot hands began on the morning of 24 June 1821 on the plains of Carabobo. The adversaries were led by a Caracas patrician, Simón Bolívar (aged 36), and a Spanish nobleman, Miguel de la Torre. The two knew each other and had married Spanish girls who were cousins (Bolívar's wife died 8 months after their marriage).

Holding the plains were the Royalists' 5,180 men, half of them Venezuelans. Bolívar summoned his forces: Urdaneta from Coro, Páez (who then was about 25) from the Llanos, Cruz Carrillo from the Andes, in all 6,400 men. Fighting under Páez was the British legion composed of veterans of Napoleonic wars. The Rifles Battalion, led by Arthur Sandes was in the third division.

When Col. Ferrier and his second, James Scott, were wounded, Capt. Charles Minchin took command. The legion's resistance is credited with giving Páez' lancers the opening needed to attack the enemy's rear. At the battle's end Spanish power was broken. Triumph was not complete, however, until the battle of Lake Maracaibo on 24 July 1823, and the battle of Puerto Cabello, 10 November 1823.

Bolívar went on to the distant Andes with Sucre, another young (29) Venezuelan, routing the Spaniards at the battles of Junín and Ayacucho in Peru, 1824. Upper Peru formed its own state, naming it Bolivia in honour of the Liberator, and voted Sucre its president.

The Campo de Carabobo is 32km southwest of Valencia on the route to San Carlos. There is a large monument and Triumphal Arch, a diorama, and several restaurants and souvenir stands nearby.

Hiking
by Paul Rouche

The trail to Chuao

From Choroní there are hourly buses passing the store or *bodega* called El Mamón on the main road out of town. If you wish, ask here for someone to guide you on the first leg (about 45min) up past the community of La Cesiva; beyond, there is no mistaking the single path.

It's 2min from the road, walking east through the cacao plantation, to reach a small iron bridge (*puente de metal*) crossing the Rio Choroní. The trail to La Cesiva first follows the river right to an irrigation canal (right, 10min), passing three small stone bridges. The way is soft and shady, leading to campesino houses, with Quebrada La Rinconada on the left. After dipping, the trail crosses the Rinconada stream, now coming from the right. At a crossroads keep left and shortly there's a steep sandy ascent to the *caserío* of La Cesiva. Ask for the way to 'Sinamaica' in a northeasterly direction. From an elevation of 200m the trail rises in earnest to a fork at 680m (about 45min from La Cesiva). Keep right; the way leads through a coffee plantation, then a banana plantation (this is called a *cambural*) to a point where you can see the Choroní road down to the left. Continue SE to the ridge at 1,000m elevation (about 1¼hr from La Cesiva).

In another 10min the descent begins and you will be able to see the Chuao-Cepe 'road' on the opposite ridge to the east. This side of the mountain is drier; you pass a cultivated plot or *conuco* and come to a house at the place called Sinamaica, 860m. Keeping right at fork below (alt.760m), it's steady downhill trail for an hour along a scrubby, sunny slope. Then the trail enters woods, crossing a stream bed several times, finally following it and descending to a large boulder (left, possible shelter); 15min. The path may be less clear; it parallels the stream bed, crossing and recrossing it and, bearing left, finally crosses the Quebrada Sinamaica, here 5m wide (20min). In the next 6 minutes you cross an irrigation canal three times and reach the clear Chuao River, 10m wide. Pick your way across among the stones, cool your feet. The path will emerge on the entrance road to Chuao, by a small crucifix on the left.

The road to Chuao (25min) is wide, and at times shaded by bamboo; it crosses the river again before reaching the pueblo of Chuao. Like Choroní, Chuao also has its long main street, *abastos*, plaza and old church. But it is set farther from the sea and there is still a 45min march to reach the Puerto de Chuao, 5km. However, the way is cooled by an immense cacao plantation and once you reach the bay, there is a house at the far right selling cold soft drinks. Fishing boats pull into the river mouth. The trip by *peñero* to Choroní takes no more than half an hour, but you should make arrangements early because fishermen do not like to leave after 15.00.

Hike from Chuao to Turmero

This is a 2-day hike with good camping in cool upper forest after a tough tramp uphill. The old trail was once a Spanish road linking the sea with the Aragua Valley. I consider this the most beautiful hike in Aragua State for its magnificent trees, shade and creeks.

Leaving Chuao, you pass the roadside crucifix where the trail joins from Choroní. Shortly after, the red earth road crosses the Tamaira River and starts to rise. From here it is a hard, shadeless walk (1 to 1¼hrs) up to El Paraiso, a *caserío* on denuded slopes at an elevation of 700m. However, the road is unmistakable and wide; the noise of waterfalls down in the Quebrada Maestra (right) follows you some distance.

Once in the sprawling hamlet of El Paraíso, ask for the *camino* ahead (SW) to Hacienda La Azucena where some of the men work at planting and harvesting coffee and bananas. It is a relief when the path enters the old plantation; the gradient is gentler, there is shade and water; the pipe runs to your left. In about ¾hr walking under beautiful canopy you come to the *quebrada* or ravine. Cross the *quebrada* two times; ten minutes later at a fork, take the left hand, going up.

From this point, depending on energy and rest stops, it is 1-1½hrs to the Rio del Medio at 1,100m altitude. The early part is called 'La Esplanada' because it is wide and straight. This leads to forest at 1,030m and continues up and down gently, on a rocky path, reaching La Cueva which is a large overhanging boulder affording possible shelter. Now sunk between steep banks, the path shows its centuries of use as an eroded mule trail. Its general direction is SW. Where the Rio del Medio (6m wide) is joined by another creek on the left there is a possible campsite.

Sometimes overgrown by ferns, the trail continues up for two hours to a spring or *manantial* at 1,800m. There are seven fern patches which you must find your way through to the trail in the woods opposite. After passing the seventh, the path again becomes an open 'tunnel', rising to the Quebrada Hierba Buena, coming from the right. The small gully has a permanent spring which is the *manantial*.

Apparent splits in the trail are not different paths; they join at the top.

Up to the ridge and over to the working hacienda called Portapán will take perhaps another 1½hr. After leaving the spring, within 20-25min the trail reaches 1,930m on the crest. It starts level, then descends. At 1,850m there is an iron cross on the left, not very tall (probably overgrown), at a spot called El Guayabo. The trail slants down to 1,520m at Hacienda Portapán where there is usually a resident caretaker, chickens and dogs.

A jeep track goes from Portapán all the way down to Turmero's outskirts, a walk of almost 2 hours. About half way at 1,460m elevation, a wide path enters from the left — this is the way to PGP Simón Machado. Shortly below is the crossroads for La Mucurita (left, an alternate route to the bottom). There are one or two gates and fences to cross, and good views of Taguaiguay Lagoon and distant Lake Valencia.

Before reaching the paving, the earth track passes an iron gate at the bottom, then a stone quarry, the *cantera*, at an altitude of 530m. From this district, called El Pedregal after the stream coming from the mountain, it is 3km to La Bodega del Chorrito where the Turmero bus stops. Turmero has bus service to Maracay and Cagua.

Parque Nacional Henri Pittier (Rancho Grande)

The main road through the national park leaves from El Limón at the NW outskirts of Maracay, bound for Ocumare and Cata on the sea. In some 20km the road passes the gates of the Rancho Grande Biological Station.

Mary Lou Goodwin, author of *Birding in Venezuela*, has for a great many years travelled widely studying the country's rich bird life, estimated at 1,360 species. Her practical, up-dated report is published by the Sociedad Conservacionista Audubon de Venezuela, Apartado 80450, Caracas 1080A, fax (582) 910716. Here's an excerpt of what she says about the nation's first park, created in 1937 through the efforts of Swiss-born botanist Pittier who loved the high, cool cloud forests in the area known as Rancho Grande. (You may find it wet, too: average humidity 92%, average temperature, 66F.)

'Henri Pittier National Park is world famous among ornithologists for the more than 500 species of birds found in the various life zones... As the Ocumare highway approaches the ridge of the mountain range, you come to the ruins of Rancho Grande in the cloud forest. This is where you may expect to see some of the endemics, include the handsome fruiteater; it is also possible to see harpy eagle (check the sky, especially around 10.00 to noon).

'To let you in on a semi-secret, there are a couple of trails behind the ruins of Rancho Grande itself that make for good birding in the early morning and late afternoon. Around the main grounds you should see blood-eared parakeets as well as white-tipped swift which nest under the balconies. From March through August there are swallow tanagers which nest in holes in the walls. When you tire of looking around the garden area, you will note that on the far side of the building there is an iron staircase. This leads to the trails, but it may be locked. Use your ingenuity. In fact, if the main gate is locked, do the same.

As you go up the trail you will come to a memorial to a young British botany student, Andrew Field, who died from a fall while studying the huge *cucharón* trees of Rancho Grande. Some 150m past this plaque is a trail leading off to the left. This is Guacamayo trail. With luck you should see white-tipped quetzal here, and in the early morning you stand a good chance of sighting helmeted curassow and Venezuelan wood quail.

'Slightly further along the highway leading to the sea there is yet another hidden trail on the left, near the statue to Henri Pittier. Just before you come to the iron gate leading to the trail there is a sign on a curve indicating "portachuelo". This pass, although only some 700m below Guacamayo Peak, is the main flyway for migrating birds and insects.'

Rancho Grande Biological Station

by Chris Sharpe

Rancho Grande lies at the top of a pass in the cloud forest of the Cordillera de la Costa. The park is of great interest to biologists, and especially birders. From the station there are numerous easily followed trails into the forest. The field station is actually atop a derelict hotel built in the early part of this century by the dictator Gómez, but never finished. Some people say that executions took place here — which makes the place downright scary at night.

A four to five day stay is recommended. You will see collared peccaries and agouti, masses of birds, both endemic and migrant (Sept to Oct), and plenty of other fauna, including a dozen species of snakes. For camping, you will need a good rainproof tent, sleeping bag (it gets cold at night), warm clothes, candles, food, etc.

The biological station is managed by the Zoología Agrícola department of the UCV Agronomy School in El Limón, Maracay, headed by Professor Alberto Fernández Badillo, (043) 450153. The station offers researchers bed and kitchen facilities. For permission to stay, you can go to the Facultad de Agronomía, or ring the Sociedad de Amigos Parque Nacional Henri Pittier whose director is Ernesto Fernández Badillo, Alberto's brother. A veterinarian, his office number is (043) 544454; fax Agrovet (043) 25204; messages 453470. The Sociedad Conservacionista Aragua is also most helpful;

(043) 831734. Their library is open from 8.30 to 17.00; Urbanización Caña de Azúcar, Sector 2, Vereda 6, Vía El Limón on the route to the park.

In El Limón there are shops and places to eat. The Audubon people recommend the Panadería near the last traffic light before the divided highway becomes a road, and La Ternera specialising in grilled meat sold by the kilo: *punta trasero*, rump steak; *lomito*, filet mignon; also fried yuca and hot maize *bollos*. You will be tantalised by smells before reaching La Ternera near the main market: turn from Av. El Limón onto Av.Casanova Godoy, then left at the first large intersection.

CARABOBO STATE

Bypassing Lake Valencia which has pollution problems, Carabobo offers travellers a busy capital city, excellent mountain park, petroglyphs, seaport and beaches. The lake, which nearly halved in size during the past two centuries (it is 34km long), is now *growing* disturbingly as water is piped in for industries. The Valencia basin has fossils of animals such as giant sloth, mastodon, primitive horse and the giant crocodile, megasaurus. Excavations have also revealed to archaeologists that the lake shores were thickly settled by Indian tribes.

Valencia

Valencia, in a valley 479m above sea level, is hot and humid. The spreading city of some million inhabitants is an important centre of light industry. At 2¼ hrs from Caracas by the *autopista*, it also makes a good springboard for western and central states. The new bus terminal is in the Centro Big-Low at the city's east entrance. Coaches and *por puestos* leave hourly for Acarigua, Barquisimeto, Maracaibo and Coro.

Valencia was founded in 1553. Streets in the small historic core have names as well as numbers, for example: Avenida 100 is now also called Av. Bolívar (heading north) and Av. Constitución (going south). *Avenidas* run N-S: Avenida 98 is Boyac, Avenida 101 is Daz Moreno, Avenida 103 is Carabobo, Avenida 104 is Soublette; *calles* go E-W, Calle 99 is Pez, Calle 100 is Colombia, Calle 105 is Cedeo.

A few colonial structures have been preserved, notably the Casa Celis, now a museum of art and history; Casa Páez, residence of general and later Venezuelan president José Antonio Páez; the much-remodelled Cathedral dating from 1580; and the Capitol, once a Carmelite convent. Although Valencia boasts a large bullring and a race course, there is little else to detain tourists.

A remarkable exception is the Valencia Aquarium which houses not only fresh water dolphins, but manatees, otters, a terrarium with snakes and a zoo with peccaries, jaguar, puma and crocodile. The piranha's dinnertime attracts attention. The Acuario Juan Manuel Seijas is on Avenida Fernando Figueredo, (041) 579815. From the terminal in Centro Big-Low, buses and *por puestos* go to Avenida Cedeño; ask to be let off at the pedestrian bridge (*pasarela*) leading to the aquarium which is all the way across town. Hours 9.00 to 18.00 daily except Monday; entrance to the aquarium Bs.50, zoo Bs.30. Restaurant. At the terrarium you can buy polyvalent snake serum, about $15, and scorpion serum when available.

Getting there

By plane   Valencia's airport is expanding services to Maiquetía, Barcelona, Canaima, Porlamar and Puerto Ordaz in the east, and Maracaibo, Mérida, San Antonio, in the west. Principal airlines are Aserca, and Zuliana, Avensa and CAVE. There are international flights to Curaçao and Miami.

By Bus   Valencia is served by a classy new line from Caracas, Aeroexpresos Ejectuivos. 'The air-conditioned buses have curtains sewn shut for screening videos, which usually take a little longer than the 2¼ hour ride so you don't get to see the end,' says Edward Paine. Reserved seats on eight daily departures between 6.30 and 19.00; fare about $9. The Caracas terminal is next to Il Foro Romano restaurant on Av. Principal de Bello Campo, (02) 339011, near the east end of Av. Libertador. The Valencia terminal is at Local No. 26, Centro Big Low, (014) 405010.

Where to stay

Services and hotels are topped by the deluxe Inter-Continental Valencia in El Viñedo suburb, (041) 211033, fax 222822. Modest downtown hotels are: the old-style Hotel Caracas, Calle 98 No.100-84, (041) 84646; 30 inexpensive rooms around a patio. Hotel 400, Av. Bolívar No.113-63, (041) 210533, 38 rooms in a converted house. The aging Le Paris, Av. Bolívar No.125, (041) 213291, 100 rooms, a/c, restaurant. The Excelsior, Av. Bolívar at Av. 129-Don Bosco, (041) 214055, 56 simple rooms, a/c. Among the modern tower hotels, more expensive, are: Stauffer, (041) 6700675; Don Pelayo, (041) 579372; and Apart-Hotel Ucaima, (041) 214853.

An English company is opening a colonial farmhouse near Valencia to tourists. The Hacienda Guataparo Guest House will be operating as of late 1993. The birding is good and there are market walking trails, Henri Pittier Park is an hour away, Morrocoy only a bit further, and guests can ride on the farm which is 9,000 hectares in its own valley just 20 minutes from the city centre. There is a lovely natural swimming pool. The house was an old coffee hacienda and there is accommodation for up to eight people. The cost per day for the whole house (irrespective of the number of guests) is $100 (self-catering). Reserations through Last Frontiers (Britain, see page 5). In Valencia phone Haciendas Guataparo (041) 670849.

Vigirima Petroglyphs

A sunny foothill in the mountains north of Guacara is known as the Cerro de Piedras Pintadas. Shallow engravings of figures, hands and mysterious maps (places? stars?) cover dozens of weathered rocks. On the slope behind this knoll rises a wall of upright megaliths. Centuries roll back as you climb the hill and wonder at the prehistoric people who, from here, may have looked over a fuller Tacarigua (now Lake Valencia). Although part of a National Park, the petroglyphs are not signposted or cared for in any way. If you bring food and water this is a beautiful airy camping spot, admittedly rocky, but often solitary. The foothills are hot and grassy, not forested until higher up.

Getting there

Guacara is 13km east of Valencia, quite near the *autopista*. From the Plaza Bolívar of Guacara, follow signs north for Vigirima. In 6km you will see Bodega La Esmeralda on the left. 500m beyond, turn left at Los Tres Samanes, another *bodega* (if you reach Bodega Los Mangos, you've gone too far). This is a broad road leading in about 2km to the shady Tronconero River. Once you have crossed the Tronconero bridge, take a right fork in ½km, passing the Escuela Rural No.49. You are now facing north on a rough jeep track running through maize fields for 1½km towards the hills. There it veers right and in ½km passes between the petroglyph knoll and the megalith hill.

Vigirima Thiis village is on an old coffee hacienda, its river deeply shaded and quiet. The pueblo is 6km beyond the Tronconero turnoff. In the hills behind at a place called Los Apios there is another large *piedra pintada*. With an early start the trail to the Montaña de Mataburro takes a half-day up and down. From Vigirima's traffic circle head north on an earth road; you pass the Vigirima River picnic area and continue along its bank. Watch shortly

Royal Road to San Esteban

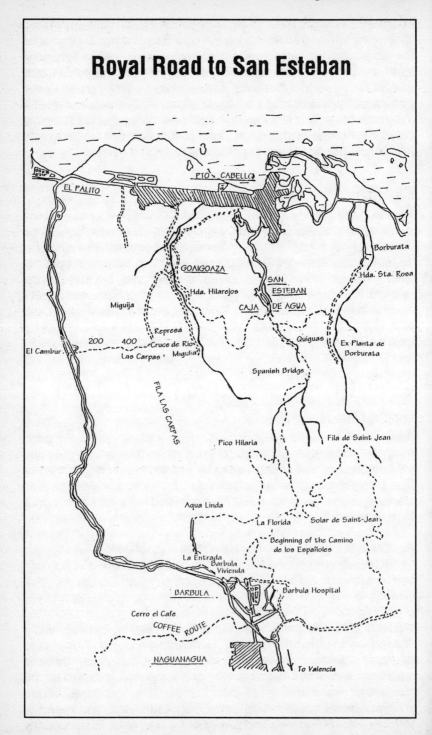

for the first petroglyphs, usually overgrown, by the path opposite a fenced hut with coffee drying patio. If you have chalk you can outline the spiral designs which are not always distinct. When the valley ends, the path narrows and trees give way to sharp edged elephant grass on hot, open (waterless) slopes. Always go N; divided trails should join up. In about an hour's climb, you pass walls of slab rocks like those near the Tronconero; these mark half way. Near the top of Mataburro the petroglyph boulder looms on the right, covered with faces, lizards, animals, perhaps a cat, spirals and designs.

Las Trincheras Hot Springs

The **baños termales** in Las Trincheras, half-way between Valencia and Puerto Cabello (by either the old road or new), attract mud devotees from many parts of the world. Remember Humboldt? He cooked a less-than-4 minute egg here — the mineral waters are HOT. Whether or not you are interested in massages, steam baths or hot swimming pools, the hotel is unpretentious and comfortable, surrounded by gardens with macaws and animals. (Non-guests may also use pools.) A modern annex with restaurant stands by the original Gómez-era building. Hotel Spa Las Trincheras, (041) 669795, has 58 moderate rooms.

San Esteban National Park

Comprising 44,000 hectares, this is one of Venezuela's newest national parks. An old Spanish road, still cobbled in places, crossing this truly lovely part of the central range, rises from the Valencia valley to a pass at 1,380m before dropping down to San Esteban. The area has long been protected as watershed of the tumbling San Esteban River which supplies the seaport of Puerto Cabello with drinking water.

Hiking the Camino Real

by Paul Rouche
Getting there   Although the easiest approach to the Camino Real is from Bárbula, a pueblo north of Valencia, a warning must now be made to avoid the district called Barrio El Hospital. As reported by Norwegian travellers Oyvind and Helen Servan, the bad reputation of *barrio* thieves is based on several hold-ups. As an alternate approach it is possible to bypass this risky entrance, avoiding the *barrio* and water line or *acueducto*. At the end of the 'Bárbula Vivienda' bus line, instead of turning right (east) past the chapel, go left to enter the Urbanización Carilinda by way of La Ruta del Este.

You pass a police post (*puesto de vigilancia*). Then take the second street to the right; where it turns, you leave it, taking a right between two houses. The path very soon goes down to a creek. Cross a wall in the river bed and you are on the right path up. This meets the Camino de los Españoles higher up.

Bárbula—Camino Real—Spanish Bridge—San Esteban

The last stop on the 'Barrio Bárbula—Vivienda' bus route is by an Evangelist chapel. Follow the street to the right of the chapel. It will change into an earth road, make a left/right dog-leg and dip down to cross the narrow Rio Cabriales, here a creek. At the first fork beyond, go up to the right; at the second crossroads (two minutes) go left. There's a water tank on your right; the pipeline runs along the earth road on your left, bringing water from the hills in the north. At the next crossroads, the Camino Real joins from the right. You have walked half an hour.

The Camino Real here is well used by peasants who cultivate coffee in Saint-Jean near the ridge. After the coffee harvest in December, I've seen burros coming down from Saint-Jean loaded with sacks of coffee in a procession which seems to have changed little in 200 years. It's one thing to come down, but going up is a hard haul best begun before the sun gets hot (you feel it by 9.00). With scanty shade, the Spanish road climbs steeply. Near the cool forest at the top, you come to a level clearing known as the 'Solar de Saint-Jean' (altitude 1200m), where a path enters from Saint-Jean on the right. But keep straight on; the Camino Real is now a path. It skirts left of another *solar*, crosses a barbed-wire fence and narrows into a trail flanking the mountain with a precipice on the left.

At last, after winding through a bracken patch, the trail reaches the ridge forest and is joined by paths coming from Pico Hilaria (1,685m) on the left. Keep right; the path improves, leading to a fresh water spring, Agua Fria. The altitude here is 1,380m, highest point on the royal road. The ascent has taken roughly 3 hours (or longer if the heat slows you down).

Now the Camino Real is so wide that you can pitch a tent in the middle. Once over the divide, the path twists down half an hour through cloud forests to another spring, Los Canales, where there are more good campsites. Altitude: 1,220m.

Continuing down for 2 hours beneath lofty forests, the royal road drops nearly 900m to the Spanish bridge. In places, the cobblestones can still be seen on the colonial road; more often, the sandy floor has been eroded 2 to 4m below its original level. Watch out for two tricky forks half way down (do not go right). The pleasant noise of the San Esteban River grows nearer on the right. Suddenly, turning left at a junction of leafy paths, you're standing on top of the

Spanish bridge. But to really see the remarkable Gothic arch, scramble down to the river's edge. Beyond the bridge 50m, a right fork leads to a large flat clearing, good for camping, while the left fork is the true path. Altitude 330m. If you do as I did, you'll make camp up here: the temperature, the water, the forest, are all refreshing.

Next day, walk down the Camino Real until it finally meets the river (¾hr). You'll pass one false fork (keep left), followed by two real ones (go right at the first and left at the second). The river, with its gleaming boulders, crystalline water and umbrella of trees, is idyllic for a dip since you have to take off your shoes to cross it anyway. The path continues (with one left fork) to the old cacao and citrus plantation of Las Quiguas. Altitude 200m.

To steer clear of false trails when leaving the hacienda, keep left of the house where the caretaker family lives, and head northeast through a tangerine grove. Soon you again see the San Esteban River on the right. In 20min walk, the path meets a major junction. Go left, ford the river below a dyke, and you will be on a jeep road built by the waterboard, INOS. This road passes a water treatment plant at the Caja de Agua and, 15 minutes on, a bridge.

Although you soon come to many cottages, this is not San Esteban proper. Keep on between the houses for 10min or so until you find a path to the right which takes you down to a ford across the river. The village of San Esteban is up on the east bank.

Practical Information

Time/difficulty   Although the net 'marching time' for this route is less than 8 hours, in practice the time doubles when you include stops for snacks, birdwatching, rest (you'll want to cool off in the San Esteban River). The Camino Real, presenting no real difficulties, is suitable for a 2-day hike, even for less-experienced walkers.

Weather   Hot. Little shade on the 3-hour ascent from Bárbula. The rainy season is said to be June to November, but be prepared for showers in May, December.

Equipment   Sun hat, insect repellent (a long-sleeved shirt will keep off most midges and mosquitoes), walking shoes.

Maps   The Direccíon de Cartografía Nacional in Caracas sells accurate maps ($2.50). Sheets 6547 and 6647 (1:100,000) cover the Valencia-Puerto Cabello area. (See *Permits & Maps-Chapter 3*.) However, maps of coastlines may be classed *censurada* as involving a national border, thus implying a delay for authorisation.

Permits   We met no parks personnel or Guardias Nacionales, but
if you are camping it is wise to get a permit from Parques Nacionales
in Caracas.

Puerto Cabello

San Esteban is 8km from Puerto Cabello but seems a world apart.
The old village, shaded by splendid trees, retains a tattered
elegance from the turn of the century when Puerto Cabello's high
society built fine estates by its cool river. Long before this, pre-
Columbian tribes also lived by the river and cut many petroglyphs
on a house-sized boulder. Ask a youngster to put you on the path
to the *Piedra del Indio*; it's on the east bank 10 minutes beyond the
village. Today, nostalgia is banished by weekend motorcyclists and
parties of bathers who arrive with canned *salsa* music and beer.

In colonial times goods were transported from Puerto Cabello by
way of the cobbled Camino Real (royal road) to Valencia. The 2-3hr
ascent to the arched Puente de Paso Hondo is a beautiful hike with
a rushing river, luxuriant vegetation and fine campsites. In the late
dry season, April/May, the loud 'kong, kong' of the bearded bellbird
(*Procnias canobarba*) reverberates at elevations between 300 and
800m. The bellbird, which clangs more like an anvil stroke, is the
forest ventriloquist. You have to be very sharp to spot these birds in
the high canopy.

Puerto Cabello is a naval base and the principal port for industries
in Valencia, Maracay and Barquisimeto. The town began life in the
16th Century as a smuggler's anchorage. Venezuela's famous
cacao, traded illegally to Curacao instead of Spain, was grown on
lush plantations bordering small rivers such as the San Esteban. In
the port's untidy sprawl today, travellers will see nothing of such
cacao, or of the coffee, cotton and indigo on which Puerto Cabello
thrived a century ago. But a few colonial buildings, including the
blue balconied Museo de Historia, have been preserved on the Calle
de Los Lanceros, a block from the seafront. These, and the colonial
fort of San Felipe, used as a prison until the death of dictator Juan
Vicente Gómez in 1935 (when 14 tons of chains and leg irons were
dumped into the bay), are worth a visit. The Navy runs free launches
across the channel to the fort. Another colonial fort, Fortín Solano,
commands the whole port from a hill behind Puerto Cabello.

More popular are the sandy beaches of Quizandal and Patanemo
Bay, 3km and 12km east of Puerto Cabello. Isla Larga, where two
sunken freighters make a coral playground for snorkellers, is 15
minutes by *lancha* from Quizandal. Ferrymen charge about $1.50
round trip. The coast road ends in Patanemo.

Where to stay

La Churuata, this area's only beach resort, is in Patanemo. La Churuata advertises a package including all food, beach, pool, jacuzzi, river, launch to more distant strands, drum fiesta and beach bonfire for about $70 a day; Caracas reservations (02) 9878198, fax 9875916. The seaside Cumboto Hotel, (042) 69362, west of Puerto Cabello, has a salt-water pool (the sea is contaminated); restaurant, 74 aging rooms, with and without a/c, about $20 single. The Suites Caribe, (042) 615556, is a business hotel on the main street near the airport; 42 a/c rooms.

One of the best *criollo* restaurants for lunch (in the country, according to some) is the popular Briceñoven on the seafront Malecón in Puerto Cabello, near Plaza El Aguila. Fresh fish, pork, goat, Falcón cheese are served until 14.30; fruit juices and arepas until 21.30.

Railway

There is train service from Puerto Cabello to Barquisimeto and Acarigua. Venezuela's only passenger train covers the 175km in some nine stops and six hours, traversing Yaracuy State. The terminal is on Avenida La Paz, (042) 271214. Service to Acarigua leaves Puerto Cabello at 7.30 and 15.00, Mon.-Fri., changing in Yaritagua for Barquisimeto. On weekends the train goes through to Barquisimeto, leaving Morón at 6.30 and 16.30.

"The day is bound to come when all forest country free from inundation will be inhabited by civilized folk, and the whistle of the locomotive and the drone of the aeroplane will be heard where previously the myriad voices of insects were the only sound." Colonel P. H. Fawcett (1907).

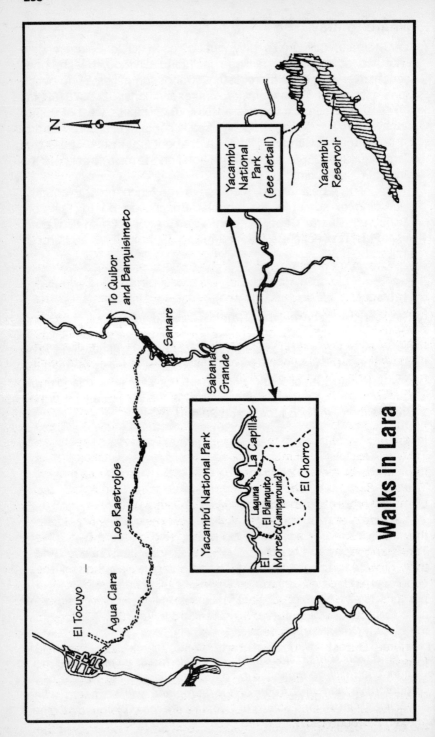

Walks in Lara

Chapter 17

Lara

BARQUISIMETO

Barquisimeto (population about 750,000) is the capital of Lara State. A busy trading and agricultural centre, Barquisimeto is on several main routes: to Maracaibo, to the Andes and Colombia via the Panamericana, to Acarigua and the western plains, to Coro in the north, and to San Felipe, Valencia and points east. The airport, 15 minutes from downtown Barquisimeto, has national flights to seven cities and international service to Miami and Curaçao. And a small railway runs 175km to Puerto Cabello.

Dotted with shady parks, Barquisimeto's centre is clean and well-kept. Streets are laid out on a Spanish pattern of *calles* which run north-south, and *carreras* going east-west. First settled in 1552, the infant town went through three moves before its present site by the Turbio River (alt. 566m). Because the city was shaken to its foundations by the 1812 earthquake, few Spanish structures remain. Today's *Barquisimetanos* prefer to go modern. Check out the Cathedral whose parabolic roof curves up like a crown.

The people of Lara are practical, lively and open. They are doers: they make instruments and play them, they sing in choirs, dance the Tamunangue, weave blankets, make pots, furniture, cheese. And they grow a great variety of fruits and vegetables: half of the country's pineapples, onions, tomatoes; a third of its sugar. Most produce is sold through a giant wholesale centre in Barquisimeto called Mercabar which covers 10 acres and moves 700,000 tons of food yearly, fresh and processed.

Andrea Bullock, who used Barquisimeto as a base, sent the following information. 'It is an easy town to get around — most streets are one way, constructed on a grid system, and buses go down one street and up the parallel one.

'Taxi drivers are friendly but have a tendency to over charge. On the trip to the airport, which I made several times, I never paid the same fare. It varied from Bs. 80 to 200. Get some idea of the current rate and agree the price before you get in.'

Lodging

Hotel Principe: Calle 23 between 18 and 19, tel. (051) 312111 or 312544. Rooms cost from $9 for an individual with ensuite bath, very clean with a reasonable restaurant and a swimming pool.

Hotel Bonifran: Carrera 19 and Calle 31, tel. (051) 316809 or 317509. Rooms from $7. Will put extra beds in room if necessary. Restaurant.

Hotel Florida: Carrera 19 No 31-51 between Calles 31 and 32, tel. (051) 24531. Rooms from $2.50 for single, $4 for double. Excellent food. Basic, but decent/clean accommodation.

Hotel Savoy: Carrera 18, between Calle 21 and 22. Rooms from $3.

Food

Carlos: An excellent *arepera* on the corner of Carrera 19 and Calle 29. Open late into the night. There is a cafe with tables in the street as well as a sit-down restaurant (inside). You can get an *arepa* and a drink (coffee) for 60p.

Reo Mar Restaurant: On the corner of Carrera 17 and Calle 17. Excellent seafood restaurant run by a Spanish family. Very friendly service. The people from around Barquisimeto come here for Sunday lunch. This is slightly more expensive than most restaurants but still excellent value for money. A meal for two with starters and main course and coffee and beer cost $5.00.

Restaurant Basil: This restaurant is in the back streets of Old Barquisimeto on Calle 19 between Carreras 22 and 23. Tel. 312706. The speciality is Arabian food and the price is very reasonable. The locals come here for lunch during the week. A meal for two with salad, entrees and drinks cost $2.15.

Hotel Hilton: The Hilton is the centre for Barquisimeto families who bring the children here to swim on weekends. The decor is clean and new and the room cost is from $15 per person. There is a swimming pool and sports club. The restaurant is excellent (though a bit pricey) and some of the waiting staff speak English. There is also a cashier who will change dollars at the bank rate.

CARORA

Lara's second city is in the central part of the state. The land is parched and many hills are fiercely eroded. Goats scramble up gullies by the road. Yet there are surprises. Dairymen here have bred a strain of Carora cows tough enough to thrive among the thorns (ask for 'Carora fuerte' cheese). A recent source of pride is wine produced by the Pomar cellars (Polar and Martell) from grapes grown on arid slopes around Carora. The old town centre has rewards for photographers: several blocks of beautifully restored houses line spotless streets with patterned tiles. There are two motels on Av. Miranda: the Madre Vieja, (052) 32912, with good restaurant, and the Complejo Turístico Katuca, (052) 32602, in a noisy shopping centre.

Other towns

South and west of Barquisimeto are intensely cultivated valleys, cool premontane slopes and unspoilt old towns. Coffee, potatoes, avocados, onions, papaya, pineapples, guavas, mangos, flowers and ornamental plants are grown around **Quíbor**, **Sanare**, **Cubiro** and **El Tocuyo**. In these towns there are modest inns: Posada Colonial, Av. Fraternidad and Carrera 8, El Tocuyo, (053) 62404, 24 rooms, restaurant, pool; Posadas Turísticas El Cerrito, Sanare, (053) 49091, 15 rooms in family homes, restaurant; Posada Los Sauces, Sanare, (053) 49219; Centro Turístico Cubiro, (051) 23985, 3 mountain cabins, 10 rooms, good restaurant.

El Tocuyo is one of the oldest towns on the continent (1545) and was provincial capital of Venezuela from 1547 to 1577. The first sugarcane in Venezuela was planted in El Tocuyo, and it is still the big crop. Long ago the town was reached by boat up the Tocuyo River all the way from the coast near Chichiriviche, so that it was a natural launching point for Spanish expeditions. The founder of Caracas, Diego de Losada, previously founded Cubiro; he retired and was buried there. Sadly, an earthquake in 1950 destroyed nearly all El Tocuyo's old churches and fine colonial buildings. For its Spanish history and much older Indian cultures, visit the Museo Arquelógico JM Cruxent in the Gobernación on Plaza Bolívar, west side, and the Museo Lisandro Alvarado on Calle 17.

Terepaima and Yacambú national parks

In striking contrast to Lara's arid regions, primary forest survives in the state's southeast where two national parks have been formed in an attempt to halt destruction and protect watersheds: Terepaima, 169km², and Yacambú, 145km². Terepaima is the lower and hotter, dropping from 1,175m to some 300m at the Sarare River. The forest here covers a third of the park only, the rest being savanna and old fields. Although animal life is severely depleted, this area is home to the ocelot and puma, deer, armadillo, agouti, opossum, monkey, kinkajou, tamandua and climbing porcupine (most of which were hunted and eaten). Turning the tables, snakes such as rattlers and corals, and ants including the infamous army ants, are feared.

The tip of Terepaima Park is half an hour from Barquisimeto by road. Old earth roads climb up from Cabudare to Terepaima village providing splendid views; the Camino Real to Río Guache Seco and Caserío Los Aposentos crosses an area of pre-Columbian burial sites. Cartography map No. 6245 covers the park. For more information (until we can make a report), check with the Inparques officer in Barquisimeto: Instituto Nacional de Parques, Parque JM Ochoa Pile, Av. Libertador opposite Complejo Ferial; (051) 530499, 512665.

In Yacambú, mountains rise to 2,200m along an Andean spur called the Sierra de Portuguesa. Flora typical of the Andes mixes with plants from the coastal cordillera and rare palms, tree ferns and local cloud forest species. Some plants grow nowhere else (such as the lovely *Fuchsia tillettii*). Rains from April to November feed rivers such as the Yacambú. The Yacambú Reservoir provides irrigation for Quíbor Valley and water for Barquisimeto.

Birding

In her travels tracking the birds of Venezuela, Mary Lou Goodwin reports that Yacambú has 'what I consider to be one of the best birding roads north of the Orinoco River...wherever you stop on this road you will find birds, but my favourite spot is the lagoon. In one short day I sighted 68 species while leisurely walking this road.' Her list includes oropendula, oriole, warbler, four wrens, eleven tanagers, antpitta, redstart, parakeet, hummingbird, toucanet....

Your starting point is Sanare, southwest of Barquisimeto, passing Quíbor. 'Sanare is another of the long, narrow towns you will have to drive all the way through.' To reach the hotel recommended by Mary Lou: 'after passing Plaza Bolívar, turn right and pass the bar-restaurant Yacambú (which is the best place in town to eat). Turn left at the next corner and left again, and you will be in front of Posada El Cerrito. This is a very modest but perfectly adequate hotel.'

From Sanare, Paul Rouche has walked along the Camino Real or old Spanish road to El Tocuyo. Today this is a questionable jeep track of some 22km, via the old and today quite dry villages of Yay and Agua Clara. His notes on a short circuit in Yacambú follow.

Hiking to Rio Negro Canyon in Yacambú

by Paul Rouche

The Yacambú National Park is little known to walkers although it has a pleasant climate, beautiful cloud forest down to about 850m, and a relatively easy trail to the Río Negro canyon. This route descending by way of Quebrada El Chorro takes 6 hours walking time, there and back (not counting a splash at the bottom). There is an excellent campground at Laguna El Blanquito at the start: picnic shelters, panorama, elegant willows and eucalyptus trees.

From Sanare (leaving town near Posada Los Sauces, a well-known inn), a paved road runs to Yacambú, continuing through the park to a *mirador* or lookout above the reservoir (30km). The entrance to Laguna El Blanquito campsite is well before this; stop at 21km and walk half a kilometre from the main road. A jeep service provides transportation from Sanare.

The earth road to Laguna El Blanquito (altitude 1,400m) is the start of the walk. However, do not enter the camp, but take the left fork. You pass a house, an old white-washed chapel, La Capilla (the track skirts the belltower), and a great millstone. Continue on, crossing two water pipes and a fence. Just beyond a huge boulder with two crucifixes is the junction of a circle trail returning NW to the highway via El Moreco. Keep left. Walking time to this junction is about 45 minutes.

The path descends past a *rancho* (alt. 1,350m). In 10 minutes you cross Quebrada El Chorro, here a small creek; 15min downhill the creek is larger (alt. 1,100m). You cross again (for the last time), and bear left. Go straight (right hand) at a fork (left for Quebrada El Chorro, 15min). Almost immediately, there is another fork: go left (right, 2min up to a peasant hut called Rancho El Chorro which has an impressive view over the Río Negro).

The descent from here takes 35min to the bed of the Río Negro. Cross a fence, then take a right fork. The trail, easy through forest, becomes overgrown at a large clearing invaded by bracken; bear SE (a path comes in from Rancho El Chorro on the right); alt.950m. Just before reaching the bottom, the path crosses a fence into a *conuco* or maize plot, to emerge at the lower right. Go left for the Río Negro; alt. 770m. Before exploring the rocky canyon mark your trail from the *conuco*. The Río Negro, when I saw it in the month of June, was a torrent. There were no pools for swimming, but we explored downstream. In 10 minutes, the canyon narrowed suddenly from 100m in width to 50m, and the river appeared to rush into a dark cave.

On the return up, you may wish to take the west route for El main path always going up, bearing left where small trails enter. You cross the little Quebrada Negra about a third of the way up. At the fourth fork (5 minutes before a wide earth road), take a right (the first), through a coffee plantation. This way brings you in less than an hour to the asphalt highway at El Moreco, 1.9km west of El Blanquito campsite (about 19km from Sanare).

Chapter 18

The Andes

PÁRAMOS AND PEAKS

This fine mountain range is a very popular hiking area showing some of the country's best aspects: charming mountain villages, friendly *campesinos* and well maintained trails. The world's highest cablecar (*teleférico*) runs to Pico Espejo, only 242m below Venezuela's highest mountain, Pico Bolívar, 5,007m. The *teleférico* can save backpackers a lot of climbing, but it deprives them of gradual acclimatisation and the beautiful path winding up the mountain below the cables.

Glaciers at one time covered the entire Mérida Valley while tongues of ice reached over to Timotes and Santo Domingo. Leftovers from this last ice age are V-shaped valleys, dark lagoons and glacier remnants such as Timoncitos (which is said to be shrinking due to climate changes). Many high-country streams are stocked with trout.

TRUJILLO STATE

Trujillo State is on the northeastern approach to the Andes within easy distance of Barquisimeto. Many country roads wind over hills cultivated with coffee and pineapple to old farming villages such as Burbusay, Santa Ana, San Miguel and Niquitao. They are worth seeing. Called the 'garden of Venezuela', Bocono, 1,256m high, has pleasantly rural hotels. Flowers and vegetables grow well as farmers rely on two rainy seasons: April-June and August-November.

Trujillo

The state capital was one of Venezuela's first settlements, founded in 1557 and moved seven times before its final site in 1572. It is

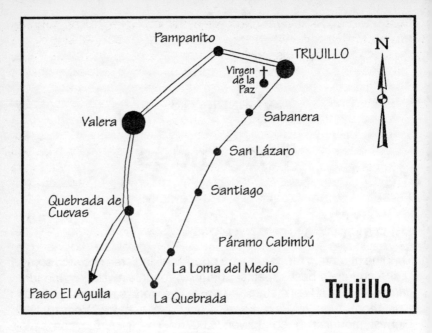

Pampanito

TRUJILLO

Virgen de la Paz

Valera

Sabanera

San Lázaro

Quebrada de Cuevas

Santiago

Páramo Cabimbú

La Loma del Medio

Paso El Aguila

La Quebrada

Trujillo

called Trujillo after the Spanish birthplace of Diego Garcia de Paredes, a conquistador who came to Venezuela from the Mexican and Peruvian conquests where he seconded Cortés and Pizarro.

At 800m altitude, Trujillo is warm, unhurried and provincial. Trujillo is not a commercial centre like its rival Valera. Two long streets lead up (Av. Independencia) and down (Av. Bolívar) the narrow valley, with Plaza Bolívar in between. You can see its colonial past in low houses and the restored 17th Century cathedral. The Centro de Historia occupies an old house two blocks above Plaza Bolívar, displaying arms, antiques and mementos of the Independence campaign. Bolívar vowed here to kill all enemies of the revolution. Next door is the Museum of Popular Art. The state is home to many self-taught potters, weavers and carvers; the museum organises a big Popular Arts event in November (on even years).

Hotels in Trujillo and Valera

Reservations may be needed for the Hotel Trujillo, (072) 33576, top end Av. Independencia, as it is pleasant, well-maintained; 32 rooms on two storeys, restaurant, bar, large pool, about $30 double. There is a park along the river in front. On a nearby side street, the Hotel La Paz, (072) 34864, has 26 large clean suites with refrigerator (no kitchen), about $20 double. People eat at the adjacent Mesón de los Cuñaos. Among economical lodgings not recently checked are: Posada Valle de Los Mucas, Av. Bolívar, (072) 33148; 8 simple rooms around a courtyard with dining tables; Hotel Palace, opposite Centro de Historia, Av. Independencia, (072) 31936, $8 single.

As Carvajal airport is closer to Valera, 7km, than to Trujillo, 22km, travellers may want to stay in commercial Valera. Hotels are busiest during the week. The Hotel Flamingo Palace, La Hoyada, (071) 41063, is nearest the airport; 30 motel-like rooms, restaurant, bar; around $30 double. The Camino Real, Av. Independencia, (071) 53795, has top rates at over $40 double. Motel Valera, Calle 2 near the Pepsi Cola depot, (071) 57511, is plain and reasonable, 143 rooms at about $20 double; sidewalk restaurant. The Albergue Turistico Valera, No 5 Av. Independencia behind the Ateneo, (071) 56997, has 19 rooms which have seen better days.

Virgen de la Paz From the top end of Trujillo, continue past the Hotel Trujillo and the Universidad de Los Andes' branch campus. Atop a hill of 1,400m elevation you see the now famous landmark of the Virgen de La Paz. Reached by a marked access road some kilometres further, the concrete monument has internal stairs for those who want a view from the Virgin's eye. At 46m, she's as tall as the Statue of Liberty and it is said you can see as far as Lake Maracaibo.

San Lázaro to Páramo Cabimbú

At this point a small country road, excellent for hikers or bus passengers, leaves Trujillo for two fine old villages, San Lázaro and Santiago. By continuing up an earth road over the Páramo de Cabimbú and down to La Quebrada, this route can bring you back to busy Valera (82km total).

The road winds through shady plantations to Sabaneta, 22km, where people go to eat Trujillo-style roast chicken and large arepas with fresh cheese. San Lázaro, 8km further, is built practically atop the San Jacinto, a mountain stream. After floods in 1987 many houses were photogenically restored and the entire village was painted white and blue from top to bottom. The people are very proud of their 355-year-old village. There is a state-run inn, the Posada Turística San Lázaro, (071) 82101, which has four plain inexpensive rooms (no hot water) in a handsome colonial house. Meals are served on order by a neighbour up the street.

Santiago, 6 km on, at the end of the paved road, is worth a stop. (A *posada* or small hotel is planned.) On the corner of Plaza Bolívar is Manuel Contreras' curio shop; you can buy a carving, or an old pot or machete. Santiago celebrates its *fiestas patronales*, like Caracas, on July 25 in honour of St. James. The road degenerates to rough earth. Trees give way to irrigated slopes and, higher, bean and potato patches are ploughed by oxen. Above this level are blackberry brambles, cow pastures and very few dwellings. In 12km, *poco a poco* the road reaches the crest and a ridge called Loma del Medio at about 2,000m elevation. The Páramo Cabimbú, somewhat higher, is to the east. To the west, the view sweeps over the Motatán Valley as far as distant Pico del Aguila.

At Loma del Medio there is a family-run *posada*, the Nidal de Nubes, with capacity for 30. 'Clouds nest' is an apt name for the ridge-hugging inn. Infant clouds puff up the abyss as hikers watch from the terrace. Big appetites are matched by hot wheat arepas and homemade jam, eggs, coffee. Señora Marita, a Hungarian, and her family built the inn, which charges about $30 a day with breakfast and dinner. They offer excursions by horse or bicycle to the *páramo*, where local sculptor Víctor González has a 'museum'. The correct telephone technique for reservations is to dial (071) 58055 and repeat '*Posada—Posada*'.

Now downhill, the road continues 11km to La Quebrada, where there is a *posada* run by María Atocha Avila. La Quebrada has an imposing twin-towered church. From this village the road is asphalted down to Quebrada de Cuevas, 9km, junction for the main Valera-Timotes highway. There remain 12km back to Valera. Alternatively, the highway SW takes you to Mérida on the Trans Andean route.

Jajó

Continuing 12km up the road to Timotes there is a left turn for Jajó (1,796m), a lovely old (1662) village hidden many curves away from modern Venezuela. It's set in a terraced valley of farms, flowers and eucalyptus. There is good hiking over a solitary páramo road to Tuñame where the rough *camino* leads on to Niquitao and eventually Boconó (about 80km from Jajó). There are many small hotels in Boconó, a mountain farming centre. The Tuñame-Las Mesitas section was a dry-weather track when I was there.

Jajó has simple white houses with red roofs, picturesque cobbled streets curving down to the plaza and church, and a dignified air. The Hotel Turístico Jajó on the plaza, (071) 57581, has good plain rooms, low prices. Peace and quiet are broken during the feast day of the patron saint, San Pedro, when locals celebrate with processions and traditional dances such as the Sebucán on June 29 and preceding days.

Astrophysical Observatory   At 3,600m altitude in the Sierra del Norte, the 3-domed observatory has four telescopes and a library (open for consultation). Situated near Llano El Hato, perhaps the highest town in Venezuela (north-east of Mérida, on the road to Barinas), the centre (called CIDA) is reached by a bumpy fork west of the Transandina, 3km above Apartaderos. The observatory, (074) 791893, is normally open to the public only on the 3rd or 4th Saturday of the month at 19.00, Bs.50. During school holidays, Easter week, and late July to early September, guided tours at: 10.30, 14.00, 15.30, 19.00 and 22.00.

Condors fly again over Mérida

Five Andean condors have been donated to Venezuela by the San Diego zoo in California. Now living on the Páramo del Buitre in the Parque Nacional Sierra de La Culata, they are Mérida's first condors since the early part of the century. The programme to reintroduce condors, twelve in all, is supported not only by the National Parks Institute and environmental groups but by the Banco Andino. The idea is to use a biological station in Mifafi for captive breeding and then release the young in the wild. Meanwhile the first adults, three females and two males, are adapting to their new home. Also planned is a breeding programme for the endangered spectacled bear. There is to be a visitors' centre in Mifafi.

Some condors were sighted in 1976 but were thought to have come from Colombia. With a wingspan of 3m, these scavengers are the largest flying birds in the world, with a range of 150km.

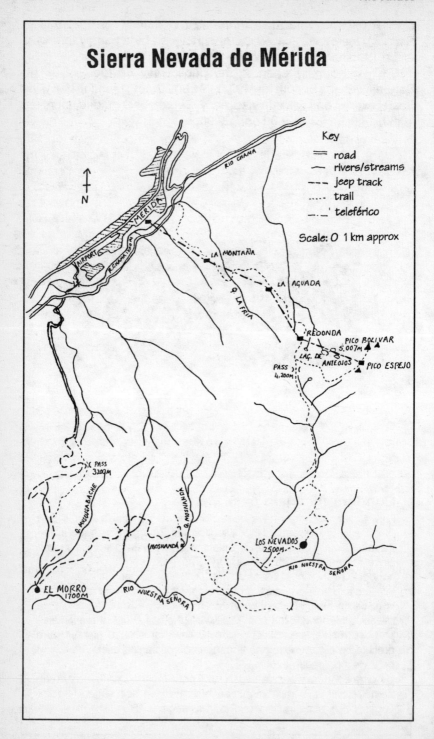

Sierra Nevada de Mérida

Key
≡ road
— rivers/streams
–– jeep track
⋯ trail
·–· teleférico

Scale: O 1 km approx

N

RIO CHAMA

MERIDA

AIRPORT

Q. CHAMA 1200

LA MONTAÑA

LA AGUADA

Q. LA FRIA

REDONDA

PICO BOLIVAR
5,007M

LAG. DE

ANTEOJOS

PICO ESPEJO

PASS
4,200M

PASS
3200M

Q. MUCUJUN-ACHE

Q. MOSNANDÁ

(MOSNANDÁ)

LOS NEVADOS
2500M

RIO NUESTRA SEÑORA

EL MORRO
1700M

RIO NUESTRA SEÑORA

SIERRA NEVADA DE MÉRIDA

The highest Andean peaks rise south of Mérida's state capital. The chain culminates in Pico Bolívar (a bronze bust of the Liberator sits up there). In a cluster to the east are La Concha (the Shell), also known as La Garza (the Heron), 4,922m; and La Corona or Crown whose two peaks, 4,942m and 4,883m, honour a pair of 19th Century naturalists, Humboldt and Bonpland, who never saw the Sierra Nevada. Continuing east is the Sierra de Santo Domingo where the massif of Mucuñuque reaches 4,672m. Directly west of Pico Bolívar is Pico Espejo (Mirror), 4,765m, served by the world's highest cablecar system. Also to the west are El Toro (the Bull), 4,755m, and El León (the Lion), 4,740m.

These peaks form the spine of the Sierra Nevada National Park. The park covers 2,760km² in Mérida State and down to some 600m elevation in Barinas State. The less freqented Barinas slopes still have some undisturbed cloud forests with deer, coatis, agoutis, porcupines, pumas and even monkeys. Ornithologists have spotted the rare Andean cock-of-the-rock near cascading brooks, as well as crested quetzals, nightjars, cotingas and collared jays.

Sierra La Culata

Opposite the Sierra Nevada is a parallel and slightly lower chain called La Sierra del Norte or La Culata (the 'butt' or rear because from Lake Maracaibo it is seen as a backdrop). Its high páramos are Piédras Blancas, 4,762m; Tucaní, 4,400m; La Culata, 4,290m; and Los Conejos, about 4,200m. In 1989 2,000km² of this northern range were declared a national park in an effort to halt degradation of habitat. The park stretches from near Timotes in the east to La Azulita in the west.

In its varied ecosystems live many endangered species. The condor has vanished and the spectacled bear (*Tremarctos ornatus*) may follow if not protected. A park study by Bioma listed 59 mammal species and 61 reptiles and amphibians, including 9 endemic frogs and toads. The park is also known for its endemic flora, particularly *frailejón* species. These plants range from ground-hugging velvety crowns to centuries-old trunks with tufted tops whose silhouettes reminded Spaniards of a procession of friars or *frailes*.

The Páramo — a high altitude garden

The páramos range from about 3,000m up to 4,300m (above this, the almost barren scree is called desert páramo). Like moors, páramos are open, windswept and largely treeless. To many plant lovers the best time to see the Andes is October to December when the páramos are in bloom. Bees, butterflies and even hummingbirds help to weave a bright floral tapestry. Insect pollination may seem a bit chancy at 4,000m, so perhaps the spectacular profusion of colours is a kind of overcompensation. One botanist compares the Andean páramos with the rhododendron belt of the Himalayas.

Some of our Andean flowers prized in Europe are the calceolaria with its yellow pouched blooms, nasturtiums, quilted-leaved gesnerias, asters, clematis, saxifrage, gentian, salvia and befaria. Lower down are beautiful begonias, fuchsias and heliconias. Dotting the páramos are violet or yellow *tabacotes* (*Senecio sp.*), blue lupins (*Lupinus meridanus*) or *chochos*; white páramo chicory (*Hypochoeris*), yellow *huesito* shrubs (*Hypericum laricifolium*), red 'Spanish flag' (*Castilleja fissifolia*) related to the Indian paintbrush, and pale lobelias called *avenita*.

The contrasts of summer-by-day and winter-by-night require special adaptation. Some plants must resist not only sub-zero temperatures and wind but radiation so intense that moisture is sucked up, stunting growth. Many species grow in rosette or cushion form as protection. With short stems and tough roots, other plants have specially adapted leaves, thick and hard-skinned, waxy or furry. The best example is the velvety *frailejón* (*Espeletia*), 'rabbit ears' to children, found everywhere on the páramo. Wool on the leaves seems to protect the *frailejónes* against ice, sun and evaporation. Most species have rosettes of soft, silvery leaves and heads of yellow flowers. This daisy relative has 65 endemic species in Venezuela and botanists think the area was the dispersal centre for all *frailejónes*. Oddly, one kind of *frailejón* is not dwarfed by great elevations (4,500m), but becomes so large as to take the place of trees. At the rate of a few millimetres a year, it reaches 3m in height and there is evidence that it lives over 100 years.

In hollows or by lakes such as the Laguna Negra grow thickets of short, red-trunked *coloradito* trees. Their twisted branches shade lichens, ferns and dark green mosses shining with dew. Such evergreen coloradito forests (*Polylepis sericea*) are not hangers-on from warmer times: they like the páramo and are said to be the highest-growing trees in the world, up to 4,500m. However, coloraditos are fast disappearing — and this ecosystem, once axed, never regenerates. This is quoted as one reason why pine trees are used for reafforestation despite being quite out of place.

Weather

Snow in July   Because snow clings to the 'rooftop' peaks of Bolívar, La Corona, La Concha, El Toro and El León, Merideños call them the five White Eagles. However, from May to November storms may buffet the páramos with snow, only to melt by day. This season is called *invierno* or winter. Campers may find the *invierno* wet and miserable or snowy and miserable. In the *verano*, the dry season or summer from about December to April, the Andes are at their most inviting, sunny and bright. December-February are the coldest months.

Caution   Because of afternoon fog, the best walking hours are in the morning. Night temperatures may plunge to freezing above 3,500m (for every 100m rise in altitude, the mercury drops about 0.6°C); by contrast the day's high may soar to 20C°. Sunburn occurs at high altitudes because thin oxygen permits more radiation. You'll see that Andinos, even small children, have leathery browned faces. Lack of oxygen may cause mountain sickness, known as the *soroche* or *mal de páramo*. There is an expression in the Andes for dying, 'to cross the páramo' — *pasar el páramo*; to feel depressed is *estar emparamado*. So go slowly, rest often and descend at once if you feel giddy, nauseous, confused.

Fiestas

In Mérida State, you may see villagers celebrating traditional festivals and saints days with street processions. January: *Paradura del Niño*, a widely celebrated search for the lost Infant Jesus, with costumed Indians, angels, shepherds, dancers. January 6: Day of the Kings in Santo Domingo, Tabay. January, last Sunday: *San Benito*, closing fiesta in Mucutujote (near La Venta-Chachopo). February 2: *Virgen de La Candelaria — Danza de los Vasallos* in La Punta. February (Carnival): *Feria del Sol*, a 5-day celebration with bullfights in Mérida City. Easter, Holy Thursday and Friday: Passion Play in La Parroquia. May 15: *San Isidro Labrador* in Apartaderos, Tovar, Jají. September 24: Archangel Michael's Day in Jají, and Mérida. September 30: *Negros de San Gerónimo* in Santo Domingo. October 24: *Fiesta de San Rafael* in San Rafael de Mucuchíes. December 28-29: *Los Giros de San Benito* (the black saint) in Mucuchíes, Timotes.

Country lodgings

The colonial-style inns (*posadas*) are worth exploring in the Andes for their charm, simplicity and usually, but not always, economy.

Most have few rooms. A few serve meals at set hours; prices may cover part board.

On the Transandina, 8km east of Mérida (passing the fork for the Sierra Nevada track) is the Posada Colonial, a remodelled hacienda house over 100 years old. Near Mucurubá, the attractive Hacienda Escagüey is now a working inn; room and board about $20. Continuing up the Transandina, the next *posada* is El Baqueano, an impeccably restored colonial house, with pricier accommodations. Just before Mucuchíes is the Posada San Román, (074) 523838, a restored hacienda house of the late 1700s. In the centre of Mucuchíes is an attractive old 2-storey house on Calle Independencia. This is the Hotel Central Los Andes, (074) 81151, which has five economical, but unheated, rooms upstairs; bathrooms across the hall. Downstairs is the excellent Restaurant Los Andes, run by the same owner, Señora Wanda.

Near the foot of the old trail from El Arenal to La Montaña Station is the large quadrangle of Hacienda La Mesa which has been refurbished as Posada Doña Rosa. The coffee hacienda was used as teleférico offices during the cableway construction. There are 10 rooms at about $45 with hearty breakfast and supper, with hot water, mountain pools, horses for hire. Posada Doña Rosa, (074) 528355 and 524084, is reached from Mérida by car, taking the eastern or Transandina exit; go 5½km until Parque Las Calaberas where there is a fork (to La Joya) and a bridge across the Chama; after crossing the river, head west 2.3km. A jeep road then climbs the last 2km to the hacienda. (On foot, see also Peter Ireland's note under paragraph 2, *Mérida-Los Nevados*.)

MÉRIDA

To Caraqueños, Mérida conjures up a town perched high in the Andes with a freezing climate. In fact, this highest state capital is situated at a modest 1,625m. Its semitropical mesa above the Chama gorge is planted with bananas and coffee. Far from being chilly, Mérida has a lovely climate with warm days and cool nights. Today, the focus is on expansion with new businesses, housing estates. Mérida is the seat of the Universidad de Los Andes known for its forestry school.

Although few historic buildings remain, the city is proud of Spanish roots dating to 1558. Mérida had two other sites before its final location where it was named Santiago de los Caballeros de Mérida. For over two centuries it belonged to the colonial province of Nueva Granada (Colombia) rather than Captaincy General of Venezuela. The Andeans are still aware that their customs are distinct (and their Spanish clearer), and they like it that way. They pride themselves on being *gente correcta* (proper).

The first Europeans to reach what is today Mérida reported that even the steepest, apparently inaccessible slopes were farmed by Indians who made stone terraces they called *andenes*, planting "roots and maize for sustenance, because the multitude of people did not allow a patch of land to lie idle, even in the cold páramos". The Spaniards, clinging to a narrow foothold along the Chama, saw the advantages of coexistence with groups such as the Timotes. Even now, Andinos are the hardest working people in the country.

What to see and do

Booths are manned at the bus and air terminals, providing many tips on pensions and excursions. The staff at the airport booth are said to be particularly helpful and speak English.

If you plan to stay a few days, visit the central market, the orchid gardens at Parque La Isla, and the small zoo at Chorros de Milla.

Alison Vickers and Tim Wainwright found the people in the Mountain Shop, opposite the teleférico, 'very friendly and helpful. You can hire camping equipment, sleeping bags, stoves, etc. They sell maps which cover the Sierra Nevada Park and Laguna Negra region.' Another tip: 'The Banco Union, just down the road from Plaza Bolívar, has a cashpoint machine which accepts Visa and gives bolívars, and saves queuing.' C. Nacher recommends as 'good value and helpful for arranging trips' a knowledgeable Merideño: Camilo Trujillo, (074) 637677.

'**Los Aleros** is a sort of theme village, modelled on a typical

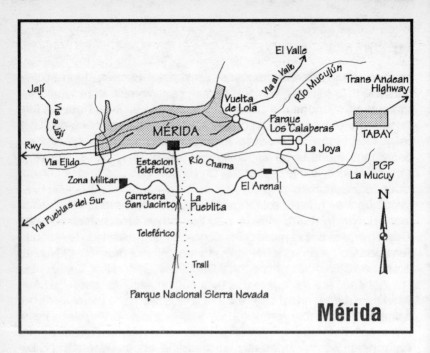

Mérida

Andean village of the 1920s. It sounds tacky but it's kind of nice, not at all overbearing. The scenery's pretty and there are all sorts of traditional and delicious foods on sale; a pleasant family excursion. Buses take 30 minutes; just go to the bus terminal and ask.' (Sandrine Tiller)

The Teleférico

Reaching 4,765m, this 4-stage cableway is the world's highest. The system covers 12.5km. Understandably, it is extremely popular and reservations, (074) 525080, are made well in advance. One way around queues is to book with a tour group; there's one in the plaza outside the teleférico. On peak holidays such as New Year's, Carnival and Easter, the teleférico is open daily. Otherwise Wednesdays to Sundays, 7.30 to 12.00 up; last car down about 16.30. Bs.300 adults, Bs.150 students ('only Venezuelans' M. Crolla was told).

'Do not go in December or January; I waited for 10 hours to go up and saw a fist-fight break out. When I did get up there I saw nothing because of the clouds.'(S.T.) However, Lindsay Griffin reported no problem. 'If you are trekking/climbing and don't want to come down, they will send you up in the empty car when they start bringing people down after lunch. No reduction if you want to get off at intermediate stages.' Peter Ireland advises that 'queues can be avoided if you arrive early. It supposedly starts at 7.30, we got there by 7.00 (during Carnival, the first car was reaching the top at 7.00). It's best to get to the top as soon as possible before clouds cover the peaks. Make sure you have warm clothes as it is very cold up there — so cold that the cablecar waits half way down from the last station. If you are asthmatic or suffer other breathing problems, take extra care. There is a doctor and mountain rescue team at Pico Espejo.'

Note   The last stage of the teleférico was closed in Dec. 1991 because of a broken cable which killed two maintenance staff. Until further notice, service is only up to the 3rd station, Loma Redonda. This is where mules wait to carry packs or riders bound for Los Nevados village.

Trout fishing

Ask about the best high altitude lagoons, most stocked with trout. The season is March 15-Sept.30 and a permit is required from Parques Nacionales' Mérida offices: Inparques, Av. Urdareta at Calle 51, (074) 631473.

Pony trekking

Rowena Hill and Andrés Fajardo are organising treks and pony treks from a farm on the south side of the Sierra Nevada. Their remote farm is 2hrs by foot from the nearest road (Los Nevados), and the vicinity offers good trout fishing and bird watching, as well as climbing. Write to Apartado 599, 5101 Mérida, ring (074) 440513, 446952.

Hotels and restaurants

Mérida has many good hotels in splendid settings, the Prado Río, Belensate and nearby Valle Grande, to mention three.

At the modest hotels mentioned here, you will not find swimming pools or discotheques. All have been recommended by readers. Hotel Gran Balcón, Av. Domingo Peña, (074) 520366: 'Clean and safe; for a small fee we left luggage while walking; cost of room was about £10 double + tax.'(A. Vickers) 'Close to the centre of town and teleférico with a fantastic view; clean, friendly and quiet; own hot shower. Good restaurant. Restaurant Comida Vegetariana facing the teleférico; nice people, great food.'(S.T.) Pensión Cristo Rey, Av.3 No.14-73, (074) 626015: 'Food and lodging for students; Sr.

Benjamin is incredibly kind.'(C. Sganga) Las Aguilas Blancas, near
Chorros de Milla: 'A *campamento*, bare but practical.'(E. Leckenby)
Hotel Teleférico, Plaza de las Heroínas, (074) 527370: 'Very close to
cablecar with double for $14, standard restaurant, steak for $2.50.
A good cheap hotel in centre is Hotel Santiago de los Caballeros,
Av. 3 entre Calles 24-25, $9 double.' (P.I.) Hotel Posada Marianela,
Calle 16 between Av. 4 and 5. 'We were treated by Marianela Núñez
more as friends than paying guests. Very, very friendly. Clean.' (J
and K Whitehead)

Enjoying fame in Mérida for some 400 flavours of ices is Heladería
Coromoto by Plaza El Llano. You name it, and Manuel Oliveira has
it or can make it — from tomato, avocado and garlic icecream, to
trout and shrimp; rum-and-coke is a popular flavour.

Getting there

Mérida can be reached by *expreso* coach (12 hours, about $10), or
jet (1 hour, $55) from Caracas. 'We went standby, but purchased
tickets 2hrs in advance; by the time plane was due to leave there
were over 20 on standby.'(A. Vickers) Various departures daily on
Avensa and Aeropostal. Flights also go from Barquisimeto, Valencia,
Maracaibo, San Antonio. If your plane is diverted because of fog
(Mérida's runway is short), you will be treated to a long mountain
drive from Táchira. 'A good reason to take the bus anyway.' (P.I.)

From Caracas, the main roads to Mérida are: the **Llanos route** via
Barinas (690km from Caracas) which rises dramatically from
Barinitas to Apartaderos; the scenic but slow **Trans Andean road**
from Trujillo State (730km) by way of Pico del Aguila; and the **Pan
American highway** via Barquisimeto and El Vigía (850km), a fast
road bypassing most of the Andes. At the time of writing no *expreso*
lines offer daytime service direct to Mérida; and none take the Trans
Andean route (you would have to start from Valera). Some lines
leaving from the Nuevo Circo Terminal are: Unión Transporte San
Cristóbal, (02) 5450004, (076) 29120, Expresos Alianza (02)
5450113, (076) 631193, and Expresos Mérida, (02) 5417935.
Expresos Mérida and Expresos Los Llanos, (02) 5411510, have
morning departures on the Llanos route, stopping in Barinas.

Via Barinas   When the Mérida flights were all booked, Peter Ireland
found a great alternative, combining air to Barinas and land to
Mérida. 'The flight from Maiquetía passes over Morrocoy, turns south
to stop in Acarigua where the plains open out, showing why
Venezuela is a beef-producing nation, and lands in Barinas (1hr
30min, $32). At an airport tourism booth, a very helpful guide gave
me a city map of Barinas and told me how to get to the bus station,

a 15 minute walk. Lots of *por puestos* (3½ hours, $6) and buses (6 hours, $4.50) to Mérida. Better view from the bus, right hand side, as the road swings around hairpin bends. Have warm clothes with you because it gets cold long before 3,000m altitude, when the *por puesto* stopped at a café by Laguna de Mucubají. The second half of the journey is down through villages; look out for the Observatory on the crest.'

Trans Andean route   From Valera, or Trujillo, the Trans Andean highway winds through cultivated valleys and hills, linking many charming villages. There are modest mountain hotels in La Puerta, Timotes, Mesa de Esnujaque and Jajó. At Pico del Aguila, the road crosses a pass 4,007m high, often snowy. The roadside inn has some lodging. Travellers pause to drink hot chocolate and view the bronze condor (not an eagle) honouring Bolívar's troops who marched this way to liberate Caracas. Behind the inn is the paved Piñango road, Venezuela's highest. And a few kilometres further the Transandina joins the Llanos route at Apartaderos, alt. 3,479m. Several hotels have been built to take advantage of the tourist trade here.

On the steep slopes, before farmers can plant wheat or potatoes children pick out stones and add them to walls. Tractors are of little use, and men or oxen pull ploughs. Wheat used to be threshed by horses and you can see the stone threshing circles. Water mills for grinding wheat still work near Mucuchíes. Today, demand for European fruit and vegetables has brought new crops — apples, artichokes, leeks and brussels sprouts — and pesticides. However, in spite of tourism-related jobs, life remains hard. In remote hamlets, children go to one-room school houses, often unheated. Their ruddy faces are wind-burnt and their clothes are too thin for warmth. To make a few pennies, kids by the road sell flowers or woolly puppies a lot fatter than themselves (white Mucuchíes puppies of a Great Pyrenees strain).

The last 62kms to Mérida spiral down the Chama Valley through picturesque pueblos such as Mucuchíes and Mucurubá. *Mucu* means 'place' in the old Indian tongue. Mucuchíes is the cold place, and Mucurubá is the place where *curubas*, a kind of passion fruit, grow.

A walk off the Trans-Andean route   The camino viejo roughly parallels the Trans Andean route as it drops down to Mérida. Alison Vickers and Tim Wainwright write: 'A pleasant amble is to follow the old track from Apartaderos to Mucuchíes, a distance of about 14km. The old track, on the whole broad and grassy, winds down the valley through the villages, occasionally joining the main road. On the map there is no clear way. We just started walking and each time we joined the main road, we headed off on the most likely looking path, which was usually the right way. Whilst it is not spectacular in scenery or challenging in walking, it is still delightful. We passed small farms, walked along the river bank and stopped and chatted to people working in fields who were all very friendly. At Mucuchíes we got the *por puesto* back to Mérida, but you could have walked further.'

Continuing west of Mérida, the Transandina descends the Chama Gorge to Estanques, hot and dry, then rises to Páramo La Negra before going to San Cristóbal, a distance of 235km, some 5 hours by bus.

HIKING IN THE SIERRA NEVADA DE MÉRIDA

The Parque Nacional Sierra Nevada de Mérida provides infinite opportunities for hiking. The following are just a few. For more suggestions buy *Hiking in the Venezuelan Andes* (see Appendix).

The Teleférico route and Los Nevados
By Hilary and George Bradt, with further information from Rowena Quantrill and Peter Ireland

One of the most interesting aspects of our five-day walk was the vegetation changes caused by altitude, the prevailing winds, and local conditions. Between the first and second teleférico stations the vegetation is lush, but reaches cloud forest richness between the Montaña and La Aguada stations. Here is the 'typical' jungle scenery everyone imagines. Everything is slightly out of hand, larger than life, and competing for air, light and moisture. In this cloud forest pocket, special plant communities complement each other. We especially enjoyed this forest because the path takes you not only through it, but above it as well. As you wind up the far side of the valley you're level with a fantastic array of air plants, ferns, mosses, and other bromeliads. I remember seeing the sun streaming down on an entire tree swathed in air plants. A few were blossoming, but all had bright red leaves highlighted by the sun against a hazy blue mountain. We could even look down on a group of wary guans, large tropical forest-dwelling birds.

After the humid cloud forest comes the dry, intoxicating smell of eucalyptus trees, but eventually these give way to scrub and bushes. From Redonda station we looked ahead at the bleak páramo in front of us, and were surprised to see a sheltered valley supporting all sorts of trees, bushes, and flowers just below the pass at about 4,200m.

From the top of the pass we could see the trail winding down into the valley of the Nuestra Señora river. At first glance the landscape was devoid of anything special, but then we realised entire hillsides were covered in pink blossoming bushes. Down from the pass the mountains became drier and drier. Prickly pear cacti were common companions bordering fields of wheat. Here on the eastern watershed, luxuriant plantlife was concentrated in the *quebradas* or stream beds. After two days of near-desert conditions it was a relief to get back onto the western slopes: bananas, grassy fields, and forests. The country folk we met along the way were friendly and always informative. Obviously construction of the teleférico had influenced the area enormously. Not only did many of these men help build the installations, but they could now get their produce to market more easily.

It was Christmas, and in the village of Los Nevados the padre organised a nativity play for his parish. With the help of several theological students from Mérida's university, the square in front of the church was transformed by the construction of a simple manger and signs posted over private houses, 'Pensión Rey David,' and 'Pensión Belén'. By the time we arrived, all we saw was a charmingly Andean nativity scene set up to the left of the church altar. No camels here, only typical beasts of burden: horses, donkeys and mules. Instead of the rich oriental robes, the peasants were dressed in Andean browns and greys. The stable was a typical thatched hut, and the terrain was not flat desert, but rugged, creased mountains. We met one of the students who told us the details of the pageant. Three hundred spectators had come, bringing their animals with them in case the padres needed more for the play. There were more than enough willing villagers for all the parts. What the play lacked in polish was made up in authenticity and simplicity.

Mérida — Los Nevados — El Morro — Mérida

The first thing to decide is whether to take the teleférico or walk up the mountain. Your decision may be made for you by the season and day of the week you make your ascent — remember the teleférico does not run on Mondays or Tuesdays, and may be very crowded when it is running. Rowena Quantrill recommends taking it at least to the first station. The first stretch is the most confusing (you're most likely to get lost here), and is hot and generally not very interesting.

Assuming you are walking, there are three ways down to the Chama River flowing past Mérida. The main road leaves Mérida's plateau behind the airport (west), while the two walking routes leave from beside the teleférico station and the eastern part of town. Each has a bridge over the river. When you get to the other side there's a road on which you turn left (north). Continue up the road until you come to telephone and electric cables strung on two sets of poles, one short and one tall. 'While still in the village, you pass a house called Villa Olga; at the next right, turn uphill — you will see a white cross 30 yards up the street. Just beyond, after crossing a small stream, a track to the *camino del teleférico* (just ask anyone) veers left at a fork and soon winds up to a ridge. After about 15 minutes, it comes to a Rotary Club cross; keep above the Hacienda La Mesa on your left). You will soon join the beautifully contoured and graded trail. We found no yellow paint markers until nearly at La Montaña.' (Peter Ireland)

There's no water between the start of the trail and the first station (La Montaña, 2,442m) four hours away. This is a convenient stopping place — fantastic view of Mérida, and a good station café with hot food (closes at 2pm). Some hikers have reported difficulty with guards requesting a special permit to camp here, but this may no longer be required. Much better to take a lovely trail, first left of the cableway, then to the right under the lines. It follows a water pipe up the mountain.

A beautiful campsite is about an hour further on — not a difficult walk and well worth the effort. It is in lush forest on a patch of grass big enough for two tents, across the Quebrada La Fría. To cross the river there's a very slippery log. We chickened out and waded. 'Make no mistake, La Fría is cold. We had spent the previous night on a bus and carried our 20kg backpacks all day; now, very soon after splashing in La Fría we had a hypothermia case; the only way we could warm him up was by zipping together a pair of bags and all three of us bundling in until nightfall.' (P.I.)

Leave early the next morning so you can enjoy the scenery without hurrying. The cloud forest is at its best here as the trail climbs through ever-more spectacular vistas. Be on the lookout for the only possible place you could go wrong on this trail. You'll recognise the spot because you actually pass under one of the *teleférico* pylons. ('The path to Loma Redonda starts just below La Aguada station, signposted to the right. Stick to high side of *teleférico* after crossing under it; the yellow markers are no longer there.' P.I.)

From Quebrada La Fría to La Aguada (3,452m) station is about three hours. There is camping near the station where water is available. ('The employee was very helpful finding us a spot within the complex and invited us into his cabin for coffee.' P.I.) The trail snaking up toward Loma Redonda (4,045m) station is clearly visible over the rocks, about four hours away (you may do it in less, but many people start to feel the altitude at this point). The best campsite here is five minutes beyond the station, with water available from the pumphouse. There are fine views of Pico Bolívar and the Anteojos Lakes. ('I would say the campsite is a good 10min from Loma Redonda station if, as we were, you are suffering from altitude sickness; it is after the lower path meets the upper path.' A.V.)

(There are more adventurous campsites below by the lagoons, which could hardly be colder than Loma Redonda where your tent will ice up overnight. Lindsay Griffin was assailed by a snowstorm on an otherwise fine year-end hike. Perhaps this is the reason for a shelter built of stone: 'From Loma Redonda, we walked via Lagunas Anteojos to the lakes of the Espejo Valley, ca. 4,000m, where we camped. There is a stone building for sleeping at Anteojos. We climbed a line on the north side of Bolívar Peak, descending the south face to Timoncito Glacier and round to Pico Espejo, where we caught the *teleférico*. This was the only time our permit was checked. This permit, which appeared to us to be a formality, took the form of a registration done at the bottom station.')

The path becomes very wide at Loma Redonda because of continual use by mules carrying tourists to Los Nevados. On the third day continue up to the pass, about an hour. Before the top you will see a path to the left, bound for Pico Bolívar and the final *teleférico* station. Pause here for your last views of the mountain if you're heading for Los Nevados.

The trail to Los Nevados is rocky, well-used (even by the occasional jeep), and downhill with plenty of campsites and (seasonal) water. You will get your first bird's-eye view of this enchanting little village about three hours from the pass. Once you've spotted the village the easiest route down is by way of the white cross to your right as you look at the village. Or you can continue along the main trail, and double back. Don't cross the river to the east.

('We approached Los Nevados from the west, following the ridge, rather than climbing over from the north. It was 5 hours from the pass before we saw the village. We saw no white cross and doubted whether an alternate route could cut the time to 3 hours. In Los Nevados, we camped in front of the school on the only flat grass, which we shared with various mules; wonderful views.' P.I.)

At Los Nevados you can buy a few basic necessities, beer, and soft drinks, and some houses offer accommodation. Or there's a lovely campsite about an hour beyond the village, by a stream. ('There are now 4-5 *posadas turísticas*. Ours was very clean and simple. For two of us in a bunk-bedded room, with evening meal and breakfast, we paid Bs.340. Los Nevados is very relaxed and we both felt we could have spent a couple of days here.' A.V.) Paul and

Tracey Weatherstone stayed at the Bella Vista where the accommodation cost £1 each per night. They write: 'It's not luxurious but the food was excellent, the beer cold and the owners both very friendly. We really enjoyed our stay there and we were given the privilege of sleeping in the double bedroom rather than in the bunkhouse.'

Before leaving Los Nevados have a look inside the church (1912): the Andean nativity scene described earlier is there.

The path to El Morro begins around the first row of houses to the right of the church. Walking west takes you above the Río Nuestra Señora canyon to El Morro, seven or eight hours away on a dusty track through hot, desert-like country (little shade). The trail is so well constructed that you'll positively sail along. There is water and several campsites, but the best combination is at Quebrada Mosnanda about half-way between the two villages, where the trail becomes a jeep track. An hour beyond this river is the Quebrada El Banco, your last possible campsite (only room for one tent here) and water for two hours as the road goes up and across several dry ridges.

As we climbed up from El Banco we looked down a ridge sprinkled with corrugated iron roofs, said, 'Ah, El Morro' and continued upward. However, the real El Morro then came into view far below us. It was charming, the bougainvillea shrubs contrasting beautifully with the whitewashed adobe walls and tile roofs. For accommodation ask for the Pensión run by Señora Adriana. ('After a long, hot day, the *posada* was bliss. Señora Adriana and her grandson play a wicked game of dominoes and we had great fun playing until about midnight.' A.V.)

From El Morro the jeep track runs to Mérida. If you go down to the village you may be able to arrange a lift. 'From El Morro we took a jeep back to Mérida. To walk back I think it would take the best part of a full day and the going looked rough and to be frank a bit tedious. Be careful to negotiate a price for the jeep before getting in — the locals paid Bs.100, we paid Bs.500. The jeep ride was suitably terrifying and worth every penny.' — Paul and Tracey Weatherstone. Otherwise you can take a shortcut across the Quebrada Mucusabache and join the road as it climbs up a long ravine. As a relief from the rather bland road we discovered a shortcut beginning on the right about halfway to a *quebrada* at the end of the ravine. Stones make up the roadbed which is still used by local traders because it cuts several kilometres off the jeep route. Not long after starting up this road you should collect water as the ridge is a long dry one, taking three hours from El Morro to the top.

Once over the pass the descent is swift, the trail joining the road at a junction. The main road curves around to the right, while another older road continues down to the left. This is the shorter, steeper route. Just keep taking the right-hand forks and heading downhill to Mérida. Plenty of water and fine campsites here. When your minor road rejoins the jeep road, you'd better start hitching. It's still a long way to Mérida, and walking it could take you the best part of a day.

Practical information

Time/difficulty   The hike described takes four or five days, but this can be shortened to two or three days by using the *teleférico* for the ascent to Loma Redonda. The trail itself is not difficult. It can be tackled by a fit person with a little backpacking experience in lugging cold-weather gear, and common sense to go slowly at high altitude.

Weather   December to March is the dry season: clear, cold, gusty. Expect fog in afternoon, freezing temperatures at night above 3,500m; rain, snow mostly from April to October.

Accommodation   By using the *teleférico* it is possible to do this hike without a tent and other backpacking equipment. Rooms and meals can be found in Los Nevados and El Morro, but you should bring a sleeping bag.

Equipment   The usual high-altitude equipment, plus insect repellent for the *bocones* (small biting insects) found at lower altitudes. Campers should avoid cutting firewood so bring your stove. Sun cream and lip salve are essential.

Maps   A Sierra Nevada 'Mapa para Excursionistas' (photocopy, about $2.50) with reasonably accurate contours is sold by the Casa de Las Montañas in the *teleférico* square. As marked trails may be old, check any side treks with a ranger. The 1:50,000 map, sheet number 5941, made by Cartografía Nacional (MARNR) covers this hike. Cost about $4. Cartografía maps are sold in Caracas by Metroguía. There is a Metroguía outlet, (02) 2391622, in the east corridor of La California subway station.

Permits   Free; easy to obtain at Inparques office at the bottom *teleférico* station, open shortly after 7.00. The permit must be returned on completion of hike. In Mérida, Inparques HQ are on Av. Urdaneta at Calle 51 near the airport, (074) 631473.

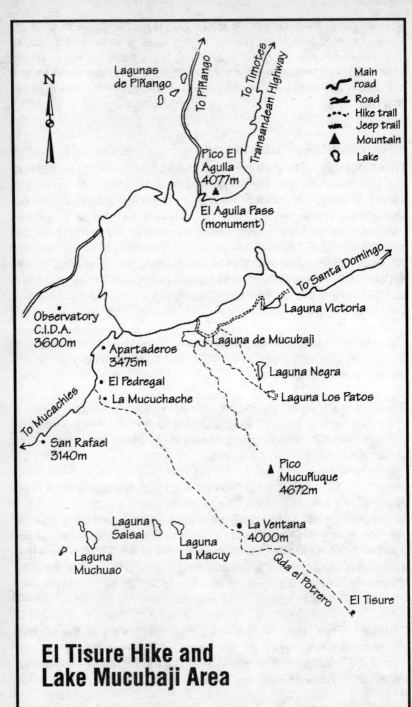

N

Lagunas de Piñango

To Piñango

To Timotes

Transandean Highway

Main road
Road
Hike trail
Jeep trail
Mountain
Lake

Pico El Aguila 4077m

El Aguila Pass (monument)

To Santa Domingo

Laguna Victoria

Observatory C.I.D.A. 3600m

Laguna de Mucubaji

Apartaderos 3475m

Laguna Negra

El Pedregal

La Mucuchache

Laguna Los Patos

To Mucachies

San Rafael 3140m

Pico Mucuñuque 4672m

Laguna Saisai

La Ventana 4000m

Laguna La Macuy

Laguna Muchuao

Qda el Potrero

El Tisure

El Tisure Hike and Lake Mucubaji Area

El Tisure — páramo and pilgrimage

by Paul Rouche

High in the Andes, Juan Félix Sánchez built a chapel of rocks and peopled it with saints carved in wood. Working alone except for his wife Epifania's help, Sánchez spent years creating a sculpture garden, completing it in 1970. Under the clouds and wind of Páramo El Tisure, beside a stone-channelled brook, Sánchez hewed figures of biblical and Venezuelan lore to form a masterpiece of naïve art. In 1989 Sánchez was awarded the National Plastic Arts Prize. He was 89. As an old man, Sánchez moved down to San Rafael de Mucuchíes. There, at the upper entrance to the village, he built a second chapel. Between this and El Tisure is a distance of some 12km or more. Mules may be hired in San Rafael (ask at the *Prefectura*) for the 5-hour trek to El Potrero, as the valley is known to campesinos. The views are enchanting at La Ventana (the window) Pass, where other peasants have placed crucifixes. Despite a headstart of some 3,100m altitude and an excellent trail, many hikers will be slowed by this stiff ascent to 4,000m.

The trail   The path starts from La Mucuchache, a community next to El Pedregal, about 4km below the Apartaderos crossroads. The concrete road to La Mucuchache joins the Trans Andean highway 0.8km from Juan Félix Sánchez' chapel in San Rafael. A crucifix (dated 17.11.84) stands by the right side of this concrete road.

The Mucuchache road soon turns into earth, climbing in a SE direction along the Quebrada La Cañada, or Mucuchache River. Still wide, the road crosses a bridge, and begins to leave behind all houses. Splendid views which open to the left over a great valley called El Pantano mark a breathing spot at 3,450m. This first stage should take 1 to 1½ hours walking time.

The next stage of the ascent to La Ventana Pass at 4,000m is steeper and quite hard going because of the altitude, although the path is always clear, at times cobbled, at times stepped. Walking time is 1½ hours not counting stops. The boulders framing the pass really do make a dramatic 'window'. The path widens again as it enters El Tisure Valley, S-SE; dropping to 3,500m altitude at a stone bridge by a sign 'Valle El Tisure'. This point is midway between La Ventana and the house of Juan Félix Sánchez: a 50-minute walk either way.

The path crosses over Quebrada El Potrero (the pasture) on a stone bridge (20min.) and continues generally level until the first farmhouse (deserted) of El Tisure (20min.); altitude 3,250m. You come to a place with a stone-walled field on either side. Just afterwards, on the right you see Sánchez' farm and low house. The path itself continues another 15 minutes until ending at the chapel. There is plenty of tenting space around, and water from streams, but little protection against wind and cold. When we left the next day, the return to La Ventana Pass took double time, but from there down to Mucuchache was just two hours without stops. Alternatively, old paths do exist (via El Castillo) which go east from El Tisure and behind Pico Mucuñque to eventually join the highway to Santo Domingo, but these require more exploration.

Hiking in the Laguna Mucabají area
by Forest Leighty

Lying some 50km east of Mérida, this Laguna (a shallow lake or pond) at an altitude of about 3,500m is one of the largest in the Venezuelan Andes. Because of its relatively low elevation it is a good place to get acclimatised while still not being too far from help if severe altitude sickness (pulmonary or cerebral oedema) should develop. There is some pleasant walking in the area.

Getting there   Buses run between Mérida and Barinas (to the east of the lake). Get off at the Restaurante Mucubají on the pass between the Barinas and Mérida watersheds. From the restaurant it is a short walk to the Park Guard Post (PGP) where a camping permit can be obtained (no charge). If entering by vehicle just for a day hike no permit is needed but it might be a good idea to check in anyway.

There is a paved road from the PGP to near an abandoned house which is about a kilometre downhill from the PGP. Just before the house there are two areas marked for camping (*Campamento*) but there are no sanitary facilities and this is a heavily visited area; you might want to camp elsewhere. Many potential campsites will be mentioned in the hiking descriptions.

Warning   You cannot leave any gear, even as big as a tent, unattended if you wish to see it again. Also gear left in a locked vehicle cannot be counted as safe unless, perhaps, the vehicle is parked at the PGP.

Laguna Negra

From the abandoned house pass the fence that closes the jeep road, head east. The jeep road has a slight upgrade and just as you are to leave it, the Laguna is visible below and to the left. On a clear, calm day you may have to look hard to see it. After leaving the jeep road, the trail drops down some 150m until rising a bit to Laguna Negra which lies at about 3,475m, nearly 4km from Laguna Mucubají. Laguna Negra is a beautiful sight on a clear, calm day. The black water forms such a perfect mirror that it essentially disappears and is replaced by the reflection of the trees on the mountainside above the lagoon. Just as the trail reaches the lagoon there is a flat area much used for camping — it even has a trash basket. The trail to this point is passable to horses and many Venezuelan tourists use horses which are available for rental across from the Restaurante Mucubají.

Laguna Negra to Laguna Los Patos   The trail continues on the right (east) side of the lagoon. The best trail stays slightly above the lake but there are numerous tracks that follow the edge of the lagoon, usually to have a steep exit back to the upper trail. When the head of the lagoon is reached, there are additional campsites. To continue, you must search out the trail which enters the woods without crossing the stream feeding the lagoon. Very shortly after leaving the lagoon there is a clearing with the ruins of an old house. The trail continues fairly steeply upward on a rocky path which occasionally skirts the cascade coming down from Laguna Los Patos. There is a total elevation gain of 275m and then a drop of about 60m. After reaching the amphitheatre of Laguna Los Patos, the main trail turns to the left — there is also a faint trail circling the lagoon basin to the right. There is still a bit of distance before actually reaching the lagoon which has a rather small water area.

Laguna Los Patos, lying at 3,688m, is named for the small Andean ducks (*patos*) which will usually be seen here. Near the mouth of the lagoon there is a rather uneven campsite with an existing fire area, but do not count on cooking on a fire. (Trees and brush cut at these altitudes do not regenerate, and this high up do not give out much heat).

Somewhat further away from the lagoon (north) there are numerous campsites.

As a diversion, while camping here, there is an unnamed 4,200m peak directly east of the Laguna that can be climbed as a tough scramble. Although this requires slight care in route finding, it does yield a good view.

Pico Mucuñuque area

Pico Mucuñuque at 4,600m is one of the highest peaks in the northern end of the Sierra Nevada Park. The north-western slope of the peak forms a giant bowl which provides considerable mountain scenery and a possible route to the peak itself. A good trail leads to this area.

From the abandoned house near the shore of Laguna Mucubají, take the trail due south that dips down through the small ravine alongside the house. There is also a trail to the west that circles the lagoon. Shortly after leaving the house a trail junction will be reached: take the right hand fork which leads up the flat meadow-like stream course of the lagoon feeder. Cross the stream twice, heading toward the head of the stream at the Cascades where the trail begins its climb. Permission can be obtained (at the entry PGP) to camp at the Cascades area (about 3,627m) or at various higher campsites (request permission for 'campamento arriba de las cascadas').

From the Cascadas the trail climbs steadily and usually not too steeply until it reaches a large headwall which is distinguished by a white gully coming steeply down the middle of it. During this climb a couple of pleasant potential campsites will be passed. Just before the headwall at about 4,023m is the last good campsite at which water is readily available.

Until the headwall is reached, the trail is very distinct and easy to follow, but here it splits with one branch going very steeply up the white gully. By searching, the other branch will be found going around to the left of the headwall, up the stream course valley. Part way up, it turns to the right to rejoin the branch up the gully. In the morning this way is dry to pass because it is frozen but by afternoon it is wet and so it is probably preferable to descend via the gully straight ahead.

From here you are really in the mountains and have left most vegetation and flat spots below you. However, there is still a reasonably well defined trail, although rather steep, heading generally southward — do not wander to the west.

Eventually, after some steep climbing, the trail ends in a saddle at 4,540m between two false summits of the Pico. The true summit can be seen some 120m higher and a bit over a kilometre off to the left. On a clear day there is an excellent view of Picos Humboldt and Bolívar to the south-west.

Although it is only 7km from Laguna Mucubají to Pico Mucuñuque (according to a signpost at the abandoned house), the steep and rough trail and the elevation makes this an exceptionally long hike to consider doing in one day, particularly since the park rules call for exiting by 18.00 when the entry gate is locked.

Laguna Victoria

This lagoon was originally formed behind a glacial moraine which later broke open. This gap has now been dammed, restoring the pretty lake. It is used as a trout hatchery so no fishing is allowed.

To reach Laguna Victoria from Laguna Mucubají, start as to Laguna Negra past the fence headed east on the jeep road. Very soon, ½km or so, there is a road leading down to the left whereas the Laguna Negra route continues on the road slightly upward and to the right. This jeep road continues downward almost all the way to Laguna Victoria which is at about 3,260m, thus a descent of around 335m. The road goes in switchbacks and is never steep. It is generally within a forested (reafforested) area with various views of Laguna Victoria, but near the lake the road turns to a trail which in one spot is not too clear. Alternatively, the Laguna can be reached via the road from Laguna Mucubají toward Santo Domingo (via Barinas route) by parking near the Km10 post and hiking up (with about 60m of elevation gain) to the lagoon.

Lodging in Santo Domingo

There are several hotels, the best known being the charming Los Frailes run by Hoturvensa, (02) 5640098. Hotel Moruco is good, (073) 881255, and the Santo Domingo is quite reasonable, family style, (073) 88144.

Crossing the Sierra Nevada to Barinas
by Paul Rouche

This exceptionally rewarding hike takes you through two states, Mérida and Barinas, starting from Mucuchíes at 3,000m elevation and ending on the southern slopes of the Sierra Nevada at about 400m. Because of the initial altitude and the very long descent, it must be considered a hard walk of some 4 days. The trail follows a road to Gavidia, then an old Spanish mule path over the Andes, down to Caño Grande and the Barinas highway.

In my view this little-known trek is one of the best because of the open páramo, abundant streams, magnificent cloud forests on the Andes' southern slopes, and absence of people. Once you leave Gavidia, there are at most a dozen farmers' cottages along the way, and many of these are uninhabited. April, the month I chose for this trek, is not the rainy season, and although higher elevations were cold, the lower slopes were hot, dry and short on shade, making the last day's hike extra tiring.

Getting there   Buses and *por puestos* to Apartaderos — leave from Mérida several times daily, stopping at Mucuchíes on the way. If you have a car, ask for the camino to Mocao and Gavidia, leaving the

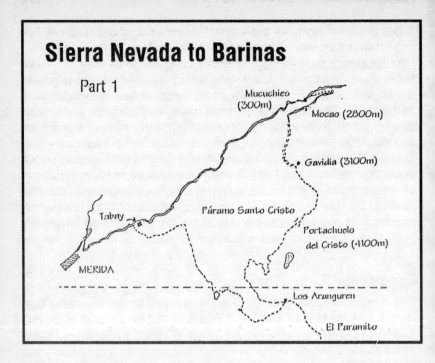

Sierra Nevada to Barinas

Part 1

Mucuchies (300m)

Mocao (2800m)

Gavidia (3100m)

Páramo Santo Cristo

Tabay

Portachuelo del Cristo (·1100m)

MERIDA

Los Aranguren

El Paramito

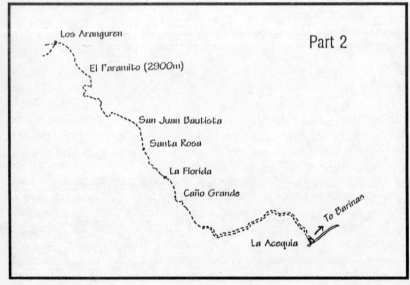

Los Aranguren

Part 2

El Paramito (2900m)

San Juan Bautista

Santa Rosa

La Florida

Caño Grande

To Barinas

La Acequia

Trans Andean highway between Mucuchíes and San Rafael. The road is steep but serviceable year-round by jeep.

The first stage, from Mucuchíes to Gavidia, takes about 2 hours walking, not counting stops. From Mucuchíes' central square where there is a hospital, a cobbled road goes down, bordering the cemetery, to the Chama River, here more like a stream. It is a short walk on cobblestones from the bridge up to the village of Mocao, alt. 2,800m. Go through Mocao, passing the chapel and straggling houses. The road parallels the valley another 35-40 minutes. You will see the small Gavidia River coming down from the left; it passes under the road. At this point, the road winds steeply up the Gavidia *quebrada* or ravine. A hike of 1¼hr brings you to Gavidia, taking the right fork at a high roadside chapel. At 3,100m altitude, Gavidia's main crops are potatoes, carrots, and garlic. Small fields, stone terraces and hilly pastures are shaded by stands of tall trees. The narrow valley is watered by Las Piuelas creek, crossed by a bridge.

Allow some 3 hours for the second stage up to the Portachuelo or pass. From Gavidia, follow the jeep track half an hour to its end at a steep rise. The trail to the páramo now borders stone walls and barbed wire fences; you go through log gates three times. Many small water courses cross the path, the way is rockier, the trees fewer and the temperature colder. A lonely cowherd is probably the only person you'll meet.

At the top a stone wall marks the pass of Portachuelo del Cristo (over 4,100m). Without crossing the wall, keep right and a few metres higher you will find a track heading SW among the low shrubs and velvety *frailejón* plants. The páramo invites tenting during the dry season, December to April, although temperatures drop to freezing. We found frost when we woke up. This is fine country for stretching your legs — you can wander in any direction over the moor-like hills.

Beginning the descent southward, allow 3 hours down to Los Aranguren where there is shelter. First, the sandy páramo track passes a large lagoon on the left; alt. 3,800m. This is just one of many glacial *lagunas*. Small streams cross the path from the right; they flow south, ultimately to the Orinoco basin as this is a watershed. At the first fork in the path (about an hour), go right; steep slopes alternate with a few level spots. After another hour, for the first time the trail crosses a small river from the left; the path soon comes to cobblestones, then drops sharply along a ravine. The next fork (left) leads to a log bridge and below is the cottage known as 'Altico de Los Aranguren'. From here down to the bridge at Los Aranguren ravine is a pleasant walk of about 1 hr 15 min. The way, at times cobbled, follows the river closely. If you are in need of shelter, you will be glad to see the deserted house which was once

Los Aranguren Inn; alt. 2,950m. In the meadow above the bridge are stone corrals, perhaps once used for mules.

The next good stopping point is at El Puente, a log bridge (about 3-3½hr). The path leads SE from Los Aranguren between two boulders; it crosses many water courses including the Sinigüís, and at least three field gates. At El Paramito (alt. 2,900m), where there is an inhabited house, for a change, go through two more gates. Below are splendid views of the Sinigüís Valley. In ½hr the trail suddenly enters cloud forest (2,600m) and skirts a small cascade. The forest track is uneven underfoot but the ferns, trees and orchids are of constant interest. There is a plank bridge over a clear, rocky river (2,000m altitude) and, just beyond, a clearing which makes a useful campsite. Nearby is a small waterfall called El Chorro.

Continuing down (another 4hr), the next stage goes to Santa Rosa community. For the first 2hr you go up and down through the forest, crossing ravines, emerging into patches of bracken only to reenter the forest. At 1,400m alt. there is a grassy spot (suitable for a tent) called San Juan Bautista, and an abandoned *rancho*. Overgrown by bracken, the path leads to the right of the hut (SE) and comes shortly to a Y; take the left hand. This reaches the hamlet of Santa Rosa in about 1¾ hours, crossing *quebradas* and fences and skirting cottages four times. Take no forks until a right hand at a Y less than 10min above Santa Rosa, a hamlet of about eight houses and one street. There is a field on the outskirts which has space for tents. At 1,000m elevation, the air is now hot.

To La Florida (about 3hr). Beyond Santa Rosa, with its *conucos* or plots of maize and yuca, the mule path dips and then rises, for a change. The countryside is less wild and you will see coffee bushes. At the first fork (30min), keep right (up); at the second in another 12min, go left; just before a house on a rise among coffee bushes (La Loma, 1,250m), go right, still climbing. 35-40min beyond is a small ravine with water; alt. 1,280m. Since no people live nearby, the water is clean. I recommend you fill your canteens here because in dry weather you may not find water for another 3hr, until you reach Caño Grande. Shortly, the trail dips through a tall and very beautiful deciduous forest, only to rise steeply to a level clearing (good tenting) at 1,280m where there is a hut. This is Los Pozos, which means water holes, although I found them dry.

My walking time down to the next deserted hut called La Florida was 70min without stopping. Shortly after leaving Los Pozos, the trail re-enters the woods and meets another path; take the left hand, going down. Within 5min at a second Y, go left along a ridge, and then zigzag down. Half an hour later, the trail, still dropping through woods and climbing again, meets a third fork; go right for La Florida.

Allow 2-2½hr for the drop from 1,100m to Caño Grande at 900m.

The trail traverses deforested slopes in a SE direction. With its ups and downs, hot sun and skimpy shade, it is wearying, although wide. You can see the Caño Grande road below on the flat. A single farmhouse marks Caño Grande.

The final stage to La Acequia on the Barinas highway is a mostly level march of at least 4hr but there are shade trees and streams — although the water is no longer pure because more people live here. Follow the old mule track past Caño Grande and continue through gates, entering a coffee plantation (there is a spring in the woods up to the right). The track meets other water courses, the occasional house, and in 50min comes to a wider cart track which becomes a proper earth road; go to the left along this (600m alt.). In 15min it fords a wide ravine, the Quebrada La Magdalena.

The next farmhouse, on the right at the top of a rise, for me marks Civilisation with a capital C because it has electricity and the owners, who grow oranges, have a car which I once hired as a taxi. (I also camped in their field.) From there, the road continues wide and flat for another 13km to reach the paved road. This, following the Acequia River, finally gets to La Acequia village (200m) on the national highway. You are 58km west of Barinas, the state capital, and there should be both buses and *por puestos*.

There is no countrey which yeeldeth more pleasure to the Inhabitants, either for these common delights of hunting, hawking, fishing, fowling, and the rest, then *Guiana* doth. It hath so many plaines, cleare riuers, abundance of Phesants, Partridges, Quailes, Rayles, Cranes, Herons, and all other fowle: Deare of all sortes, Porkes, Hares, Lyons, Tygers, Leopards, and diuers other sortes of beastes, eyther for chace, or foode. It hath a kinde of beast called *Cama*, or *Anta*, as bigge as an English beefe, and in greate plenty.

Sir Walter Raleigh, writing on the wildlife of Guiana (Venezuela) in *The Discoverie of the Large, Rich and Bewtiful Empyre of Guiana*.

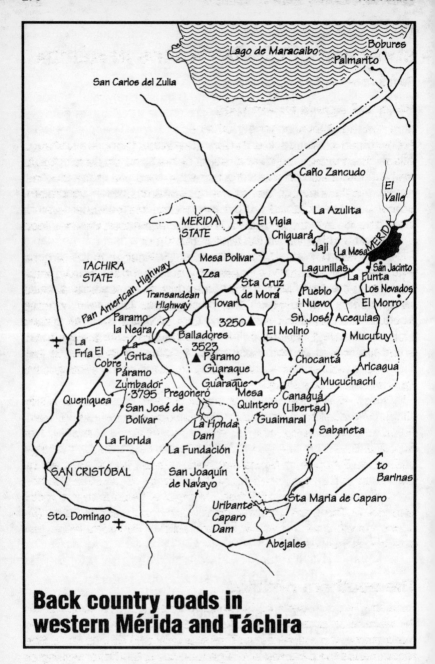

Back country roads in western Mérida and Táchira

SOME BACK COUNTRY ROADS IN MÉRIDA

Based on notes by Edith Steinbuch

Paso del Aguila to Piñango

Map: Cartografía sheet 6042 TIMOTES.
A 47km road winds over the Páramo de Piedras Blancas to Piñango village. The first half, asphalted, starts behind and above the Aguila inn (4007m), making it surely the highest — and one of the loneliest roads — in the country. Drivers may complain that their car radiator appears to overheat, but in fact the altitude makes water froth or 'boil'. The inn at Paso del Aguila is a popular *parador*. Besides food and hot chocolate, hikers can find a bed there.

On the páramo called Piedras Blancas (or Piñango depending on your map) you will see few passers-by, perhaps a *por puesto* jeep. Above tree level the wide glacial valley has three lagoons stocked with fat trout, say anglers. The road, at first fairly level, passes lagoons and descends northwards with splendid views of distant Lake Maracaibo. El Hatico, an old stone dwelling with a huge patio, is the first house on the road; about 3,000m alt. Below it, at Las Tapias, the road splits and although both routes end at Piñango, the Tapias route is less steep.

Piñango, in a green valley at about 2,480m elevation, is a tidy village where leathery-necked farmers plough with the help of oxen. For food and lodging, ask for the house of Señora Araujo. Her husband Saturnino Araujo will provide horses for treks to the large Laguna de Piñango, to Santa Apolonia, or even for the descent by mule path to the Pan American highway south of Lake Maracaibo.

It is also possible to go SE from Piñango to Timotes over a rocky jeep track. The track crosses three páramos in about 25km (an hour's drive), and the views are incredible. The road ends just beside Las Truchas Hotel.

The southern pueblos

From the Trans Andean highway west of Mérida, jeep roads cross the serrana to small *pueblos del sur*. Edith Steinbuch has visited many remote communities such as Mucutuy and Mucuchachí. She recommends the páramos and high farms as splendid for walking or driving. Moreover, today a network of rough side roads (not on most maps) links the N-S routes, largely enabling you to avoid the highway. The country people are hard-working farmers; you have only to ask for help to be given shelter. (Map 5941 of Mérida State.)

Mérida—El Morro—Aricagua

Many hikers do the *teleférico*-Los Nevados route, circling back by way of El Morro where there are *por puesto* jeeps once a day to Mérida. However, El Morro's road also continues south to Aricagua.

Por puestos from Mérida to El Morro all leave by the bridge over the Río Chama west of the city. Take the avenue out past the airport, turn south to San Jacinto district; the bridge is near a petrol station (this may be the last place to buy gasoline). The first stage up the mountain is partly paved. A good 2hrs by car, it rises steeply on arid slopes to the forest proper at 2,400-3,200m elevation. Beyond the pass the southern road is hot and dry, descending to the farming village of El Morro at 1,700m. (Ask in El Morro about another jeep road leading west to Acequias and San José on the Mucutuy road.)

South of El Morro the road dips and rises to the cultivated slopes of Aricagua, about 1,500m alt., centre of a prosperous coffee-growing valley. In all, the drive from El Morro takes six hours. Beyond, it is possible to work your way west by first heading south on an even less-travelled road to Mucuchachí.

La González—Mucutuy—Mucuchachí

A good but unpaved route leaves the Transandina at La González, a junction beyond Ejido, 49km west of Mérida. Here a bridge spans the Chama River. The first part parallels the Tostós ravine up a steep sandy road, hot and dry. At the first fork, keep right. (A rutted road joins from the east, coming from Acequias and El Morro.) The road improves as it climbs to San José, the first village, and some trees give shade. Higher, at about 3,000m alt. on the cloudy, cool Páramo de San José, plants make a colourful carpet of different species of *frailejón*.

The road now descends the cordillera's southern side by way of La Veguilla hamlet and continues to Mucutuy. Guest rooms are to be found in Mucutuy, and Señora Uzcátegui prepares meals, given notice. From the well-kept village of Mucuchachí, a further 22km, a dodgy road leads west to Canaguá, also called La Libertad.

Estanques—El Molino—Canaguá

The gorge of the Chama drops dramatically to 442m at Estanques, quite a hot pueblo. Here the Chama turns north to Lake Maracaibo. To the south, slopes are heavily eroded where a 'rain shadow' keeps the land arid. In Estanques look for a paved road up behind the little colonial chapel. Asphalted as far as El Molino, the road (which is joined by the Santa Cruz de Mora route) ascends through four climate zones: baking scrubland with cactus, subtropical slopes cultivated with bananas, coffee and pineapples, evergreen cloud forest, and páramo often chilled by dense fog.

At El Molino a gravel road winds south to Canaguá (Libertad), district capital. Canaguá has a gasoline pump. There is a pensión, too. From Canaguá, you can circle back to the Trans Andean highway via Mesa Quintero (west) and Guaraque-Tovar (north). The last part of this route is paved. It crosses beautiful cloud forests on the Páramo Guaraque, 3523m.

Towards Táchira State

Also from Guaraque, a jeep route heads south then west through the cordillera, leading eventually to San Cristóbal. Reports say the road is primitive between Guaraque and the small town of Pregonero in the high Uribante Valley of Táchira State. However, once in Pregonero you will find a newly paved road going north to La Grita. Southward, this paved road skirts La Honda dam on the Uribante and goes all the way down to the Barinas highway, emerging about 50km from San Cristóbal. This junction is close to the new airport called Santo Domingo (daily flights to Caracas).

A back country road links Pregonero and San José de Bolívar. From San José, return to the Trans Andean highway by way of the paved serpentine road to Queniquea and Páramo Zumbador. Ornithologist Mary Lou Goodwin has birded this 'wonderful' Zumbador route and reports that the beauty of its birds and forests is well worth the arduous road.

An alternative for jeep drivers, or hikers, is an unpaved road which heads for the high country due north of San José de Bolívar and crosses straight to La Grita.

An Abstract taken

out of certaine Spanyardes Letters con-cerning Guiana and the Countries lying vpon the great riuer of Orenoque: with certaine reportes also touching the same.

An Aduertisement to the Reader.

Dear Readers,

We invite you to send certaine reportes touching your travels in Venezuela. Updates and new information are particularly welcome.

You can write to England or Caracas:

Hilary Bradt
41 Nortoft Road
Chalfont St. Peter
Bucks. SL9 0LA
England

Hilary Branch
Apartado 60182
Caracas 1060A
Venezuela

Appendix

READING AND REFERENCE

Everyone's heard of *The Lost World* by Sir Arthur Conan Doyle and *Green Mansions* by W.H. Hudson. Here are books of a more factual interest.

Birding in Venezuela by Mary Lou Goodwin, Sociedad Conservacionista Audubon de Venezuela, Caracas, 1990. The second edition covers the haunts of more species than most ornithologists could hope to see. Practical, updated and with maps.

Birds of Venezuela by Rodolphe Meyer de Schauensee and William H. Phelps, Jr., Princeton University Press, New Jersey, 1978. 52 colour plates make this book an invaluable companion on travels, especially in the Llanos region where bird lists approach 320 species.

Churún-Merú, the Tallest Angel by Ruth Robertson, Whitmore Publishing, Pennsylvania, 1975. The expedition which measured Angel Falls and put it on the world map in 1948. Some good details on jungle travel, Jimmie Angel and old-timers.

Climb to the Lost World by Hamish MacInnes, Hodder & Stoughton, London, 1974. Very readable account of the British expedition which climbed Roraima's north prow in 1973 from the Guyanese side. Good background on Everard Im Thurn's 1884 ascent, climbing techniques.

Guide to Venezuela by Janice Bauman and Leni Young, Ernesto Armitano Editor, Caracas, 2nd edition 1987. An invaluable background source on history, architecture and geography, as well as on roads, local sights and customs of a large part of the country. The first Venezuelan guidebook written by people who actually went to the places themselves. Clear maps.

Hiking in the Venezuelan Andes by Forest Leighty, Venezuelan Andes Press, Miami, 1992. A small, practical book written by a long-time resident in the country who has walked the trails and graded them for difficulty. Many maps. Available in Caracas, Mérida.

Humboldt and the Cosmos by Douglas Botting, Michael Joseph Ltd., London, 1973. This is a fascinating account of Alexander von Humboldt, said to be the last 'universal man': geographer, botanist, geologist, explorer, diplomat and writer. He reached Venezuela's Casiquiare Canal, fixed the height of mountains and latitude of rivers and collected thousands of new plant and animal specimens.

Out of Chingford, Tanis and Martin Jordan, Coronet 1989. Subtitled 'Round the North Circular and up the Orinoco', this is an interesting and entertaining account of the Jordan's travels by their own inflatable boat. The Angel Falls area was one major expedition.

Personal Narrative of Travels to the Equinoctial Regions of America 1799-1801 by Alexander von Humboldt. Trans. from the French by Thomasina Ross, London, 1852. The second of three volumes details explorations in Venezuela: Cumaná, Guácharo, the Apure, Orinoco, Atabapo and Casiquiare rivers. Humboldt studied everything he could see, touch or measure: electric eels, curare, it's all here. And still valid today.

Los Aborígenes de Venezuela, Walter Coppens, editor, Fundación La Salle de Ciencias Naturales, Caracas. In Vol. III (1988) anthropologists write about seven contemporary ethnic groups including the Warao, Yanomami and Piaroa. Clear maps. Vol.II covers six groups, among them the Paraujano and Pemón. In Spanish.

The Explorers of South America by Edward J. Goodman, Collier-Macmillan Ltd., London, 1972. The journeys, sometimes quite fantastic, of Columbus, Vespucci, Ordaz, Raleigh in Venezuela, and later naturalists Humboldt, Bates, Spruce. Plus the famous Andean and Amazonian explorations. Concise reference.

The Jaguar by E. Mondolfi and R. Hoogesteijn, Gráficas Armitano, Caracas, 1993. A thorough survey of the jaguar in Venezuela. The many colour photos show a wide variety of wilderness habitats in the Llanos, Guayana Highlands and Amazonas.

The Last Great Journey on Earth by Brian Branston, Hodder and Stoughton, London, 1970. A British hovercraft expedition crossed from the Amazon via the Casiquiare to the Orinoco in 1968 and rode the great Atures rapids.

Neotropical Rainforest Mammals by Louise Emmons, Univ. of Chicago Press, Chicago & London, 1990. Very good field guide with illustrations by François Teer of some 500 species.

Venezuela's Islands in Time by Uwe George, National Geographic, May 1989, pp 526-561. Travel among tablelands, with spectacular photos and illustrations of how the Guayana Shield came to be. Mandatory for those with 'tepui fever'.

Venezuela: World Bibliographic Series by D.A.G. Waddell. Clio Press, Oxford and Santa Barbara, California, 1990. An annotated listing of 815 books concerning Venezuela. *The* source for anyone wanting to study a particular aspect of the country.

OTHER BOOKS ON SOUTH AMERICA FROM BRADT PUBLICATIONS

Backpacking and Trekking in Peru and Bolivia by Hilary Bradt
Sixth edition (1994) The classic guide for walkers and nature lovers.

South American River Trips by Tanis and Martin Jordan.
How to explore the rivers of South America in your own boat. Full of anecdote and humour, as well as information. The Venezuela section covers the Jordan's expedition in their own boat up the Carrao and Churun rivers to Angel Falls.

Backcountry Brazil by Alex Bradbury.
Three areas are covered in depth: Amazonia, the Pantanal, the north-east coast.

Climbing and Hiking in Ecuador (second edition) by Rob Rachowiecki and Betsy Wagenhauser.
The definitive guide to the volcanoes, mountains and cloudforest of Ecuador, by two former residents, plus general travel information.

Backpacking in Chile and Argentina
Spectacular mountain scenery, well-run national parks, excellent food and wine, good transportation and safe cities. A hiker's and traveller's paradise.

Plus maps of every Latin American country.

This is just a selection of the books and maps for adventurous travellers that we stock. Send for our latest catalogue.
Bradt Publications, 41 Nortoft Rd, Chalfont St Peter, Bucks SL9 0LA, England. Tel: 0494 873478.

Index of Place Names

For the reſt,which my ſelfe haue ſeene I will promiſe theſe things thatfollow and knowe to be true. Thoſe that are deſirous to diſcouer and to ſee many nations, may be ſatisfied within this riuer , which bringeth forth ſo many armes & branches leading to ſeuerall countries,& prouinces,aboue 2000.miles eaſt and weſt,and 800. miles ſouth and north .

Sir Walter Raleigh writing about the Orinoco in *The Discoverie of the Large, Rich and Bewtiful Empyre of Guiana.*

NOTES

NOTES

5000
1800
——
3200

NOTES

NOTES

NOTES

NOTES